KEEPING KIDS IN THE HOME AND OUT OF THE SYSTEM

KEEPING KIDS IN THE HOME AND OUT OF THE SYSTEM

LISA A. HILL, PH.D., LMFT

To order additional copies of this book, contact:
Xlibris
1-888-795-4274
www.Xlibris.com
Orders@Xlibris.com
747814

CONTENTS

Dedication

To my mother, Evelyn R. Charles (1930–2004): Thank you for doing the best you could, all the time, with the resources you had. What you provided was more than enough. I love you to death, literally.

To Grandma (1911–1995): Thank you for *filling in* and giving me persistent and consistent unconditional love. I love you to death, literally.

To my husband Charles of thirty years and counting: Thank you for being my co-laborer on the parenting journey. I love you until death do us apart.

To my daughters Charlisa, Chellsee, Chancler, and Cherrish: Thank you for loving me in spite of myself. I love you in life and, ultimately, death.

To Milaya, Marlee and Nyla, thank you for allowing G-mommy to study and brag on your all-around brilliance. I love you more than I could ever demonstrate.

To my son and grandsons in love, Dontae, Dontae Jr., and Syncere, thank you for stepping into my heart. I love you.

To my sisters, Deborah, Danette, Brenda, and brother Kenny (1955 – 2014) thank you for being there for me, literally, as soon as I came out of the womb. Growing up with you was a blast. I love you.

Introduction: The Criminal Justice System: The Road to Destruction

The United States has the world's largest prison population in the world. Three percent of the adult population is in prison. The United States imprisons more of its citizens than third-world countries. I was inspired to write this book after serving thirty years in county and federal probation departments. One of the biggest service areas of the departments I worked for was in Oakland, California, which has been ranked among the top 10 deadliest cities to live in the United States. It was my experience that living in a violent city contributed to kids ending up in the criminal justice system. Parenting kids in high-crime-rate areas contributes to the dysfunction of the parent-child relationship. Many of the parents that I served had lost control of their children. *Many parents felt they had lost their children "to the streets."*

The juvenile justice system was established to provide substitute parents for wayward children who were at risk of danger. *Parens patriae is a Latin term that means "parent of his country."* Legally, the term refers to the court's authority to intervene against abusive or negligent parents. When parents demonstrate an inability to care for their *children*, the juvenile court is legally obligated to step in and protect the child. The inability to care for a child can be demonstrated by the parent's inability to provide the bare necessities of life, including food and shelter, resulting in harm to the child.

When parents have demonstrated that, in spite of their best efforts, a child is unmanageable in the home, the state can intervene. Finally, if a child's behavior is posing a risk to themselves and others because they are engaging in community misconduct, the state can also step in and make parental decisions. Probation officers and social workers carry out the state's parental responsibility; the former is responsible when the child has committed a law violation.

After working three decades in the criminal justice system, I concluded that once children enter into the juvenile justice system, their lives are negatively impacted. As soon as a child enters into the detention facility, sometimes irreversible trauma will begin. In the true sense of the term "trauma," kids exposed to juvenile justice facilities will encounter shock, disturbance, distress, pain, and overall emotional and physical suffering. There is rampant, documented physical and emotional abuse in juvenile facilities all over country. *The staff who are charged with the "care, custody, and control" of juvenile offenders are not prepared to deal with the behavioral manifestations of the trauma that precede the youth's arrival to the detention facility.* This trauma is perpetuated by the subsequent detention; therefore, a vicious cycle of harm occurs. The juvenile institutional officers, sometimes called counselors, view the emotional problems of the offenders as aggressive, confrontational, and overall negative behavior that accompanies the children into the facility as further proof that the juveniles are bad and deserve to be locked up. When I was a group counselor working in juvenile hall, I too believed that many of the youth were inherently dangerous. I was routinely called out of my name, threatened, and physically assaulted on a few occasions. I recall a young offender, who feared being returned to his native country, attempted to take me hostage as a last-ditch effort to prevent extradition. I was called the "B" word so many times, I started turning around every time someone used the derogatory word.

I would later learn that trauma can be triggered and that sometimes, through no fault of my own, negative feelings would be triggered by my engagement with a detainee. Sometimes it was the detainee transferring negative feelings on to me because perhaps they saw me as the mean or abusive older sister, aunt, or even the mother that had caused the traumatization. I had to learn not to take the abuse from detainees personally. Just like parents, kids utilize whatever resources they have at their disposal at any given time to deal with their current situation. Some kids have not learned how to deal with disappointment, stress, delayed gratification, structure, or direction from an adult figure so they will use verbal or physical aggression to communicate those uncomfortable feelings. Kids need to be taught to control those emotions.

When kids enter detention facilities, they come with whatever skills they have and will utilize those skills to adapt to the detention facility. While serving as a superintendent of a detention facility (camp), I learned pretty quickly that profanity was the chosen vernacular of the detainees and staff! Although the staff would refrain from using profanity when I was visible in the program or within earshot of the staff interfacing with the youth, during unannounced and chance encounters, I would hear staff verbally abusing the detained youth. Not only did the line staff engage in this behavior, I soon discovered that the first- and second-line supervisors condoned the behavior by their silence. Within two months of being promoted to the top administrator position, I held a shift meeting with all line staff and supervisors. My directive that staff refrain from using profanity was met with resistance initially by sighs, rolling of the eyes, and overall looks of disappointment. Thankfully, one of the institutional officers was bold enough to verbalize the sentiment of some of the staff. The vocal staff member said that profanity was the only language that the kids understood and that many of the youth would only listen to them if they used profanity: *"You have to use their language." I* found that many of the staff did not really believe the department's mission statement or core values that stated all people had the potential to change. Many of the staff truly believed that the youth that they served were dangerous, unredeemable, and predators. This distorted view of the juveniles that we served was supporting and justifying the abuse. I had to reconcile the fact that people do the best they can at any given time with the resources they have. Many of the people who work with juvenile offenders are merely misinformed. I would later learn the etiology of this dangerous misinformation.

The Coming of the Super Predator

I was so concerned about the preconceived notion that an overwhelming majority of juvenile offenders were predators, I had to research further. It was apparent that this view was pervasive enough that I felt like it had to have some historical significance. What I found was that in 1995, criminologist John Dilulio wrote a paper in which he described the coming of the super predator. *According to Dilulio, because some kids were not being raised properly, children were growing up with no respect for human life and no sense of the future. Dilulio claimed that these children would eventually kill or maim on impulse without motive.* Dilulio hypothesized that super predators were incapable of valuing another life; therefore, they lacked remorse. Dilulio reported that juvenile offenders would naturally rape, rob, assault, deal drugs, and engage in gang violence and a number of other dangerous behaviors. Because these youth would have a natural inclination to commit crimes, rehabilitation, which is the primary foundation on which the juvenile justice is based, was futile. The only recourse for combating the super predator was to incapacitate them by putting them in custody where the community would be protected. Many people, even previously conscientious human service workers, believed that Dilulio's projections would materialize. There was an overwhelming fear. Although some human service workers like institutional officers, group counselors, probation officers, and social workers still believed in their work and the ability to rehabilitate juveniles, they could not be sure. The only way to assure that Dilulio's predictions would not materialize was to have those predators disarmed, even at the risk of harming them. It was either harm the predator or risk harm to innocent victims. Although many of the innocent juvenile offenders were not a risk to the community or themselves and were only in the system because of what would have been a single mistake, these nonrisk and nonviolent youth were sacrificed. Dilulio had initiated a war, and like all wars, it is anticipated that there will be collateral, albeit innocent, victims. In the words of Marcus Tullius Cicero, *"In times of war, the law falls silence."* When the law falls silent, so does justice. Mr. Cicero also said, "Times are bad. Children no longer obey their parents, and everyone is writing a book" (*smile*).

Dilulio would admit that he had erred in his prediction of the birth of the super predator. But the damage was done. His theory is forever entrenched in society's mind. And the fact that parents were not raising their children effectively was never retracted. Society continues to value incapacitation over rehabilitation because with the former, there is a guarantee that offenders will not re-offend in society; however, with rehabilitation there is always the risk that a free offender may commit additional crimes. This fact is confirmed by the high recidivism (return to crime) rates of offenders.

Training, policy enforcement, and later progressive discipline did little to eradicate the verbally and physically abusive culture that had become the cultural norm in detention facilities. The institutional officers, who saw their primary role as controlling the behavior of the youth in their custody, were unwilling to shift their focus to one that emphasized care and understanding. Training would be no avail. I recall a union representative telling me that if I directed his members to take part in training that had been proven to reduce the number of violent incidents in detention facilities, he would encourage the members to participate in the training as directed but not to apply the principles learned. My further research into abusive behavior in detention facilities would reveal that my facility was no different from many other facilities across the nation, and like many other facilities, the top administrators, who got their direction from political boards or other elected officials, were not prepared to address the harms that were occurring on a day-to-day basis. I soon learned that to address the abuses could make probation departments liable. More to my dismay, changing the culture of detention facilities meant taking on bargaining unions and calling judges into question, and overhauling a big system. *I would later learn that my request to address the dysfunctional practices in detention facilities was likened to physically turning around a 100,000-ton and 900-foot cruise ship in the middle of a lake.* I reached out to presiding judges, supervising public defenders, and district attorneys who had expressed an interest in alternatives to mass incarceration, the attorney general's office, and legislatures. The abuse was not high enough on a high-enough official's agenda to address.

From time to time, egregious cases of abuse will grab the attention of the media; however, in a culture of abuse, which amounted to youth being shamed, verbally abused, threated, manipulated, and suffering broken bones, those cases would end at a critical incident report or package. I recall a youth who had his arm broken by a staff member. When I came into the office, I noticed he was holding his arm cautiously. When I asked what happened, he indicated a staff caused the injury. I asked the staff on duty whether the minor had seen the medical staff. When it turned out he had not been given medical attention, the staff member called the person who had allegedly caused the injury to transport the minor to the medical unit.

I would learn that it was not only the culture of abusive staff that was driving the ongoing trauma in the detention facility but also a code of silence that precludes even well-meaning staff from speaking out.

Los Soplones Obtienan Suturas

As I pointed out, in detention facilities all over the country, verbal abuse and emotional degradation is the norm, and physical abuse is not uncommon. *What perpetuates the systemic abuse is the no-snitch code that is immediately adopted by juvenile and adult detainees as soon as they enter the lockup.* This code of offender ethics is unrivaled by the same no-snitch policy that all new staff are indoctrinated into when they first arrived on the job in lockup. In essence, it is well accepted that snitches will get stitches. If you tell on another detainee, you will experience ostracism, at the very least physical assault, or even death at the worst. This rule applies to detainees, inmates, and staff. Therefore, even new institutional officers who come into the job with the goal of making a positive impact on the youth soon learn that their allegiance to their peers, even if their peers are engaging in abusive and illegal behavior, is the only way of assuring a "good shift." Since many urban, at-risk youth have been indoctrinated into the no-snitch code of ethics prior to coming into the facility, it is easy to transfer that value system into their life in detention facilities. The experience in most detention facilities is far from rehabilitative.

As a result of the trauma, re-traumatization, and poly-traumatization that come from the rampant verbal and physical abuse, youth rarely reintegrate back to their communities rehabilitated. In addition to the traumatic experiences that may have contributed to the youth ending up in the juvenile facility, the abuse that ensues from the youth's detention results in not only re-traumatizing the youth but adding more trauma. The youth may come out of the facilities worse than when they entered. During my tenure as a superintendent, I saw too many youths who entered the system as first-time offenders who had committed minor violations. Some of those offenders matriculated into the adult system for very serious offenses.

The Criminal Justice System: A Criminal System

It was not until I had spent almost three decades working in the criminal justice system and I had begun teaching in the Criminal Justice Department at a University that I realized that the criminal justice system was not a justice system at all. In researching the field, I realized that at its inception and after a period known as enlightenment, the smartest penology minds had determined that people who committed crimes were actually just people who sometimes make mistakes. In other words, they make decisions based on the resources, usually information, they have at any given time. During the period of enlightenment, society came to understand that the offender was just like them. Therefore, it seemed masochistic or even sadistic to chop off offenders' hands and heads or brand them with a scarlet letter. The criminal justice was established to offer humanistic services to offenders who, in some cases, made a mistake due to a deficit in judgment. The leaders in the 1800s who started the humanistic justice system understood that long periods in jails and prisons, and all that happened as a result (overcrowding, emotional and physical abuse, substandard food, lack of programs, idleness, etc.), actually resulted in offenders coming out of prison worst. So, how did we, as a civilized society, come back to mass incarceration? Most criminal justice agencies, in order to get mass amounts of funding, will claim loudly that they are utilizing evidence-based practices. That just means that the agencies are only providing services that, through rigorous research, has been proven to reduce recidivism. So how come recidivism rates are still high? Did the research point us back to mass incarceration as a solution to crime? Is that the best we as a technologically growing society can do to address community misconduct? Perhaps incapacitation (prison) is a viable option for habitual and predatory offenders, but unfortunately, our prisons are not filled with violent offenders.

Another discovery I made during my teaching of courses such as restorative justice is how ironic our current system of justice, which is based on a retributive and just-desserts philosophy, is referred to as a criminal justice system. Is it called that because it is believed that everyone who comes into contact with the system is a criminal? Isn't society's goal to rehabilitate offenders, in other words return them to a productive level of functioning? Why are we referring to them as criminals? Think about it, the system that is charged with rehabilitating offenders is referred to as a criminal justice system. The title implies that the "criminal" will get fairness and what is deserved. Is that an inherent contradiction? Do we really want fairness for a person who has done wrong and, in some cases, committed very serious acts? Or do we want them to get just desserts, retribution? Why not call the system that responds to criminal behavior the criminal retribution system or the criminal punishment system because, in effect, that is exactly what happens? But if our society is really interested in rehabilitating offenders, how come the name has not evolved to something like the criminal advocacy system or the human justice system. Have we neglected to change the name because it still fits because people who end up in the criminal justice system will get a criminal standard of service? Yes, that fits because once you enter the system, there are crimes that will be committed against them. People in jails and prisons all across the country will be abused emotionally and physically. Minorities, especially the poor, will continue to be vastly overrepresented in the criminal justice system and even though we have the ability to keep large amounts of data, no one has figured out that the disproportionate number of minorities in the criminal justice system defies rational statistics? Many people will be falsely convicted, and we accept this by our deliberate indifference because somewhere in our psyche, we know that what we are providing is criminal services not humane justice.

Why else would our research-driven, technologically advanced society accept poor outcomes with offenders who are served in the criminal justice system? The research shows that the outcomes, as measured in recidivism rates, are poor. It is estimated that as high as 80 percent of those who enter the criminal justice system will commit another offense. What other system or organization could stay in business year after year, decade after decade with that failure rate? How come the criminal justice system has not gone out of business or at least filed for bankruptcy?

But then it hit me during one of my lectures, perhaps the criminal justice system is not doing that bad after all. Perhaps I have been reading the data incorrectly. Perhaps that recidivism rate of 80 percent is actually success. Perhaps the system is meeting its mandates and business is flourishing. Then I saw the budget. Nationally, almost 30 billion dollars is spent on criminal justice. I don't think most of that money is being spent on rehabilitation of offenders. Yes, criminal justice.

Why I had to write this book: My quest to shut down the criminal justice system

Toward the end of my career with a county probation department, I found out how sick the criminal justice system was because I began to prick it and it bled. By pricking it, I mean that I started to question why we were not *really* providing evidence-based practices, and I was told that, like the offenders to whom I had read their Miranda rights, I had the right to remain silent and that anything I said would be held against me. I didn't keep silent and it was held against me. I had to take another approach. Instead of being part of the system, I decided that I would make sure that only those who needed the system would enter its doors.

While serving over three decades in the criminal justice system, I encountered so many extremely talented people—people whose talents were literally being wasted because they had become entangled in the criminal justice system. *I served talented youth in the juvenile justice system who had natural writing, reading, singing, dancing, oration, mechanical, technical, and artistic skills. Some of these kids could take an issue and debate it better than the most experienced orators. I met youth who had natural musical abilities with perfect pitch. I saw youth who could clean better than the most seasoned Mary Maids professional.* These children had something important to offer if given an opportunity to share. I remember one of my clients taught me the art of highlighting! One of my male clients watched me highlight information in an article I was reading. My line was consistently crooked. Exasperated, he took the highlighter and through frustration said, "Ms. Hill, if you turn the highlighter around this way, you will be able to highlight more precisely." I can honestly say that *every time* I pick up a highlighter, I look at it and turn it around to the fine point to assure that I am highlighting correctly. Unfortunately, in all too many cases, it was not until the youth arrived at juvenile hall that their skills were manifested. Even more pitiful for some youth, the beautiful traits lay dormant and are never revealed. Parents must reveal the talents of their children. I served adult offenders who could build anything without written plans/drafts, competent draftsmen, plumbers, and mechanics. Those skills were being utilized for literally pennies per day in the jails and more egregiously, the talents were being used in exchanged for a king-sized candy bar, a burrito, a "Chinese plate," or a 12-ounce can of soda that would be provided by the institutional staff who requested the service. When I was the superintendent of a detention facility, I displayed the youth's artwork all over the facility to make sure that the work was visible not just for the youth, who were very proud of their productions; displaying the work reminded me and anyone else who came into the facility the caliber and potential of the youth that we were serving. They were not just juvenile offenders, but young artists and visionaries who should not only be defined by the behavior that brought them into the system, but also by what they could potentially produce. However, to my sadness, the talents of many of these juveniles ended up on the dead-end road to which the criminal justice system leads. I don't want to completely eliminate the criminal justice system. I would like to return the system to its good intentioned roots. When the juvenile court was first established, it was with the goal of acting on behalf of youth and assuring that they did not suffer the negative influences inherent in the jail and prison milieu. At the conception of the juvenile court, there was a concern for youth to assure that they were distinct from adult offenders. There was a belief that children could not form the mental schemas (mens rea) to commit crimes. Even with the expanding research on the ongoing maturation of the brain well beyond the age of majority, children are increasingly being treated like cold and calculating predators to be feared, therefore locked away. My goal is that only people who require the services of the criminal justice system will enter its doors. For everyone else, it is my goal in writing this book that parents will raise their kids in such a way that they do not end up in the criminal justice system

A Parent's Plan to Avoid the Criminal Justice System

When I first started working for the probation department, I was young, single, and without children. I had a lot of extra time. I took a job working for a residential youth treatment center. The program focused on children, five to twelve years old, who were beyond their parental control. I would often leave that job and immediately go to my probation job. I could not help but notice that many of the youth in the residential treatment center demonstrated similar behavior to the adolescent delinquent youth at the detention center. They were, in fact, the same kids. Later, I would find some of the kids I had worked with at the residential center in the probation detention center. I became burdened with one question: What happened to these kids in six, ten, twelve, sixteen little years that sent them on the path of delinquency? I would ponder, "Not too long ago, these kids were some parent's infant, toddler, little boy/girl. What event changed them?" I started paying attention to parents and their babies. Most parents are so careful and attentive to their newborns, babies, and toddlers. New parents usually demonstrate so much pride. Novel parents smile at their children a lot. Although I never was bold enough to do so, I knew if I approached a new mother and asked them if they planned for their child to be incorrigible or even arrested and detained in juvenile hall, I would probably risk being assaulted or thought of as crazy at the very least. The fact of the matter is that no one plans to have trouble raising their children; something happens or something does not happen, and kids become incorrigible, or beyond the parents' ability to control the child. Many of the parents I served in probation were surprised their child was in trouble. They would lament, "Not my child." They always thought that it would be someone else's child that would end up in the criminal justice system. After working with several surprised parents, I drew a very important conclusion that *it is not enough to plan for your child not to end up in the criminal justice system; parents must have a well-thought-out plan to prevent their child from ending up in the criminal justice system.*

My other observation from working with juvenile-justice involved youth was that *one way or the other, parents will put in the time with their children.* For some parents, the time will be spent talking to their kids, taking them to the park, going to playdates. Some parents will be very involved with their kids' school, going to back to school night and open house. Some parents will volunteer in their kids' classrooms and chaperone field trips. Some parents will make sure that the child has well checks every year and cheer their child on at school events, whether that means sitting in cold bleachers for a game, or spending all day at a track meet to see the child run in one event. Some parents will sit for hours at debate competitions, waiting for the opportunity to see their child make a one-minute speech, or a spelling bee, only to find out your child missed the first word. However, some parents will miss these events because of other seemingly more important events in their lives. But the absentee parents won't get off the hook. The time they missed will be waiting. The missing parents will ultimately spend a lot of time on the phone because the school is constantly calling about the child's behavior or the parent must show up at the school in the middle of the day to pick the child up after a suspension. Absentee parents spend a lot of time in counseling offices attempting trying to find out why their child is struggling socially. Absentee parents spend time in court after their child has been detained and bringing food to the detainee during visiting hours at the detention center. When I worked as a counselor at the juvenile hall, I will never forget this mother who used to visit her son who was in custody. The mother did not drive, so she would have to catch the bus. The buses only ran on a limited schedule on weekends so she would have to get off the bus a mile away from the detention center and walk the rest of the way, uphill! The mother was not in the best of health and so she had trouble making it up the hill. She would have a few bags in her hands containing food and books for her son. By the time she reached the facility, she would be sweating profusely. As part of my role of group counselor, I had the pleasure of monitoring the visiting hour so I would watch that mother and other parents visiting with their kids. The probation department also allowed visits from grandparents, aunts, uncles, and siblings over eighteen years old. All the parents brought their kids favorite food and some would bring card and board games. The kids would tell the parents about the dramas of detention life, and the family members would fill the detainee in on all the drama that was happening in the family and the community. Many of the families looked so happy. It was obvious that the detainee was enjoying all the attention that came with the family visits. I could not help but wonder what would have happened had the parents and family members spent this level of quality time with the kids before they were arrested. Instead of spending time hiking up the hill to a detention facility, perhaps the family could have spent quality time, going hiking together when the child was younger. I realized that when raising kids, you are going to put the time in one way or the other. You can either spend quality time engaged with your child in the home, or waste the time sitting in principal's offices, babysitting your child at home after they have been suspended from school, visiting at detention centers and later adult jail and prison facilities. Some of you that are reading this book are saying, no, not my child. It is my hope that after reading this book, no, it will not be your child. However, if you are reading this book after your child has entered the criminal justice system, my advice is that you do whatever you can to get your child out!

I was more than inspired to write this book, I was urged to write this book to enlighten parents and prospective parents on the dangers that await their child if parents do not take an active role in raising their children.

The Intended Audience for the Book

There are so many unread parenting books in publication. So in writing the book, I was really hoping that I could produce something that parents would want to read. That sounds simple but it is not. Parents are in a constant state of multitasking so they rarely have time for extracurricular activities such as reading. If a parent finds his or herself with a little extra time, rarely will they desire to fill that time reading a self-help book. Therefore, prior to writing the book, I conducted a review of the literature. I wanted to know what had already been written on parenting. Why re-invent the wheel. I found hundreds of books and realized that there were actually really good works out there; however, based on my experience with literally hundreds of parents, I didn't find anything that to which I felt my parents could relate. I didn't have an *A-ha, here is what my parents need* moment. The books ranged from parenting for dummies, which implied that parenting could be accomplished in such a way that even a person who lacked knowledge could be a successful parent. At the other end of the spectrum, some of the parenting books were very technical and written in such a way you would need a biology, psychology, or physiology degree to understand the concepts. Again, all of them provided good information; nonetheless, what was missing was a down-to-earth, easy-to-understand, reader-friendly, keep-it-real, honest conversation for parents. As a probation manager, I used to tell my probation employees that they must be willing to have tough conversations with parents. The department provided probation institution officers and probation officers with enormous training, some of which provided officers with skills on how to handle themselves if threatened with physical violence. At the very least, probation staff could protect themselves from assault. Therefore, they were in a unique position, unlike social workers and therapists, to have tough conversations with parents that may result in, if nothing else, verbal assault. I would reason that probation staff may be only ones positioned to tell the truth to parents. Therefore, if parents were not handling their parental role appropriately, and that was leading to acting out behavior by the child, probation staff, in carrying out their due diligence, were responsible for honestly communicating this fact to the parent.

This book is not being written to sit on the shelves. I want to make sure anyone who could benefit from the information in this book has an opportunity to get a copy. It is my hope that this book will be given out to every parent that enters the doors of probation and social services agencies. I would like school site councils to pass out the books to parents. I would love to see hospitals give out the book in the mommy (or daddy) bags when new parents leave the hospital with their new babies. When adoptions and foster agreements are finalized, I hope the book will be part of the exit package. Perhaps judges could have the book on the bench and strongly suggest parents read it. I would like to see the book given out at back-to-school night. Even people who do not have children or are beyond childbearing age should buy a copy of the book to gift to other parents. *I hope people keep a copy of the book with them so when they see parents acting badly, they can hand them the book like a business card.* Perhaps your children are all grown up and your relationship is not what you would like. Reading this book may provide some insight into what may have gone wrong. Finally, to my parents who are behind bars and at some point will resume their role as mom or dad when released, it is my hope that you will spend a little time reading this book prior to your release date so you will be armed with parental knowledge as your reenter society and take on your role as parent.

Once I achieve my first goal of producing a book that parents would want to read and making sure that the book is made available so all parents have access to the material, I will be well on my way to accomplishing my long-term goal, to drastically reduce the number of kids who end up in the juvenile justice system (and ultimately the criminal justice system) and departments of children services. Once people enter the criminal justice system, they become entangled in a vicious cycle that sometimes takes generations to break. Good parenting will go a long way in reducing the number of kids who enter the juvenile justice system. Since I spent so many years serving families in the justice system, I encountered multiple children from the same families and even multiple generations. On more than a few occasions, I encountered the child of one of my former clients.

"The future destiny of a child is always the work of the mother."
~Napoleon Bonaparte

Parents: The Gatekeepers

Napoleon Bonaparte is only half right. He leaves out the father. Although mothers are responsible for carrying a baby in the womb until delivery, at postpartum, the father is equally responsible for raising the child. Kids, if they are not provided with the proper role models, instruction, and direction, could certainly develop some of the characteristics of a predator. Studies have consistently concluded that many personality disorders and more serious mental disorders are believed to be the result of dysfunctional family relationships, and very often stem from the parent-child relationship. This makes sense; children initially learn important behaviors from their families of origin. For example, parents are the first ones to socialize their child so they can teach their children socialize and to say please and thank-you, take turns, be patient, etc. The primary purpose of this book is to assure that parents have the information they need to properly raise children who have the skills necessary to be successful adults and not end up in the criminal justice system. By the time youth end up in the juvenile justice system, it may be too late. They become labeled an offender or maybe even a predator. That label gives society the right to lock the youth up during which time they will be traumatized.

Sometimes well-meaning, uninformed, and frustrated parents perpetuate their children entering the criminal justice system and even of child-serving agencies such as social services. When parents are faced with children who are incorrigible, at-risk, or the parent is unable to care for the child due to their own personal problems, some parents will welcome the intervention of the criminal justice system for support. After their child has been taken into custody, I have had parents tell me, "You raise my child because I cannot do it." Some parents believe that having access to a probation officer with a badge and powers of arrest gives them the relief and respite they needed to address their child's destructive behavior. My three decades of experience working with youth and parents in the criminal justice revealed that, in most cases, probation and social services intervention do not make youth better. Conversely for most youth, their experience with social services and probation departments has resulted in ongoing delinquency and the youth transitioning into the adult criminal justice system. However, *good parenting is the gatekeeper to the criminal justice system.*

In Honor of Parents

My quest to change the abusive system that was under my purview would prove daunting at times, isolating, and finally exhausting. My journey to fix a broken system eventually ended with my early retirement, but not without what I feel was a courageous battle. For the role I played in further traumatizing youth due to my lack of information, I apologize to the families and I hope to honor the families I attempted to serve by telling their stories. My data for this book comes from the thousands of youth, parents, and families that I served in over three decades of working in probation, clinical practice as a licensed marriage and family therapist, and raising my own four children. Although I could never recall all of the people by name, I give special recognition to all the people that inspired the writing of this book. These parents had to learn from trial and many errors.

Throughout my tenure as a probation officer, therapist, and parent, I have had the opportunity to witness many parenting decisions that have resulted in dysfunctional families and traumatized children, many of whom have ended up in the criminal justice system. Those parents were frustrated and exhausted by the time they made it to my office. The parents' annoyance wasn't solely because of the trials with the children, but also because life can be tiring. Add having children to an already overtaxed life can easily result in emotional challenges. When I recall some of the misinformed decisions I made while raising my four children, I cringe and shake my head at my lack of knowledge. However, as I will affirm many times in this book, "Parents do the best they can, at any given moment, with the resources they have." Sarvesh Jain said, *"Admitting your mistakes makes you humble. But not repeating your mistakes makes you clever."* I hope this book makes clever parents out of my readers.

In writing this book, I hope to honor all the parents and children whose stories will be used to illustrate uninformed parenting. Many readers will recognize that these stories are not so uncommon, but in spite of this, and fortunately, many families don't end up in the criminal justice system. Although I have encountered some unique circumstances, I can honestly say that the unifying theme to all the stories is that parents merely lacked the appropriate knowledge, skill, or ability in the moment to appropriately address their child's behavior. The point in writing this book is not to blame parents or remind them of the mistakes that were made. Because as the saying goes, when you point one finger, there are four pointing at you. Yes, I would have to confront my own mistakes. My goal for writing this book was to assure that parents and caretakers have the knowledge, skills, and abilities they need, and therefore, they are clever enough to provide intelligent parenting so their child will not end up in the criminal justice system. The families I served in probation demonstrated the same challenges of families in my private clinical practice and in my own family. What was unique about the probation families was the lack of resources to address their children's challenging behavior. For all the parents who are already on the parenting journey, I say to you that no matter how far you are on the road, from one day to fifteen years, you can go forward more successfully. No matter how many mistakes you have made, I say to you with much respect: **Parents do the best they can at any given moment with the resources they have.** This book will increase your parental capital and assure that you have the knowledge, skill, and abilities you need to raise kids who do not end up in the criminal justice system.

Not My Kid

At this point, you may be wondering why a well-meaning, good parent would want to read a book that uses research and data collected from parental mistakes, especially the parents of "those" at-risk youth or delinquents. Shouldn't I read a book narrated by successful parents who raised successful kids? Let me respond to the parents who are thinking in that vein by adding one final note on the value of learning from mistakes. Ponder this question:

If you were confronted with a choice of two equally trained surgeons, would you select the one who has operated on over 100 people and never lost a patient, or the doctor who has performed the same number of procedures, but lost one patient? Most people want a flawless doctor. As a matter of fact, most people only want a flawless role model, someone who has demonstrated competence without failure. However, a person who has tried and failed has a lot to offer. As a matter of fact, some people will tell you that there is a miracle in making a mistake. Even the research has revealed that there is growing evidence to suggest that innovation flourishes when people *are given the space to make mistakes. Mahatma Gandhi attached value to experimentation; he believed that **a person is not free unless he is free to make mistakes.** Once a person has made a mistake or been unsuccessful, she must confront, address, and work through the error.*

This book is being written with the same level of humility as a doctor who has lost a first patient. The data comes from parents who have made mistakes in parenting and in the clear, perfect and retrospective vision that can only come from hindsight, their stories will help other parents to avoid the errors in judgment, the missed opportunities, and the overall mistakes made while raising their children. As indicated previously, much of the data drawn upon for this book comes from people who did the best they could with the resources they had to raise their kids, and somewhere along the line, something went wrong. Whenever I would tell people that I served as a probation officer, they would respond with "I bet your work is challenging." Most people only associated probation with juveniles and jails and prisons with adults. For the juvenile offenders, people would respond to my career choice with, *"Those kids are murders, rapists, batterers, liars, and thieves."* People would ponder why I would choose a field that meant I would come into contact with "those kids." I would respond, yes, the job can be challenging, but not for the reasons you are thinking. My challenges mostly stemmed from a lack of understanding. I would tell my friends and associates that the youth I worked with in probation were just like any other kid. The response would always be the same, "Not my kid!" My kid would never do some of the horrible things that "those kids" do. Of course, on the rare occasion that the person did not subscribe to the theory that the kid was inherently bad or evil, the child's criminal behavior would be ascribed to the parent. After spending three decades serving in the criminal justice system working with hundreds of parents and hundreds of co-laborers in the field and collaborating fields, *I have never encountered a parent or heard of a parent who, early on in the parenting process, thought that their child would end up in the system. The majority of the parents I served, at one point, had very high aspirations for their child.* I want more parents to be able to say, not my kid. In, *Keeping Kids In The Home And Out Of The System,* I outline nine habits of law-abiding people that parents must internalize, model, teach, nurture, and reinforce in their children to prevent them from ending up in the criminal justice system. By utilizing the real-life stories of families that I encountered in the probation and private clinical practice over the past thirty years, I demonstrate how important it is for parents to learn and adopt the habits into their own lives first and then those skills can be easily implanted on to their children. The organization of the book is simple. First I lay a foundation to prepare parents to revisit their role of parents. I will introduce the skills of law-abiding people. Once parents understand those habits, I will operationalize them into three broad but critical development phases of childhood development. Parents will be introduced to the phases, and it will be clear that parenting infants, school-age children, and adolescents require different strategies. Finally, I will have a chapter on courageous conversations. In this section, I outline several issues that parents must confront that may be impeding the parenting process.

Chapter One

Parenting 101: What You Need to Know

Parent Defined

How would you define "parent": If you Google the term, you will learn that a parent is a person who has a child; that a parent is something out of which something has developed; a parent is a mother or a father. Most parents easily meet this description, and they feel that they have achieved the title of parent because a child developed as a result of them. However, a further review of the definition of parent provides the information that excludes some people from earning the full distinction of parent. The full definition of parent includes a person who raises a child. Raising a child is different from parenting a child. Raising a child is like any other job that you would begin. You should research the job description, talk to other employees to get the true picture, measure your knowledge, skills, and abilities with the job description and what other people doing the job say the position requires. Reading this book will provide you with the job description. One of the primary goals for writing this book was to assure that parents fully understand what it means to be a parent. Becoming a parent means you are fully and unapologetically caring for a child or children. It is important that parents understand what I mean when I say unapologetically caring for a child. This means that you are caring for your child in a manner that does not acknowledge or express regret and committed to raising a human being between the ages of one-minute-old to eighteen years old. I will never forget the parent who told me that her biggest regret was that she "did not close her legs [and suffocate her son] during delivery." That is the ultimate form of regret. Raising a child is different from merely parenting a child. Parenting a child is limited to possessing the title and providing the bare minimum care; however, raising a child requires consistent, active, and tireless effort and engagement. Parenting is an adjective and, as such, an action word. Not unlike prospective employees, prospective parents should research the job description prior to embarking on the job to determine if the job will be a win-win. Let's look at the full job description of parent. Napoleon Bonaparte's famous saying is "Give me good mothers and I shall give you a great nation."

> *Give me good mothers and I shall give you a great nation.*
> *~Napoleon Bonaparte*

Parents: The Givers of Life

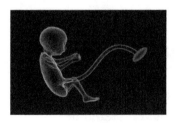

As I indicated before, Bonaparte only had the value of the mother half right; it is the parents that are the givers of life. There is a lot research on peer relationships and the importance of assuring that kids are socialized, hence the advent of the "play date." Later research confirmed that not only should parents make sure that they socialize their kids to have friends, parents should also make sure that kids associate with prosocial peers. Many parents get on preschool waiting lists during the pregnancy because they want to make sure that their child is accepted in the best preschools so they will be socialized in the best environments. This is a great example of **proactive** thinking; however, it is my belief that the most important relationship that a child will have will be with his or her parents. The parent-and-child relationship is the most critical relationship in the life of a child. Understanding this fact will be a better example of the skills of **putting first things first**. The parent-child relationship will determine, unequivocally, the outcome of the child. The parent-and-child relationship will determine whether a child will make it to adulthood successfully emotionally and physically. It is my belief that if parents truly understood how important they are to their child's eventual success in life, they would take their role much more serious. I believe many parents appreciate their status as mother or father, but I don't think they accept and acknowledge how critical it is for them to consciously, unequivocally, and without compromise accept their role as mother or father. Parents are the giver of life! Let that sink in for a moment. I mean really give thought to the fact that if it were not for the parents, the child would not have been conceived nor come into the world. Conception, in the event of a viable pregnancy, always means life will result. It does not matter whether the birth resulted from longtime planning or poor planning; either way, two people are going to become parents. How a parent raises a child must not depend on how the child was conceived. Babies don't decide, regulate, or schedule their birth. As my second oldest daughter reminds me every time I am resistant to granting her requests, "I didn't ask to be born!"

Although my daughter provides a good example of parental manipulation, she actually makes a good point; it is only because of the intimate union between her dad and I that she was born. In spite of all the medical and fertility advances that have occurred throughout the ages, the fact remains that conception can only occur after a male sperm and female egg have come together and fertilization occurs. The owners of that sperm and egg are physically accountable for the birth of the child. I would be remiss if I didn't acknowledge that there are circumstances that can occur that would result in forced conception. In those instances, the most responsible person carrying the sperm or the egg must make the best decision for the child. If the decision is made to raise the child, there must be a commitment to take full responsibility for raising the child and the means of conception must never be a factor in the efficiency of raising the child.

Parents must take responsibility for the conception and ultimate birth of a child. One of the clearest messages I learned during the three decades I served in the criminal justice system was that accountability and responsibility are not the same. To be accountable means that based on a certain fact (parentage), there is an obligation similar to a legal contract. Contracts are binding because people chose to enter into an agreement to be responsible for something. *Some parents raise their kids as though they are just being accountable and it is the thing to do to avoid being charged with neglect or suffer other emotional and financial liability. To be responsible is to recognize a duty to exercise control and power over someone.* In some cases, obligatory parenting is enough in that it is better than no parenting at all; however, in all cases children will do better with conscientious responsible parenting.

The Parent Journey

The parenting journey begins at the very moment that the first child is born. Some may argue that the journey begins at conception because how a woman treats her body when she is pregnant will impact the physical and mental life of the child. I agree with that; however, depending on what you believe, God or nature usually takes care of most of the physical and emotional development in utero. Therefore, even under the worst of circumstances, most children make it out of the womb. I was born during a time when women did not have many options. In the 1960's, if a woman became pregnant, should would more than likely only have a few legal and healthy options. Therefore, unless the mother decided to give the baby up for adoption, ten months after conception, the baby would go home with the birth mother, no matter how many other children were already in the home. That being the social climate that I was conceived under, when my mother became pregnant with her fifth child, she was not happy to say the least. My dad was not a help meet; he was a bartender alcoholic, bless his heart, so my mother was not only unhappy, she was disappointed and frustrated. But my mother was very bright so very early in my mother's pregnancy with me, she climbed on the roof of my grandmother's house and jumped off. Luckily the house was a single-story because I survived and my mother was chastised harshly by my grandmother who wanted as many grandchildren as she could get. My mother made the best decision she could with the resources she had. I often laugh when I think about my mother jumping off the roof. I have images of myself in the womb being tossed to and fro, and while I am hanging on to the umbilical cord I am yelling, "Whoa,

Mommy, what's going on out there?" But true to my beginning form, I am stubborn and don't give up easily. I survived a jump and several decades later, here I am writing a parenting book.

The most important part of this story is assuring that parents understand that they are on a journey. As is the case with all journeys, there is a beginning and ending. *You become a parent with responsibilities as soon as the child comes into the world; however, your parenting goal must be to parent the child in such a way that he will ultimately leave home and live independent and productive.* Parenting is not an indefinite responsibility. The relationship is determinate, but the parent's role moves from one of parent, who is taking full care of a child, to ultimately a consultant. The consultant allows the once-child, now adult, to make his own decisions and live his own life. The parent of an adult only consults when invited to do so. "Mom, do you think I should have another child? What do you think, son? What would it be like to have another child financially? Socially?" Alternately, a parent of an adult would not respond to that same question with, "Why would you want another child when you can't afford the ones you have . . . don't ask me to babysit . . . you are crazy for even considering having another child." I was forty years old when I had my last child. After confirming the pregnancy, my husband and I went to my mother's home to tell her the great news. My husband said, "Guess who is having another baby?" My mother looked at me with disgust and said, "I know you are not pregnant again!" I left crying. I later understood that my mother worried that if I continued to have children, I would not be able to take care of her during her elder age. My mom was not behaving as a consultant; she was acting like a mother who found out she was about to take on more responsibility. My mother became ill two years later and that two-year-old toddler and I took great care of her during her final days. I, along with that two-year-old that my mom worried would prevent me from caring for her spent many nights, doing just that. I nursed my mom while my two-year-old entertained my mother. Yes, life is a journey, and when you come to the end, you realize just how short the road was. Parents must begin the journey immediately so as soon as the child is born, the work must begin.

The Parent Potter

In January 1504, Italian sculptor Michelangelo completed a world-famous sculpted statue of the biblical character David (who slayed Goliath, the giant). What is impressive about the piece of art is the fact that Michelangelo created the 17-foot piece of art with a single block of marble. Two artist had refused to work with the marble because there were too many imperfections. Michelangelo is applauded for taking a flawed piece of marble and turning it into one of the most famous pieces of art. Interestingly, some people believe that the work of art was already in the marble and Michelangelo merely chipped away at the outer layer until he revealed the final piece of art. Evidence of the latter theory is supported by the cases of children who are geniuses or prodigies who appear to be born with artistic and intellectual gifts. There have been cases where children have demonstrated the ability to play the piano proficiently the very first time they attempted to play and children who master a language at the first exposure. Very young children have graduated from high school in spite of the fact that they have not been in school long enough to complete the twelve years of curriculum. Michael Kearney reportedly graduated from high school at six years old and graduated from college at ten. Tanishq Abraham received his high school diploma at age ten and graduated from community college at eleven. These cases support the theory that a child is born with an innate blueprint and parents are responsible for revealing the true character and abilities of the child. In spite of the above two kids'

academic gifts, their parents could have elected not to pursue their talents further.

Nurturing the natural abilities of a child is not the only challenge facing parents. Many parents enjoy bringing out the best in their children. The bigger task facing fallible and mere human specimens, who are affectionately known as mom and dad, is to avoid adding more layers of stuff that could interrupt or even stop the development of the child masterpiece. The more layers that are added, the harder it will be to get to the predestined person waiting within. Since evidence supports that geniuses are born, it stands to reason that all of us are born with a predestined amount of innate potential. In other words, at birth, our DNA has already established the blueprint for our potential. So, just like the statute of David may have already been underneath the layers of marble and waiting for Michelangelo to chip away and uncover the famous piece, children already have the potential to be great at birth. *Babies are born with a set amount of potential. When babies leave the womb, they are just waiting to have their ultimate or maximum potential revealed.* The uncovering of a child's true potential comes from living and growing in a nurturing environment; one that is rich with resources, that will allow the child to thrive. The resources I am referring to do not come with a price tag. I am not talking about "things" such as expensive cars, big houses, expense accounts, yearly vacations, top-notch schools, name brand clothes. Although those material things are great, they will not guarantee a child will become a productive adult. The things that I am referring to are emotional resources that validate the child such as unconditional positive regard, love, patience, and positive presence.

The Child: Not a Second Opportunity

Parents' pre-contextual ideas is the antithesis of unconditional positive regard. In opposition of accepting the child for who she is and will become, some parents have a preconceived idea about what their child will become. Don't get me wrong, the main purpose of this book is to inspire parents to actively raise their kids in such a way that they nurture specific thinking and behavior patterns that lead to them becoming effective adults. These traits are generic and include planning, prioritizing, organizing, socializing, learning, and collaborating. *However, where some parents go wrong is when they have a very specific preconceived life already planned for their child. For some parents, the child becomes the parent's second chance at a life that they did not achieve.* We will discuss how naming a child after someone could potentially typecast the child into being a smaller version of the namesake. However, there are other subtle ways that parents can groom a child to their own preconceived destiny. Some parents dress their kids like smaller versions of themselves. I have seen one-year-old hip-hoppers, punk rockers, gothics, and nerds. These babies sport the look of the popular culture. They may have multiple piercings by two years of age. Pop culture babies wear sagging pants; some have green hair. The planned lifestyle that parents have designed for their children may be driven by their own unfinished business. Parents may be motivated by their own life's desires or talents that lay dormant and never materialized. In this case, parents are hopeful that their child will fulfill their dreams to become medical doctors, dancers, musicians, and famous athletes, to name just a few. I recall a television commercial where a young man had won the lottery. He said that his dad had always wanted to see him graduate from medical school, so after winning the lottery, the son paid for his father to attend medical school. In other words, winning the lottery allowed the son to avoid having to live out the dreams of his dad.

Instead of shaping the child into a junior or second version of the parents, the parent must recognize that at birth, the child is a new creation who has his own destiny. The parents' responsibility is to allow the child room to thrive while chipping away at some of the traits that don't lead to success and nurturing the traits that lead to adult success. A great visual analogy of this is a potter on a pottery wheel. The potter is working with a glob of clay. As the clay spins, the potter is shaping and forming the clay just like parents will shape behavior. In addition, the potter is pulling away and removing all extra clay that is not needed for the end product. Parents must also remove parts of the child's behavior that will be contrary to the child forming into a productive adult.

Guard Your Masterpiece

The time that we have raising our children goes by very fast, especially when parents understand that it is really only the first few years that have the biggest impact. Research has demonstrated that the personality is established by first grade. That means that parenting during the first six years are extremely important. From about six years old forward, parents are responsible for refining the personality; thus like Michelangelo, mom, dad, and the responsible caretaker are just chipping away raw and unnecessary components of the personality in order to reveal the hidden ideal personality. Parents work really hard during the first few years to develop the maturing child, teaching, directing, and modeling. Once the personality is formed, children continue to be highly influenced by outside people and events. Also, after six years old, most children start attending school full time and spending less time with the parent and in the family milieu. By six years old, children are proficient communicators so even the most precautionary parents will begin to allow their child more freedom. By six years old, parents allow kids to attend birthday parties alone, have playdates and even sleep over at their playmates' homes. By eight years old, when children are able to handle hygiene needs, some parents allow their children to go on chaperoned camping trips. Although this newfound freedom should be based on the maturity level of the individual child, parents should also stay on the parent path and make sure that they continue to control their child's environment. When parents allow their child to be under other adult's care, they should make sure the care is consistent with the values, morals, and ethics of the parents. Parents should vet the adults that will care for their kids.

Lessons from the Field

When I was case manager over a community day school, there was a young man who seemed to be very upset all the time. I met with his parents, who were divorced but amicable and committed to raising their son, albeit separately. During a meeting with the parents and the young man, I noticed he was very angry at both parents. When the parents left, I asked the young man why he appeared so angry. He responded, "I hate them!" After initially being resistant to sharing the reason, he told me that when he was a child, he was molested by his father's best friend. He said that his parents went out very often and the molester was the go-to babysitter. He hated his parents because he felt that every time they went out to "have fun," he was molested by the substitute caregiver. So any time the young man saw either of his parents smiling, it fueled his hate for the parent. I convinced the young man to reveal this ten-year secret. When the parents returned to my office and we disclosed the story, the mother broke down in tears. She could not understand why her son had not shared the abuse before. The mother reported that the friend had been sent to prison after it was discovered that he had sexually abused his own son. After learning that man had molested his own son, the parents ended their relationship with the offender. When I asked the mother and father whether they had any clue that at the time, their friend had been sexually assaulting their son, both said no. Upon further reflection, both acknowledged that their son had regularly protested going to the friend's house but they didn't view his resistance as serious. The parents acknowledged that during the time their son was young, they enjoyed going out often. Because I was a mandatory reporter, I had to determine the whereabouts of the man who raped my client years earlier. It was at that time I learned that the man was in fact in prison for raping his own son. Even after learning that the man had raped his own son, the parents never thought to ask the son whether he had been abused by the perpetrator. I think, on some level, they were afraid of the answer.

My young probationer who was molested by his father's friend is an extreme case; however, there are lesser evils that parents must protect their children from such as substance abuse, pornography, profanity, domestic violence and certain religious and secular practices. Parents must consistently protect their masterpiece.

Like Michelangelo, parents are the initial designer of their children's character. When one becomes a parent of a newborn, the parent inherits a malleable piece of clay that will ultimately become a finished human creation. Allow that idea to sink in for a moment. The life of that newborn is in a parent's hands. Think about the most valuable thing you own or want to own. What if someone gave you a crystal ornament that you learned would be worth millions of dollars in eighteen years? It is not worth anything in its present form but will reach its potential in eighteen years only if it is preserved and taken care of. During the maturation process, you had to do certain things like clean, buff, and shine. Would you do it? Most would take good care of their appreciating treasure. A treasure that will increase in value is how parents should view their children. Parents must conscientiously clean, shine, and buff their children like a valuable piece of crystal so that it will appreciate in value. Who knows, they may even appreciate you one day.

Active and conscientious parenting requires making the choice to take on the several years long obligation to create an individual that will ultimately possess, at the very least, the nine habits of a person who does not end up in the criminal justice system. It was reported that Michelangelo worked very long hours while sculpting David, and he rarely slept or ate. Although it is expected that parents will get the prerequisite amount of nourishment while raising their children, sleeplessness often characterizes the parenting process, especially at different developmental stages like infancy and adolescence. Parents have the single responsibility to pull the greatness out of their child. In light of this huge responsibility, parents must prepare for the journey for the path of creating a masterpiece. When parents fail to protect their child from harmful environments, additional extraneous layers are added to the masterpiece as opposed to being chipped away as a result of conscientious parenting. Consider Michelangelo chipping away at the stone while attempting to reveal the masterpiece, and as he removes pieces, more stone is added. If additional layers are added, the chef d'oeuvre will never materialize. Traumatic events add layers to the child's personality. Instead of chipping away at some of the extraneous character traits to reveal the true self, those additional layers change the blueprint. That blueprint could very well include spending time incarcerated in prison.

Planting Good Seeds

By now, parents are probably scratching their head wondering if they are prepared for this role of parent now that they understand the full job description and qualifications. As you can see, there are so many variables, most of which parents will not have any control over (especially during adolescence). That is why providing conscientious parenting is so important from the start. Ultimately, you will be able to control what is within your parental purview and your sphere will decrease as the child gets older. When your baby is born, you have all of the control and authority. Parents even decide who the baby will associate with such as day care providers. Your job is to plant the seeds, in such a way that they will ultimately sprout independent and productive adults. A parent's job is likened to that of a farmer. The environment in which the farmer plants his crops and how well she takes care of the crops will determine the outcome of the harvest. If the farmer does not plant good seeds and don't take care of the seeds planted, the harvest will be compromised. Reaping a bad crop is exactly what happens when parents neglect to properly care for their children. Planting good seeds in parenting consists of consistently caring for the child, modeling good behavior, and being available for consultation as the child gets older. Children whose needs are not met or are neglected or abused will not have good outcomes. What is most important is that parents understand the need to provide purposeful parenting from the moment the child leaves the womb. There is no time to waste. Keep in mind that the totality of the childhood experience will ultimately be a story that the child will tell over and over. It is not uncommon for people to ask me even today, What was your childhood like? Sometimes I offer stories on my childhood, especially the good stories. Our stories define who we are whether we want them to or not. What will your children's stories tell about you?

Family: The Incubator

Parents should be mindful of events that may result in trauma to the child. What is trauma? I am glad you asked. Trauma is a type of damage to the mind that occurs as a result of a severely distressing event. Very often, trauma is the result of an overwhelming amount of stress that exceeds one's ability to cope. Overall, trauma is an emotional response to a terrible event such as violence, physical or sexual abuse, death of a loved one, domestic violence, natural disasters, or an accident. Childhood trauma often refers to trauma that occurs prior to six years of age. Trauma can result in the person having flashbacks, may lead to troubled relationships, and even physical symptoms such as head or stomach aches.

When children under twelve are brought into juvenile hall, probation intake workers work very hard to release them as soon as possible. It is believed that removing young children from the detention center quickly would prevent the negative exposure that results from interacting with older and possibly more sophisticated detainees. Unfortunately, in the haste to release young offenders, probation workers miss the opportunity to [thoroughly] assess what social, emotional, or physical issues may have led the child to act in such a way to bring them into juvenile hall. Many of the youth that I served in the juvenile justice system were repeat offenders. Even during the first contact with probation, in most cases, the youth would disclose that they committed community misconduct at least one other time before being arrested and referred to the probation department. Therefore, it is important that parents are *proactive* in addressing juvenile delinquency, by acquiring the knowledge, skills, abilities, and resources to prevent delinquency instead of waiting until their children became involved in the juvenile justice system. By understanding normal childhood development stages, parents would be able to anticipate developmental stages and milestones, and respond appropriately when challenges arise.

Understanding normal childhood development will prevent the chances of negative childhood occurrences. Research has shown that adverse childhood experiences (ACE) results in emotional problems such as stress, anxiety, and depression as well as physical ailments later in life. Very often, these emotional problems are manifested by acting-out behavior. Adverse experiences are different from mere uncomfortable events. For example, children are punished for acting-out behavior. They may have their toys taken away or not permitted to attend a classmate's party after failing to clean their rooms. These losses of privileges scenarios are undesirable and disappointing but will not cause a traumatic reaction. However, examples of adverse childhood experiences, which include domestic violence, divorce, substance-abusing parents, death of a loved one, and sexual and physical abuse, may potentially cause emotional problems. Accordingly, it is very important that parents have as much information at their fingertips as possible to permit them to conscientiously raise their children in the most favorable environments possible. Throughout the decades that I spent serving families, many of the youth and their parents shared traumatic experiences that preceded the youth's involvement in the criminal justice system. The parents did not recognize the events as traumatic, and even some childcare professionals may not have identified those events as harmful either. Therefore, many of the parents did not even consider getting counseling for their child. During my tenure as a probation officer, I recall three siblings that witnessed the death of their father during a domestic violence incident. The father was stabbed and the children, who were in another bedroom at the time, came into the room where the father lay bleeding to death and crying out to the children to not let him die. Because the kids panicked, they did not call emergency medical teams; instead, they called their grandmother, who initially didn't answer the phone. When she finally answered the repeatedly ringing phone, she implored the kids to call 911. By the time the medical team arrived, the dad had bled to death. The death of the father was traumatic for the children. This event classifies as an adverse childhood event. The children—nine, twelve, and sixteen—at the time, never received counseling. All three were subsequently engaged in community misconduct.

A great percentage of juvenile-justice-involved youth have a history of trauma and suffering from post-traumatic stress symptoms. One study found that 90 percent of youth in the juvenile justice system had experienced at least one traumatic event, but many have suffered many traumatic events in different areas of their lives (poly-victimization). Interpersonal trauma or traumas that occur in the home are highly detrimental. An example of interpersonal trauma is physical or emotional abuse and domestic violence. Many of these traumatized youth meet the criteria for post-traumatic stress syndrome as defined in the Diagnostic Statistical Manual (DSM-V) of mental disorders. The juvenile justice system is not prepared to respond to youth with mental health problems nor should they be. These youth need targeted, assessment-driven services that have been proven to effectively address trauma. Traumatized youth, who end up in juvenile justice detention facilities, are retraumatized. Juvenile detention staff who are not trained to recognize and address post-traumatic stress symptoms such as irritability, arousal, and reactivity may respond punitively, thus further traumatizing the youth. According to the Diagnostic Statistical Manual V (DSM V), children who have experienced trauma may act impulsively, are easily triggered, and constantly in fight-or-flight mode. While in detention facilities, juvenile corrections officers often respond harshly to these manifestations of trauma.

It is important to note that although parents are answerable for providing the best environments that will permit a child to thrive and ultimately mature into a productive adult, during my tenure in the criminal justice system, I became keenly aware that all parents did not have equal access to the knowledge and resources that would decrease the chance that their child would not be traumatized. Some parents had easy access to the necessary tools and resources that will assure positive outcomes for their children, and some parents were restricted due to time and finances. Accordingly, the parents I served did the best they could with the resources they had. When I served as an intake probation officer, I recall that by the time some youth would appear for their first detention hearing, some parents would have secured counseling and even an alternate school program for their child. These actions would reduce the need to further detain the youth. These parents could satisfactorily show the court that they cared, they were involved, they were willing to invest time and finances, and they were present. However, some parents would not have the resources or knowledge to provide the needed resources, so some children would remain in detention longer to allow probation to arrange those services that would minimize the risk of further community misconduct or trauma. I recall reaching out to some parents to advise that their child was in custody, and would get no answer. The parents would be unavailable and very often it was because the parent was at work. Some parents had jobs that would not allow them to take off easily. In addition to understanding developmental milestones additionally knowing the impact of how negative events impact childhood development will reduce the amount of trauma children experience. As noted in the story of the three kids who witnessed the death of their father, trauma is often the gateway to the criminal justice system. Parents must raise their children in such a way that adverse experiences are minimized.

Improving the familial and childhood experiences for youth is consistent with my goal of reducing the number of kids entering the juvenile justice system and later the criminal justice system. The re-traumatization that occurs in detention centers results in a vicious cycle. Children who may be responding to adverse childhood experiences may end up in juvenile hall as a result of not getting their needs met in their family of origin. Once in juvenile hall, they are re-traumatized, which exacerbates their problematic behavior. Therefore, youth who would have naturally transitioned out of the juvenile justice system end up remaining in the system longer. Instead of being integrated back to their families and communities better emotionally equipped to deal with what may be an adverse environment, youth are further traumatized in juvenile detention facilities and later end up in the criminal justice system. Involvement in the criminal justice system is like a dead-end road that leads to destruction people who get involved in the criminal justice system have a difficult time getting back on track and often return to crime. Educating parents on how to raise highly effective children will ultimately reduce the number of people entering the criminal system. An incubator is an enclosed apparatus providing a controlled environment for the care and protection of premature or unusually small babies, an apparatus used to hatch eggs or grow microorganisms under controlled conditions. Just like an infant who spends time in an incubator, parents, along with the family, must be the enclosed all-encompassing and controlled environment that provides the protective factors needed for a child to grow emotionally and physically, and to assure the child gets all the nutrients needed to thrive.

The Childhood Story

While serving probation clients, I routinely asked them about their childhood experiences. Many of the clients reported that they did not have a stable or consistent relationship with their parents when they were young. Very often, one or both of the parents were not consistently present during the client's younger years. Some of my probation clients have told stories of longing to have their parents around. According to many of my probation clients, their parents' absence resulted in a variety of traumatic experiences. Kids have gone days without food; they had to wear dirty clothes and they were teased. One person reported that because her mother was not home to comb her hair, she had to wear a hat to school. On one of those occasions, at some point during the day, someone pulled the hat off, resulting in a team of laughter at her frayed hair. I have had some children report that they were often embarrassed because their parents did not show up to an important event. Kids have missed field trips because parents were unavailable to sign the permission slip. Some kids report that on Halloween, they had to sit in the office during the parade because their absentee parent had religious beliefs that did not support wearing costumes. However, the religious tradition was not explained or practiced due to the parents' absence. All the kid understood was that they could not participate in the parade. I have had probation clients tell me there were times when they were in so much emotional pain and all they wanted was for their parent to ask them what happened. Several of my probation clients revealed to me that there were times when they arrived home with black eyes or scratches on their faces, but the parent never asked what happened. These experiences are traumatic and register in the childhood story as painful memories that had a negative impact on the child's development. In many cases, traumatic experiences can change to trajectory of a child's life. I have interviewed families who describe a child as very gifted in school and talented in other areas of their lives. However, the parents or child will point out that "all of a sudden" things changed and the child started "acting out." As a therapist, it is usually my job to figure out what was the "all of a sudden" event that happened. Unfortunately, all too often, "what happened" is never revealed to the probation officer, therefore continued delinquency is the means in which the child will act out their pain.

Ideally, prior to having kids, parents should understand what trauma is and its impact on childhood development. Some parents believe that their kids are too young to understand or be impacted by negative experiences. Parents erroneously surmise that kids are not even paying attention during negative domestic events. However, the research supports that trauma can effectively delay or permanently stop childhood development. Again, examples of traumatic events that can negatively impact development are family violence, substance abuse, death of a parent, witnessing a murder or violence, divorce, and moving out of a long-established residence and neighborhood. Although it is understood that some of these events are unavoidable, it is important that parents identify stressors and traumatic events and support the child through the process. Parents should not wait until the child begins to act out before they address stressful events.

Parents should be proactive, and if the need arises, the parent can execute a plan of action. Oakland, California, was the largest service area in the probation department where I served. Oakland has been ranked as one of the deadliest cities in the country. For many of the kids I served, violence and death was all too common. Although some of the kids would describe these traumatic events as commonplace, even if my client minimized the event, I was aware that hearing about a friend whom you had just "hung with" a day or even hours prior to their murder is traumatic. Having your friend die in your arms while bleeding out is traumatic. Playing around with a firearm and accidentally discharging it and killing your friend, or watching a friend kill him or herself is traumatic. However, many of these kids have never sought out support because it was not the masculine thing to do or parents were oblivious to the repressed pain. Parents should have a big role in the childhood story. As children get older, the parents' part in the child's story will become smaller. As kids get older, their friends become more important. However, parents must check in and if they see a change in the child's attitude and behavior, they should be prepared to intervene. Three of my children are adults. When we are together, they enjoy telling stories and some fables about their childhood. Usually the stories cast dispersions on my parenting in the moment. Usually the stories end in a burst of laughter. I have had to apologize at the end of some of those stories because even though they are told in amusement, sometimes there is a hint of pain. I will discuss the need to apologize in the section entitled "Courageous Conversations."

A lot of information has been shared. It is likely that for some people reading the book so far, parenting seems multifaceted, daunting, overwhelming, burdensome, tiresome, and anxiety-producing, to name a few adjectives. You are right, parenting is all of the above and more and must be taken seriously. However, parenting is manageable. The knowledge, skills, and abilities of parenting can be learned because parenting is an art and not a science. Allow me to provide some tangible information that will make the parenting journey more adaptable.

Parenting: Art vs. Science

Although I am far beyond childbearing age, I would be an awesome parent today if I would start my parenting journey with the knowledge that I learned while on my parenting journey. It is true that hindsight is perfect vision because I now see clearly what needs to happen to raise successful children. It would be wonderful to start all over again with all my acquired knowledge. Unfortunately, if I had a baby at my age, all the media attention and interviews that would result from the unlikelihood at the very least, and the overall freakiness of a person of my age having a baby, would not allow me the time to raise the kid. I would have to sign countless autographs, take many pictures, and alas, prepare my biographical sketch for the *Guinness World Book of Records.* Therefore, I will have to settle for writing a book and giving my readers the benefit of my valuable experience and the experience of thousands of parents I served in probation and clinical practice. And like the surgeon who has lost at least one patient, the shared experience of my parenting journey and that of others has resulted in my being more informed and deliberate in my parenting skills. Therefore, I would like to share the art of parenting.

My experience taught me that *parenting is not based on rocket scien*ce; so there is no need for the instructions manual that many parents wish they had. *Parenting is more akin to an art that parents can study and easily acquire.* An art is distinguished from science. Wikipedia defines science as any systematic knowledge base or prescriptive practice that is capable of resulting in a prediction or predictable type of outcome. When parenting children, there are no precise rules to follow that will lead to predictable outcomes in every situation. There is no precise formula that identifies the right amount of love, affection, discipline, etc. Science requires that a behavior be repeated over and over with the exact same quality and results. Raising children will never lend itself to the exact same level of quality consistently for eighteen years, especially if a parent has more than one trial (child). Parents and life circumstances change. There are too many variables, including age, mood, climate, culture, peers, and society, to name but a few. Many parents of multiple children cannot understand why one child or maybe all but one child appears to adjust well, but then one will come along and appear to be alien to the family. I explained to many parents that children are different, in part, because circumstances are different in the family's life. What was happening when one child is being raised may change during the early years of another child. For example, the socio-economic status of parents change. One child can be raised during a time when the family's financial resources are limited, and another child may be born during a time when the family has gained wealth or vice versa. Other circumstances that may impact the development of a child is the marital status of the parents. Parents who are together when one child is born may have separated by the time another child is born. Single-parent families have different dynamics. Understanding the fact that family structure changes and other dynamics of family life is part of the art of parenting. Webster's dictionary defines art as "skill acquired by experience, study, or observation." A skill is the ability to use one's knowledge effectively and readily in execution or performance. Parenting is an art in the true sense of the word. This is great news for parents who are asking for a parenting manual. You don't need a manual, you just need to understand the many components of the art of parenting.

The Power of the Relationship

You probably have seen advertisements promising to show you how to shed 20 pounds in just four hours without changing your diet or walking one mile. You get so excited because eating thousands of calories a day and losing weight at the same time is a dream come true. However, you have to sit through an hour's presentation watching someone draw pictures of what they are saying all the way to the end and then you get the answer. Oftentimes, in order for you to get the answer, you have to pull out your credit card and buy a product that you can only get online in the next ten minutes and the clock starts clicking down. I promise this will not be one of those books. I will give you the answer upfront. The single most effective strategy, resource, or tool a parent has at his disposal for successfully navigating their children through childhood to adulthood and assuring that they don't end up in the criminal justice system is . . . wait for it . . . *the parent-and-child relationship.* That is correct. There is nothing to purchase because everything a successful parents needs is present at birth. Initially parents will have to gain an understanding of the developmental phases of childhood. Once parents learn the changes that occur during each phase and how to handle them, parenting becomes easy. Books that teach parents what will happen in a certain situation are usually very successful because people want to know what to expect. The parent-child relationship is like money in the bank.

The Currency of the Parent-Child Relationship

The parent-child relationship can be compared to a bank account. The amount of money in the account at any given time is dependent on the deposit and withdrawal history. If there are more withdrawals than deposits, that could ultimately bankrupt the account. To put it plainly, if you take out more than you put in, there will not be any money in the account. As soon as parents begin their parenting journey, they begin adding and subtracting from the relationship (account). Parents have the potential to begin their parent-child relationship with a lot of currency. The added currency comes from responding to the child's basic needs (not wants) and consistently being available. However, also similar to the checking account, if you don't put love, energy, attention, respect, or presence into the relationship, then you will not have love, energy, attention, respect to take out. There are specific times during the month when my checking account is used more often. At a certain time of the month, my mortgage and insurance bills are due and I grocery shop. However, there are other times when my account is inert. During that time, I cannot spend. My suggestion is that parents seize upon every opportunity they can to add money to the relationship account. That means you should be there for your kids when you can, catch your kids doing something nice, no matter how rare the occurrences, and compliment them. Listen to them when they want to talk. Be nice, compliment their hair, their choice of colors even if the outfit is hideous. Look for reasons to say nice things. If they finally cut their hair but it is still too long, compliment that at least the hair is going down (or up) in the right direction. Remember how you complimented your young kids for *everything*. Remember when kids were really young and you complimented them on how well they could hop on one foot. Recall how proud your child was when you would say that his drawing was beautiful—although you had to ask what it was—you still managed to tell that little child that it was beautiful? Remember how excited you were to see how well they could write their names even though the letters were all different sizes and some were backward and still others were unrecognizable? Remember you complimented your child on how big their poop was? Go back to that. Kids still need validation. Even adults want to hear that their work is above average. When I worked as a probation officer, I was pretty confident about my performance; however, I looked forward to getting my annual appraisal and seeing all the good things my supervisor had to say about my work. I would offhandedly mention to my colleagues that I had earned an "exceeds performance standards" evaluation. Kids need to be validated, especially by the people that mean the most to them. As Charles Swindoll stated, "Each day of our lives we make deposits in the memory banks of our children." Barbara Johnson also understood the need to have extended periods of quality time with your children. She wrote, "To be in your children's memories tomorrow, you have to be in their lives today." Parents, you will decide the amount and the quality of your child's childhood memories. Put currency in the relationship account.

Chapter Two

PARENTAL ROLES

Next, parents should understand that the art of parenting involves three responsibilities, role model, teacher, and consultant. A *role model* is someone who is exhibiting positive traits in an effort to influence the same behavior. A good role model is someone looked at by others as one to be imitated. When kids are born, a parent's initial responsibility is to be a good role model because kids ultimately do what you do, not what you say. Recall that one of the primary premises of this book is that parents do the best that they can at any given moment with the resources they have; however, conscientious parenting requires parents to walk the walk that they talk. Mahatma Gandhi understood what it meant to be a role model; one of his most popular sayings is, *"Be the change you want to see."* This could not be more true than when it comes to raising children. Parents must start the parenting journey with a vision of their child becoming a productive, self-sufficient, law-abiding adult. The blueprint to making that vision a reality is in the parent or primary caretaker. The parents' ability to adopt and model the habits of highly effective people will determine if the children will internalize the habits. By adopting the productive habits, parents will automatically model the behavior for their children. The parent, who is usually the first and the most consistent person in the child's life, becomes the model for behavior. Children will imitate the parent's behavior similar to how birds imprint on their parent or whoever becomes the most consistent person in the child's life. I will discuss this topic further in the book.

Patience is an important skill that kids need to learn. Like the imprinting duckling, kids learn patience from their parents or primary caretaker. How do you respond when you have to wait in long lines? *Do you shrug it off and say, it is what it is, or do you complain the whole time as thought life should not involve waiting?* Ideally, you will verbally strategize on how to avoid situations that make you uncomfortable. For example, while waiting in line, you could say, I wish I had brought a book to read or next time, I am going to grocery shop when the store is likely to be less crowded. By saying this, you are modeling the habit of proactivity. I know this is a stretch for some people, but you could also use the time as a teachable moment for your kids or forget about the line and the people and use the time to have a conversation. By doing this, you are offering you and your child a win-win experience.

Patience can also be modeled by parents when faced with everyday problems. I recall when I was very young that if I would hurt myself on an inanimate object such as a bedpost, my grandmother would hit the bedpost and say, "Bad bedpost . . . don't you hurt my baby!" My mother and grandmother would consistently do this with me and all of my siblings. We in turn responded the same way when our children would get hurt. It was not until years later during my training as a therapist that I learned that blaming inanimate objects for my pain was transferring responsibility for my behavior. By ascribing blame to a non-thinking, non-acting, and basically a non-human, I may have learned to be angry at an outside entity when things hurt me. This is just a non-empirical hunch. However, what I do know is that sometimes when I get hurt, I look for outside blame. For instance, whenever I trip and almost fall (which I do more often than the average walking adult), I look at the floor with disdain for a few moments. Oftentimes, there is nothing there that could have caused my stumble or that could have impeded me from walking upright. In spite of this, I look at a perfectly even ground or floor and roll my eyes. Recently I dropped a bottle on my toe. Obviously it hurt very bad and I found myself very angry at the bottle. After getting air back in my lungs, I picked up the bottle and threw it aggressively in the trash. After going to the doctor and learning I had fractured my toe, I thought very negatively about that bottle. I even showed people the type of bottle that had broken my toe as if I were trying to get everyone else to be mad at the bottle. The bottom line is, initially I ascribed full responsibility for the pain in my toe to that lifeless bottle when I should have been angry at myself for trying to carry more to the recycling bin than I could handle effectively. It was entirely my fault for dropping the only heavy and glass item that I had in my hands at the time. It was also my fault that I didn't put on shoes prior to going outside. There was no bad bottle. Positive role modeling is an important strategy to raising kids. Role modeling is the first skill that parents will utilize when raising kids. Role modeling starts at birth, at which time the imprinting process likened to that of ducklings begins.

Students learn what they care about, from people they care about, and who they know care about them.
~Barbara Harrell Carson

The next role that a parent will find themselves is that of a *teacher.* A teacher is also known as an educator, tutor, or instructor. Parents are a child's first teacher, and the teaching begins as soon as kids leave the womb. However, once kids are school-age, they are influenced by outside teachers so the parent needs to turn into an earnest and consistent instructor. I don't mean passive teaching; parents need to really be "in their kid's faces" and engaged with the child. A teacher is someone who guides, mentors, directs, and, of course, teaches. The role of teacher requires a parent to be very active. Once kids become school-age, they will come into contact with many other adults and power figures that will have an effect on the child's development. Parents must neutralize these new authorities. At the very least, parents must be mindful of the contact that their kids have with other people because these people can impact their lives. At school age, kids are soaking up information and they will draw from any available source, good or bad. I know it sounds like I am describing solar panels, but it's actually a great analogy.

To respond to the child's desire for persistent information, parents need to gird up and get ready to constantly give out information. Parents are in the best position to provide the information to their children because as Barbara Harrell Carson stated so eloquently, *Students learn what they care about, from people they care about, and who they know care about them.* If you know any teachers, you are aware of how exhausting the job is. *I am reminded of little Joey whom I met in a hotel hot tub while on vacation. When I arrived at the hot tub, my desire was to relax and enjoy the jets pulsating against my aching back. Within a few minutes, a man got in the tub along with his son, who I would soon learn was little Joey. After smiling and exchanging pleasantries, I resumed my relaxed position. Soon, the teaching began. Joey asked how come the water was so hot. Dad explained, in detail, how the hot and cold water operated. Joey asked where the bubbles came from. Dad explained the jets and how the electricity caused the operation of the jets. Of course Joey wanted to know exactly what jets were. Dad did his best to really explain. Of course, Joey, finally decided that he needed to know who was sharing the bathtub with them. Dad explained I was a guest in the hotel just like they were. Joey asked my name. I opened my eyes and told him. He wanted to know where my dad was and why I was alone. The best part of the conversation happened when the dad interjected quickly and asked Joey, "What did I tell you about invading people's space?" Joey said that, "It was inappropriate?" Dad confirmed and Joey immediately apologized. What most impressed me is that Joey understood, albeit at a basic level, that inappropriate meant unsuitable. Wasn't that a great vocabulary word on which to build? As a hotel guest wanting to relax in a hot tub, I was exhausted by the time the questioning stopped. But as a parent educator, I was pleased with the job Dad was doing in the teacher role. Joey's dad was doing exactly what he should be doing. Joey had a young brain that was soaking up all that great information on water, jets, electricity, and the social skill of appropriateness to boot. Joey needed all that information because he will assimilate and incorporate the information into life skills later in life. As for me, because I am old[er] and my brain is no longer a sponge but more like an impermeable pumice stone, my brain shut down and I wouldn't or couldn't take any more novelty so I had to leave the warmth of the hot tub. I told Joey that it was nice meeting him. I complimented Dad on how well he was teaching Joey and I got in the bathtub in my hotel room.*

Joey's dad was on duty. Unlike schoolteachers, for parents, there are no weekends, fall, spring, or summer breaks. Parents must stay in the role, more like character, at all times. In addition to the teaching, the parent of a school-age child must also spend a lot of time directing, re-directing, and guiding their child. Although the child may appear to be independent, the parent must be very vigilant and constantly monitoring their child. During the teaching stage, parenting, when it is done right, is exhausting!

The role of *consultant* is the final role that parents will undertake while parenting their children, and it is a role that some parents find most difficult into which to transition. Why? I am so glad you asked.

Consulting is difficult because, unlike teaching, consulting is hands off and parents experience a void in their own lives because they are so used to teaching and directing. Once parents transition into the consultant role, they fear a loss of control. *A loss of control for parents and an increase in control for adolescents is actually a developmental milestone.* By the time your child reaches adolescence, you have put in a lot of work laying a strong foundation, and now it is time to sit back and watch your kids maneuver their own lives by putting the teaching tools into action. A consultant offers expert advice. Unlike the professional consultant, parents gained their expertise from experience, not books and education. I have told every young person that have consulted with me that I am only an expert because I have experience and not because I am any better than they are. I tell my advisees that I have been the age that they are already and have mastered it as evidenced by my being alive to tell about it. For the teens that I have advised, I say that the only reason I know what I know is because I have had fifteen, twenty, or even thirty years on the road of life longer than they have. Some of the things that kids, adolescents, or young adults are experiencing, I have addressed and either mastered or learned by trial and error. Parents must make sure their kids understand that they are only in a position to advise and consult because you have experienced life and similar issues that are confronting the child. A word of caution. Don't lead your kids to believe that you always did the right thing because that would be dishonest. The truth will come out of the closet at some point. Emphasize all the good decisions you have made and talk about the bad ones if necessary. Tell your kids that because you have had some successes and made some mistakes, now at the ripe old age of now, you can attest to the fact that "you know what you know and you are sharing it with one of most important people in the world." One final note about consultants, they are similar to clinicians in that the goal is not to tell the person what to do; instead, you are hoping to lead them to discovery. Consultants, like counselors, empower their clients by allowing them to discover their own meaning and solutions. Likewise, once a child reaches adolescence, parents must allow them to discover their own way with guidance.

There are some cases when parents find themselves in the position of role model, teacher, and consultant all in the same encounter; however, all parenting behavior should fall under these three rubrics at the appropriate time. Therefore, when parents are engaging with their children, they should be able to identify whether they are being an effective role model, teacher, or consultant. If, upon examination, you are engaging in another role, such as friend, adversary, or business partner, the parent must reposition themselves. I must add a concluding comment about parents as friends. Many parents have asked me whether it is okay for their kids to be their friend, or best friend, or only friend. My response is always the same: no, you will never be your child's friend, especially best friend for life (bffl). Friends are defined as companion, soul mate, intimate confidante, playmate, schoolmate, workmate. You must always remain in the parent role. It is okay to be friendly, have fun times together, socialize and share hobbies, but you will always do these things from the perspective of a parent-and-child relationship. Don't expect your child to share everything with you. He or she should have friends to share with.

Lessons from the Field

When I was the superintendent of a detention facility, one of the young men shared that his parents had been together since middle school. As a matter of fact, the mother was fifteen and the father was fourteen years old when the young man was born. This was bittersweet for the young man. Although the parents had never married, and both were in subsequent relationships, the parents made a conscientious decision to co-parent their son. The parents attended all meetings and visiting hours. The mother always dominated the conversations, and the young man rarely spoke in her presence. However, in the detention center program, the young man was actually quite verbose. One day I talked to the young man and told him of my observation of his dual personality. He volunteered that he didn't like to talk a lot around his mother because she always takes over the conversation. He went on to say that she is always hanging around his friends and even likes to go out with them to parties. I asked the young man whether he had ever discussed his feelings with his mother, and when he said he had not, he invited me to talk to her. When I discussed the issue with the kid's mother, she conceded that she enjoys spending time with her son and his friends because she didn't have an opportunity to "party" when she was younger since she became a mother so soon. She said that most of her friends no longer wanted to go out and party, so instead she spent time with her son's friends. I had to explain to her that parents must remain in the parent role so that their children will respect their authority. However, if she and her son were "going-out buddies," it will be difficult to discipline him when necessary. The mother reluctantly agreed to separate her parent and partying roles.

Four Premises of Parenting

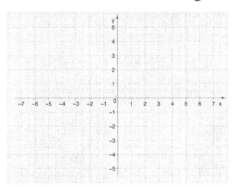

Up to this point, the information that I have provided so far was provided to prepare you for your role as parent. I am hopeful that by defining the parent, their role as the giver of life, the critical nature of the parent-child relationship, and the primary roles that parents play that parents would be prepared for the role they will play as parent.

I want to conclude the discussion on the parent role by giving you four facts. During the three decades that I spent serving families, I learned four undeniable truths. First, although it has been supported by research that parents and caretakers play a critical role in assuring that children come out of childhood with the knowledge, skills, and abilities to become highly successful adults, this is not a book that judges parents. The most important and main premises of this book is that *parents do the best that they can at any given moment with the resources they have.* Therefore, informed parents will provide wise parenting, and ill-informed parents will offer less-than-effective parenting. My goal in writing this book is to level the playing field between effective and not-so-effective parents. The information provided in this book will assure that all parents who read the book will be exposed to information that will allow them to provide effective, age-appropriate, and courageous parenting strategies.

It is also supported by research that actions speak louder than words. In other words (no pun intended), a person's actions say much more about their message, beliefs, values, intentions, etc. than their words. The point that actions are more profound than mere words has been advanced in many wonderful quotes such as: "Actions prove who someone is. Words just prove who they want to be." "Don't fall in love with someone who says nice things. Fall in love with someone who does right things." "Characterize people by their actions not by their words." My favorite is "People who care use words to express. People who care more use their actions." This last quote is most poignant when it comes to parenting. I guess to put it plainly, when you are parenting, you have to be authentic and, as my probation kids like to say, "You have to come correct." Kids recognize inauthenticity or what they refer to as fake. So parents who present one way in speech and another in action will have kids who ultimately act like they do. Accordingly, the second premise to the book is that *kids will do what you do, not what you say.*

The third premise to this book is that *kids must be raised not parented*. If you look up the definition of a parent, you will find that it means *to be or act like a mother or a father*. The definition is a noun as it gives a title. The term implies that you don't have to do any more than be given the designation of parent or take on the role of mother or father. However, if you look up the term "to raise (a child)," you will see an action definition that means to bring up, look after, take care of, rear. To raise a child, parents must commit to actively engage with the child and stay in the parent role until they are successful young adults. In most states, the age of majority is eighteen years old. Eighteen years sounds like a long time; however, having raised three to adulthood, I can say from experience that the time goes really fast.

The final premise of this book does not need much elaboration. **Your children come through you, not to you.** It is your job to raise them in such a way that they are capable of leaving home and living on their own productively, successfully, and not remain in your care or end up in the criminal justice system.

Before you move on to the next chapter, I want you to google the song "If I Could" by Regina Belle. This song epitomizes the parent's dilemma, and yet the lyrics offers the appropriate role parents must adopt at the very moment the child is born. I am adding a few of the lyrics that capture the message of the song:

> "If I could
> I would try to shield
> Your innocence
> From time
> But the part of life
> I gave you isn't mine
> I'll watch you grow
> So I can let you go"

Chapter Three

THE NINE HABITS OF PEOPLE WHO DO NOT END UP IN THE CRIMINAL JUSTICE SYSTEM

Now that you know your roles, you are ready to know exactly what skills you must model, teach, and nurture via consultation in order to raise effective adults that do not end up in the criminal justice system. In 1989 best-selling author Stephen Covey authored a book called *The 7 Habits of Highly Effective People.* It was promoted as a self-help book for parents. The book outlined seven internalized values or habits that, if followed, would result in children matriculating into productive adults: Be proactive. Begin with the end in mind. Put first things first. Think win-win. Seek first to understand and then to be understood. Synergize. Sharpen the Saw. I didn't read the book until I was well into adulthood and I was already working in corrections, my chosen career field; therefore, I felt like I was an effective adult. However, I thought, what the heck, it is never too late to learn. As I read through the seven habits, I realized that I understood and even possessed the same values; however, I did not consistently and conscientiously follow the seven habits. As I incorporated the habits into my life (albeit, it started out slow and I fell off the wagon many times, okay, I still fall off the wagon), I realized that I was more productive when I applied the skills. I also found that I experienced less stress, and using the skills definitely helped me avoid a lot of trouble. For example, one of the values are to put first things first. This skill required that I prioritize big and small details of my life. What a lifesaver that skill has been for me. Sometimes I have so many competing responsibilities. I use to try and complete them all. However, reading *The 7 Habits of Highly Effective People* taught me that some things are more important than others, and I should start with the most important things, and then if I get to lesser important tasks, I feel successful; however, if I don't make it to the least important tasks on my list but effectively manage the important items, I feel a sense of success at the end of the day. In other words, I feel effective and I don't stress. Usually the items positioned at the end of my list are the inconsequential. Lo and behold, in 1997 I read another life-changing booked entitled *Don't Sweat the Small Stuff* written by Dr. Richard Carlson. In that book one very important lesson I learned is that every day could be my last day alive. I realized by reading that book that on my very last day on earth, there will not only be things left undone, but also none of the things I thought mattered will matter. *There is one thing that I could not rationalize away because I was sure that on my very last day on earth, I will want my relationships with my family, especially my children, to be intact. I don't believe that I will be at peace with regrets regarding raising them.* That knowledge put everything in the right perspective for me and helped me become a more effective person and an even more effective parent.

After having been enlightened by the skills necessary to become an effective adult, I was eager to share the habits with my clients and the parents of my juvenile clients. Once I became a probation manager, I shared the skills with my staff. Convincing adults to change their attitudes and behaviors with respect to raising their kids requires courage. Adults don't like other adults telling them how to parent their kids, no matter what authority you are working under. I often shared with my staff who were working with juvenile offenders that they would have to have courageous conversations with parents. Some of my staff resisted because they tried to avoid confrontation. Some of my staff felt these conversations were futile as adults are "set in their ways." Still others held the view that some parents were just unfit to raise kids and the conversation on appropriate parenting skills would be to no avail. In response to my staff who resisted to avoid the likely angry and perhaps aggressive confrontation with parents, I would remind my staff that the Probation Department had spent a lot of money training them on crisis diffusion, verbal judo, self-defense, and other ways of protecting themselves so they may be the only ones courageous and equipped to have the tough conversations. In spite of the annual hours of training that probation counselors and probation officers receive, some of my staff were still not convinced that they could handle the reprisal that may result after advising very angry parents that they, in fact, was contributing to their child's delinquency in one way or the other. So I would tell my staff that if it were truly not received as a teachable moment and all civility and professionalism failed, at least they tried and as the saying goes, "No harm no foul." For some that were just scared to have the conversation, I would offer that they should rely on my last resort, but lifesaving strategy, put the information out there and run!

In Covey's book, he offered seven habits of effective people that I found useful; however, in addition to the seven habits, there were two habits that many of the youth and adults I served were also to be lacking that were directly responsible for them ending up in the criminal justice system. One these habits was delayed gratification, and the other one that was closely aligned was the ability to be content with the word "no." I will outline all of the habits and how parents can incorporate these habits into their attitude and behavior during the parenting process. As is the case with adaptation of other skills that kids will have to learn, parents will initially model, then teach, and ultimately consult and advise their kids on the nine skills.

Habit One

Be Proactive: Know What to Expect When You Are Expecting

Most, if not all, of my probation clients did not expect to end up in custody. Some had given some thought to their behavior but did not think as far as getting arrested, and they especially never visualized that their behavior would result in being in custody. The first habit that Mr. Covey identified in effective people is proactivity. Proactive people are grounded in their values. Accordingly, responses to situations are grounded in the values they hold, and they readily apply them in any given situation. That is why parents must begin to model, teach, and reinforce this skill as soon as the baby comes out of the womb. Being proactive is more than having a plan; being proactive is manifested in action. By reading this book, you may be acting proactively because your children are young or perhaps you don't have children but are planning to someday and you are proactively learning strategies to address the inevitable issues that you will face during the parenting journey. At some point during the parenting process, you may even use reading this book as an example to your kids of how you were being proactive in parenting.

Proactive people create situations by causing something to happen rather than responding to it after it has happened. Being proactive simply means having a plan at all times and to be constantly in pursuit of that plan. We pursue goals all the time without even knowing it. If we are expected to be at work at a certain time each day, we plan our day accordingly, taking various intermediary action steps to proactively reach the goal of getting to work. Therefore, if the plan is to arrive at work at 8 a.m., the decisions regarding what time we get up, prepare to leave, the mode of transportation and the distance must be predetermined to accomplish the larger plan, which is to arrive to work on time. People who fail to plan end up not achieving the larger goal, and in the case of arriving to work on time, run the risk of being late, being written up, or even fired.

My oldest daughter models a lack of proactivity for her children, without even knowing it. I call her each morning when she is en route to take her children to school. Very often, in the middle of our conversation and often midsentence, she will blurt out, "Oh my gosh, what are you doing . . . get out of the way . . . why are you driving so slow . . . people act like they don't have anywhere to go!" My favorite is her response, "Why is it so much traffic out here?" Although there is commuter traffic every morning, my daughter acts surprised that she can't speed to work when she is late. Since she is an adult and my role is simply to be a consultant, I respond, "If you would just leave a few minutes earlier . . ." Her response is typically, "I know, Mom, I planned to but I woke up late."

Planning is not the same thing as proactivity. Planning is a mental state; proactivity is an action. But all is not lost; even if she decides not to be on time and continue getting up early and traumatize her kids while speeding to work, she can say to them, Mom needs to get up and leave earlier. I never know what the traffic is going to be like, so if I get up earlier, we can relax and have a better ride each morning. Modeling proactivity requires that you possess the skill yourself first and then you can be a viewed as a viable teacher and consultant of the skill with experience. So proactivity starts with you, parent. Being proactive means planning ahead for what may come.

Being proactive is the opposite of responding reactively as the latter is usually utilizing the best option in the moment. In my daughter's case, speeding is her only option if she wants to get to work on time. Of course, no one can plan for all things; however, for the things that are inevitable, being proactive is a skill of effective people and a skill that prevents a child from entering the criminal justice system.

Let's start with how having the skill will assist parents to raise effective adults. Having children is one of the life events that parents can model proactivity even prior to conception. Prospective parents, therefore anyone who has the ability to produce a child should start out by conscientiously making a decision to have children. That means birth control must be an important consideration. Barring extenuating circumstances, people are in complete control of whether they will become parents. The absolute means of avoiding having children is abstinence. Other forms of birth control are viable, but none provide the complete certainty of control of conception like abstinence. However, for those people that did not abstain and conception occurred, proactivity is still very important and an effective habit in which to engage.

As soon as expecting parents learn of their impending parenthood, they should begin to plan for the full journey that lies ahead.

Lessons from the Field

The popular book, What to Expect When You're Expecting, *continues to be a best seller for expectant parents and even people who are only contemplating becoming parents. The book reportedly sold over 17 million copies and is hailed as the bible for pregnant woman.*

It is estimated that 90 percent of pregnant women have read the book (I am one of them). The book gives the reader a month-by-month glimpse into what will happen during the pregnancy and the development of the growing fetus. Parents want to know when to expect the fluttering feelings that indicates the baby's movements. Parents want to know what symptoms they will have so they know what is normal. Parents don't only read What to Expect When You're Expecting so they know what to expect; they want to know how to prepare, what they should do, and what to avoid. People read the book to be proactive.

Having an understanding of what to expect when you are expecting should not end at the birth of a child. Parents should keep the momentum going and understand what to expect at each succeeding developmental phase as the child matures to adulthood. Once the baby arrives safely, parents must understand how children process the world during different phases of their lives outside of the womb. There are some parents who are reading this book who conceived very easily and without effort [outside the sexual act itself], and there are some who are reading this book who went through great lengths to conceive or adopt a child. For those parents who prepared, they were likely very careful in how they treated their bodies inside and out. Some parents prepare for pregnancy by changing their diets, exercising, taking in more vitamins; some expectant parents avoid certain chemicals, litter boxes, and once they become pregnant would carefully consider whether they should be in certain areas that could be dangerous for the child, such as crowded places. Examples of proactive thinking during the pregnancy stage may include taking into consideration all the needs of the child: shelter, clothing, food, protection, etc. How will these needs be addressed and by who? Who is in the circle of caretakers? Infants' immune systems are developing, which means babies sometimes get sick often. Parents should have an idea of who will care for the sick child in the event that the parents are working and the primary caretaker is not available. How will medical needs be addressed? Becoming pregnant requires that parents prepare for the next eighteen years. I am not talking about minor plans like what to name the child or how to decorate the nursery. Expectant parents must plan as preparing for an imminent national disaster because having kids will result in many catastrophes, even when raising the best kids. To begin with, some kids are born with challenges. Some kids are born with physical and developmental problems that must be addressed immediately. Most parents don't plan for kids with problems. When we learn we are expecting, most of us assume our children will be perfect, although they are the product of a union of two imperfect people. Children who develop asthma will likely spend many nights in an emergency room. Children who are born with autism will need special care, and the parent will need more respite than parents of children without autism. Don't get me wrong, children with special needs are a gift and beautiful, and they are no better or worse than children without special needs; they just need specialized care. Some children are more active than others so their parents will need to be willing and able to keep up. Some children will not sit in a movie theater for a two-hour film so their parents will need to have a trusting care provider or wait on the parents' favorite movie to come out on DVD. Children with special needs may have to attend special schools. For some parents, this may mean uprooting and moving to an area with schools that are best suited for their child. Parents who have jobs that only offer graveyard shifts will have to arrange evening childcare. I have seen parents who raise their children in shifts. One parent will work during the day and the other at night. This takes a toll on the union because the couple has limited time together; however, the alternating shifts may be the only option. It doesn't matter when you begin to plan ahead; planning ahead can happen at any time your goal is to move emotionally or physically move forward.

In order to avoid ending up in the criminal justice system, children must learn the skill of being proactive. Being proactive is equivalent to having a plan, and parents should introduce this skill to their children sooner than later. The skill will become increasingly important as the child gets older. Parents can demonstrate the proactivity by having the car serviced prior to a long road trip. In anticipation of a storm, parents can go to the grocery store. Demonstrating proactivity can be as little as preparing school lunches the evening before to avoid running late in the morning. Reading a book on parenting demonstrates proactivity. The main point is that the parent engages in a conversation with the child and let them know that all of the actions are for sake of planning ahead. Once children enter the period of adolescence, they will naturally have more freedom and mobility so the value of having a plan will need to be firmly grounded. The following is an example of how to teach and encourage proactivity.

Four year-old Marcus says to his dad, "I want to climb that big tree over there. It looks like it is 100 feet tall! Can I, Dad, please?" Dad replies, "That tree is really high and the branches are far apart. How will you reach the branches?" Dad also asks, "Once you get to the top of the tree, how will you get down?" After a few fictional exchanges, including little Marcus suggesting that he fly from branch to branch like his favorite hero, Dad can finally convince little Marcus that there is no efficient plan for climbing the tree.

An example for an older child may proceed as follows: Fourteen-year-old Megan asks her mother if she can go swimming the day before a wedding where she will be a junior bridesmaid. Her mother responds, "But you are getting your hair specially styled for the wedding the day before the wedding. Swimming would destroy the hairstyle. What is your plan for maintaining the hairstyle while swimming?" Megan draws her own conclusion that swimming the day before the wedding is not an option.

Proactive thinking is a gateway skill to forward thinking. This type of thinking involves planning for the future. Successful adults must live for today but plan for tomorrow. Forward thinking is contrary to the adages, "Living for the moment, or live for the day," which are philosophies embraced by many people, especially in today's younger generations. **However, living for today while planning for tomorrow** (and even later) is a better option if, by some chance, tomorrow does in fact comes. The problem with only living for the day is that you don't take into consideration that there may be a tomorrow, and if tomorrow shows up, there needs to be provisions.

Being proactive also means having an alternate plan, also known as plan B. It makes sense that plan B is an alternate plan since B comes after A in the alphabet, but I digress. Having a plan should include having a backup plan if in fact the well-thought-out plan A is no longer an option. Another way parents can develop the proactive skill in their children is to often ask the question, "What is your plan B?" Let's return to the tree climber. Once Marcus indicates he will fly from branch to branch and learns that humans don't fly, you can ask, how else can you navigate that tree using real-life human skill? At some point, the parent will guide Marcus to the conclusion that he will not be able to climb a tree. For Megan who wants to swim before the wedding, she may suggest getting up very early the next morning and having her hair re-done in spite of the fact that it costs a lot of money. When you explain that you will not pay for a second hairstyling, Megan will likely conclude that swimming the day of the wedding is not an option. The point is that the skill of proactivity is a learned behavior and parents should take advantage of teachable moments. One final note on proactivity; kids must understand the full consequences of their choices. So while explaining the consequences of behavior, parents must outline the good, bad, and the ugly.

Lessons from the Field

Whenever I conducted an intake on a new probation client who was in custody for the first time, he or she would always say that if I would release them, they would never commit the offense that resulted in them being in custody again. My clients always learned their lesson after the fact. They would acknowledge that they had not been proactive and did not foresee the negative outcome of their crime. Because I know that the ability to think abstractly and foresee cause and effect is a skill that develops with maturity, if my client did not pose a risk to the community or themselves, I would often take my new client at their word and release them. However, for my clients who had been arrested on more than one occasion, and sometimes for the same type of behavior, I could not give them the benefit of the doubt. Even young concrete thinkers can make the connection that action "A" results in outcome "B" after one adverse experience. Therefore, whenever I would encounter a repeat offender client in juvenile hall tearfully begging for me to release them, I would usually help them to make the abstract connection that they were in fact being proactive, but they failed to take the full consequences of their behavior into consideration. You see, many of my repeat offender clients limited their plan of securing the fruits of their crimes but neglected to factor in the possibility of being caught.

In the late 1980s and early 1990s, many young men were being arrested for drug sales. My young clients would spend many hours each day on residential corners waiting for people who wanted to purchase crack cocaine, a controlled substance and felony offense. My clients could make several thousands of dollars in a short period of time selling drug. However, if they were arrested, this was a major social and financial setback. Not only were my young clients unable to make any more money, they would have to spend time in custody. For some of my adult offenders, having a felony conviction meant the loss of many privileges such as the ability to apply for certain jobs and the loss of the constitutional right to vote. I would always remind my clients that they must be proactive, and in doing so, consider all of the possible consequences of their actions. If any of the possible outcomes were not favorable, they should not engage in the behavior.

When my clients would engage in forward thinking but would not consider the full ramifications of their decisions, I would reinforce the principle using my favorite adage, *"If you do the crime, you must be prepared to do the time."* In other words, live for today, but plan for tomorrow even if tomorrow results in a loss of freedom. In order for parents to assist their kids in avoiding the criminal justice system, parents must teach their kids the principles of proactivity, including having a well-thought-out plan and an alternate plan if needed.

Habit Two

Begin with the End in Mind

Because most of my clients never thoroughly planned out their crimes, they obviously did not have the end in mind. The next habit of people who do not end up in the criminal justice system is closely related to the first habit of proactivity. Effective and productive people consistently begin with the end in mind. Once there is a plan in place, the planner must have a clear picture of what success looks like; in other words, what is the desirable end. In the same sense, parents must have a clear picture of what it will look like when their child reaches adulthood. The familiar cliché, "A means to an end is an idiom that is usually applied to an activity (such as an undesirable job) that is not as important as the goal you are hoping to achieve." Most people work for two weeks because they have an opportunity to receive a paycheck at the end of the two weeks. Although most people are conscientious about how they perform their jobs, some people robotically perform their employment tasks. Parenting is not a job that can be performed robotically because the means on which they perform the job could result in a disastrous end. Therefore, as parents raise their children, they must always have the end in sight as they proceed. Most parents don't want their kids to lie and steal or commit any law violations. I watched a mother use her seven-year-old daughter to steal a shopping cart full of groceries. She literally directed her to leave the store and go to the end of the parking lot to an awaiting car. When the store clerk confronted her, she said her mother told her to take the groceries. What this mother taught her child was the skill of thievery not realizing the fact that the child will eventually utilized the same skill later. Parents want their children to have high self-esteem; however, when that child makes a mistake, *sometimes the larger plan (to have high self-esteem) is lost in the parents' disappointment.* I have seen parents verbally abuse their children in public. These behaviors are antithetical to nurturing confident and honest children. Parents must connect the end to the means they utilize in raising their children. Instead of negatively equating the mistake or error in judgment with deficiencies on the child's part, parents could reaffirm the big picture or end plan (successful adult) and describe to the child how the mistake did not align with the big plan. The most efficient means is to model the behavior they are hoping their children will acquire. Beginning with the end in mind means that parents tell their kids consistently of the positive plan they have for their children's lives.

Lessons from the Field

One of my favorite probation experiences occurred while I was the superintendent of a residential detention camp for delinquent boys, ages fifteen to eighteen years old. These youth had been removed from their homes due to ongoing delinquency. Removal from their homes was a last resort as it had been determined that remaining in the family home would result in further risk to the youth and or the community. I had not raised boys, so supervising the case management boys in a 24-hour facility allowed me to gain valuable information and experience about the physical, emotional, and social characteristics of boys. As superintendent, I spent countless hours engaging with the boys. To my staff's dismay, I was often the judge and jury after allegations of ill treatment by my staff. One of the things I learned early was that when kids are in custody, they don't believe they are ever treated fairly. Therefore, every day, one of the boys had a story of inequity. In addition to the story of the day, I was able to learn about his story (History) that ultimately landed the young man to the criminal justice system. I would ultimately learn about his relationship with his parents which more often than not was a source of the reason he was now in custody.

Because of the history of the youth at the camp, making through a structured program was challenging in the least. However, graduation from the program meant returning home. Prior to graduating from the program, camp youth could earn the privilege to go on home visits, whereby they could spend 24 to 72 hours at home before returning to the program on Sunday evening. One young man returned from his home visit late and was facing the consequence of not being able to go home the next weekend. The resident's mother, who was very eager for her son's coming home the next weekend, requested a meeting with me to appeal on her son's behalf. During the meeting, the mother began describing the reason her son had not returned to the camp on time. It became embarrassingly apparent that the story the mother was telling was new information to the camp youth. He had a surprised look on his face. Midway through the story, the minor began to try and corroborate the story and then the mother tried to hide her confusion because obviously, she had not witnessed the parts of the story her son was adding. The two began to shamefully talk over one another until the minor had to admit that he and his mother had not told the truth. I asked the mother, What is it that you want from your son in the long run? I explained to the mother that although I understood her current motivation for the short-term goal of getting her son home for the weekend, I courageously explained that by modeling untruthfulness, she may have taught her son that in the long run, lying to avoid consequences is a viable option.

Lessons from the Field

Ending up in jail usually epitomizes not having the end in sight. While working as a probation officer, I was assigned the cases of many juvenile offenders who had been arrested for shoplifting or burglary. They would walk into stores and select an item that they wanted and proceed to the exit, passing several cash registers without making any attempt to pay for the items. This behavior is consistent with the legal definition of petty theft, a misdemeanor offense. Sometimes my clients would enter the store with backpacks in anticipation of concealing the items they planned to steal. Entering the store with the intention of committing an offense raises the crime to a higher level, burglary. Very often, my clients would get caught because the censors that were placed on the merchandise to detect theft would sound an alarm. Other times, the undercover security guard would catch my client before she exited the store. In either case, the juvenile or adult would be arrested and the case would be referred to the probation department. Whenever I would interview a youth who had been arrested for shoplifting, petty theft, or burglary, I always asked the same question: "What made you think that the store would not take efforts to protect the merchandise and how come you thought that you could just walk in the store and select what you want and then walk out without paying?" Most juveniles would respond, "I don't know." In an effort to make it more personal, I would say something like, "What made you think Mr. Macys or Ms. Target did not think to protect the merchandise. Don't you think that if there were not security on the merchandise that someone else would beat you to the merchandise and there would be nothing for you to steal?" Again my young client would say, "I don't know, I really didn't think about that."

It was clear that my young offenders did not have the end in mind when they planned their offense. Most of my young offenders only thought of the beginning, getting the merchandise. They did not think of the end that could include jail or prison, wearing recycled underwear, eating bad food, and the dangers of that were part of incarceration.

Habit Three

Put First Things First

"You have to decide what your highest priorities are and have the courage – pleasantly, smilingly, non-apologetically – to say 'no' to other things. And the way to do that is by having a bigger 'yes' burning inside."
~Stephen Covey

Stephen Covey's third habit puts the first two habits in the right order. Habits one and two instruct us to have a plan and always keep the plan in the forefront. Habit three makes sure that we take our many competing plans and put the most important one first. In other words, we should prioritize our goals and the things that are most important should come sooner than later. Probation clients are consistently disorganized, but because of their immature brain, disorganization makes sense. To arrange mental images in such a way that the most important thing is ranked number one requires that you are able to see the big picture that includes all the things on the list at one time. For some people, especially young thinkers, they only see what is directly in front of them. Parents can begin to teach this skill early along with early education. When kids learn their ABCs and number order, they are ready to learn the skill of prioritization because they understand that A comes before B and one always precedes nine, so they are ready to understand priority and that first things comes first.

Many children get into trouble with schoolwork because they fail to put the most important things first. I know many of the kids I served did, especially my own kids. I recall being up late assisting with the completion of an assignment that was assigned weeks before and now due the next morning. Although most students desire to earn good grades, some students find it difficult to put in the study time that is required to earn the higher grades. Some children put off doing school projects because they prefer to play video games or get on social media. I have heard it said that in order to say yes to your priorities, you have to be willing to say no to something else. There lies the problem. For most young people, even adults, delayed gratification and self-denial are a challenge. However, I think that schools have caught on to the idea of prioritization because many schools provide date planners at the beginning of the year so students will write down important obligations such as assignments and project due dates. Children need to learn early that they should prepare a daily, weekly, or monthly schedule. Parents can also model this skill by maintaining a schedule. The most concrete way to teach prioritizing is through the use of a budget. Parents should share their budgets with their children so they understand early in life that bills must be paid before extracurricular activities. Parents may want to show their children that they must pay their household bills first and then if there is money left over, the family can afford a vacation or a new car to replace the old but functional one. A perfect means of modeling that first things comes first is to show the child that their needs come first. Parents must demonstrate what is important. However, parents must first identify what is important. This point becomes poignant with respect to working parents. Parents may have an important event on their agenda for the day; however, if the child becomes ill, it is important that parents demonstrate that the child's health and the parent's responsibility for caring for the child is most important. Kids should hear you say to your friends, "I will not be available because I am going to my daughter's or son's event." Don't say, "I am sorry I can't attend," you merely can't go because you desire to go to your child's event more than going out with your friend, Priority!

Lessons from the Field

As a juvenile probation officer, I had the pleasure of working in and later supervising a unit called the Family Preservation Unit. Unlike other probation units, the Family Preservation Unit allowed the probation officer to work with the entire family as opposed to the identified client that had been arrested. The Family Preservation Unit took into consideration that most people do not operate independent of the social system with that they are associated. Therefore, not only was I engaging with my juvenile client, I was able to serve older and younger siblings and the parents if they were available. Since I was a licensed marriage and family therapist, this was a wonderful assignment and experience for me. I was even able to meet with grandparents who often were great historians for the family, and some grandparents enjoyed "telling on" the parents "who they never liked anyway." Sometimes grandparents became my secret informant. It was during the family preservation assignment that I was able to witness many parenting styles. As a deputy in the unit, I had access to grant money, which allowed me to buy the family-needed supplies and pay for basic necessities such as rent deposits, overdue utility bills, clothing, beds, groceries, and hygiene products. The goal of the unit was to provide families with what they needed in an effort to prevent removing the delinquent youth from the home. At the beginning of supervision, the family had to disclose any financial aid that they received and all of the family's debt. Since I had to provide an account of the money I spent on the families, I consistently measured the family's funding requests with their reported finances and debts. In the event of discrepancy, I would ask the parent to justify the request. On more than a few occasions, I would discover that parents would overextend their budgets to buy the child something that they obviously could not afford. For example, I had a family of *five who had a total income of $800 each month. The family was living in subsidized housing, but by the end of the month, there was not enough for extracurricular activates. However, one month, the mother requested money for groceries. When I asked the reason she was short on funds for the month, she disclosed that she had spent $200 to purchase her son a pair of Michael Jordan athletic shoes. The mother said that her son had asked her several times and that "all the other kids had Jordans." I asked the mother whether the other kids' families were living off $800 each month and whether they owed restitution and fines for an offense that their son had committed (I was a young probation officer and upon reflection, I realize my response was harsh. I attribute it to a lack of empathy). Most important, I explained to the mother that she had literally spent 25 percent of the family's monthly income to purchase a pair of shoes. I also told her that Jordan shoes were trending; therefore, another version of the shoe would come out and her son would likely want another pair. I further explained to the son that his mother needed to prioritize and put first things first. I also reminded my young client that because of his actions, there was a victim waiting to recover their loss from the crime he committed. Therefore, before he paid for his tennis shoes, he should pay his victim back.*

Habit Four

Think Win-Win

In Covey's book, *The Seven Habits of Highly Effective People*, he refers to thinking of win-win as being self-confident and refraining from competing with and comparing oneself to other people. Children must learn to be self-assured in who they are. A child's worth should not be based on the standard established by other children. Avoiding the inclination to compare oneself to another is a challenge today and will become increasingly challenging. When I was growing up, I only had people in my immediate environment to compare myself with; however, today the number of people a young person can come into contact with is countless with television and all of the reality shows and social media. To avoid perpetuating the need for your child to compete, parents should never say to their child, "James can play the piano, so how come you can't play the piano?" Parents should not look at how other kids dress or style their hair and tell their child they should imitate the same behavior. There are two primary reasons parents should avoid comparing their child to other children or even lead their child to believe they should compete with others. First, when parents compare their child with another child, the parent sends the message that the person that is being compared to is of a higher standard and the other child needs to improve in some way. Second, when parents compare their child to another child, the parent runs the risk of being viewed as a hypocrite. Parents usually will not accept the same response or justification from their child that they engaged in the same negative behavior as "so and so."

A sure way to be in trouble with my mother was to offer as the reason I did something was because someone else had done it. Even if that was the reason, I had better proactively prepare a plan B reason if asked to explain my behavior. If I even slipped and suggested that someone else had motivated my behavior, my mother would ask, "If your friend jumped off a bridge, would you follow?" Sometimes I wanted to say, well, yes, if it looked fun, but of course I understood her point that even if I jumped off a bridge, it should be my idea since I would have to deal with the consequences. So if my mother had asked me to join a basketball team like all the other tall girls my age, I would have viewed her counsel as hypocritical. Following the crowd works both ways, for the good and the bad. So if a child is caught using drugs, drinking, stealing, cutting school, most parents would not accept the response from their child that they engaged in the behavior because that girl that you liked with the pretty hair, who played the violin and was a star basketball player, was doing it so I thought it would be acceptable to you.

Like it or not, competition is part of the fabric of our society; however, until children are mature enough to handle fair competition, they should be taught the win-win habit. This thinking habit does not compare one person to another. Competition mandates that there is at least one winner and one or more losers. A win-win attitude and behavior asserts that there is a third and better alternative, that everyone can win or gain something. Instead of it only being a small piece of the pie that is up for grabs, children should be taught that there are several pies and if you don't get a slice of one, go after another pie. Another example is with respect to ideas. Everyone has an idea; some are good and another is better, but there is one that is the best idea for a given situation or moment. Children should be taught that the best idea does not cancel out the other good ideas. In a race of three runners, there are fast, faster, and of course, the fastest runner in that race. All three may have good times but the winner had the best time [in that race]. The other two runners still ran a good race if they did the best they could.

Another way to explain the win-win habit to children is to use the body as an example. There are many different parts to a body. Each one has a specific purpose. The heart is not more important than the lungs, because without the lungs, it would not matter if the heart was pumping blood if the person did not have air.

Another benefit of the win-win habit is the ability to reach consensus. Parents play a big role in this attitude change. Parents must change their strategic goal from negotiation to reaching consensus, or win-win. Negotiation results in each person giving up something in order to reach an agreement. Neither parents nor kids like to negotiate at times (kids, especially adolescents, never want to negotiate). Many parents refuse negotiate because they have the attitude that they are the parents and the kid is living under their roof so they are not giving up anything. In the below scenario, the student enjoyed school but didn't want to be the smartest in the school. The mother wanted her to be the top student. Consensus would have resulted in the student attending school and doing her best. With win-win or negotiation, both parties describe what they can agree with. Both parties feel empowered because they both win to a certain degree.

Lessons from the Field

As a juvenile probation officer, I had the opportunity to supervise a unit of probation officers assigned to abate truancy. Most of the kids had been identified by their school administrators as missing more than the average number of days or course periods. After attempts to rectify the truancy failed at the school level, the case was referred to the probation department for mediation and possible referral to the district attorney's office for filing of truancy charges, a violation of the law for people under the age of eighteen. Every case that came across my desk was for a young person who was resistant to attend school regularly. However, one case was unique. I recall a sixteen-year-old girl who flat-out refused to go to school regardless to what action was taken. She volunteered to go to jail if necessary. The case was sent to my unit for mediation. The probation officer's job was to determine what obstacles were preventing the student from attending school. The probation officer was charged with looking for social, emotional, or physical impediments to school attendance. Based on my interview with the minor's mother, I learned that the student had been a gifted and talented student throughout her earlier school years; however, when she reached high school, she started to become truant. The mother disclosed that previously her daughter attended a prestigious school where all the students were bright but then her daughter had "started embarrassing" the mother by earning low grades. To the mother's dismay, she finally dis-enrolled her daughter.

When I interviewed the student alone, I learned much more. She disclosed that when she was younger, her mother would verbally abuse her if she did not understand the work. Her mother often compared her to other children at school and flat-out asked her why she could not be smart like the other kids. Her mother told the student on many occasions that she was an embarrassment. Once the student was old enough to make her own choices about school, she stopped attending school. The young lady was smart enough to know that in California, compulsory education ended at sixteen years old. She no longer wanted to be compared to other students or be an embarrassment to her mother. Although the student viewed herself as smart, she understood that there would always be students who were smarter and she could not stand the pressure of being constantly compared to other students. Once the judge realized that holding the young lady in contempt of court for not attending school was futile, the case was dismissed. The mother was furious and blamed "the system" for giving up on her child. It was always my hope that the young lady would someday return to school.

Consensus, thus win/win, would have meant that although the student wouldn't be top student, she would do her best and remain in school.

Curfews are a good example of an area where win-win thinking would be important. Mom wants 10 and the teen wants to return home at 11. I often negotiated with my kids so if I said 10 and they said 11, I would say, "Oh, I'm sorry, did I say 10? I meant 9:30!" My kids would always go back to 10. What I described was forced negotiation, not consensus. Consensus would have resulted after we both decided what we could agree with. If I wanted my children to come home at ten o'clock, I could probably agree with 10:20 or maybe even 10:30. Giving my kids thirty extra minutes would have made them feel more empowered.

Habit Five

Seek First to Understand and Then to Be Understood

As the title implies, people who do not end up in the criminal justice system know how to listen and empathize. Suffice it to say that most of my clients did not consider the loss to the victim prior to committing the act. Most kids who cause emotional or physical harm to other people don't think about the resultant harm prior to the act; an offender is usually reacting to their own feelings in the moment. Parent sometimes teach this skill by telling kids that they must learn to walk in someone else's shoes before they pass judgment on someone's situation. This analogy is actually good advice for an abstract-thinking adult. However, as Brian Tracy so eloquently writes, "In order to walk in someone else's shoes, I must first remove my shoes." Here lies the problem. This skill is next to impossible for children to learn. Until children reach a certain maturity level, they are egocentric and incapable of understanding another person's perspective. Accordingly, children will not take off their shoes especially if it means putting on a less desirable pair. You think a sixteen-year-old will trade in his new Air Jordan tennis shoes for an old, no-name-brand shoe that was purchased at a garage sale? You think if given the opportunity, a young girl will trade her one-of-a-kind prom dress for one that was purchased off the rack at a department store where there are several made in all sizes? Until they have reached a certain maturity level, empathy must be modeled, taught, and nurtured.

Empathy requires abstract reasoning ability. Until children reach a certain age, they may not be able to think abstractly. Simply stated, young people are self-centered. The inability to take on the perspective of another is one reason that many people end up in the criminal justice system. Most people will not rob or assault themselves, so they can't see themselves in a victim. It is very difficult to take on another person's viewpoint when you are focused on your own perspective. Parents can model empathy by taking on the child's perspective. Parents can model empathy while watching television and empathizing with the characters on the show. When kids are school-age and beyond, asking the question, "How do you think that person is feeling?" is an easy way to introduce, teach, and nurture empathy and get the child used to taking on the perspective of another. Parents can also play a huge role in a child not taking on the perspective of another by always ignoring the fact that there may be another perspective. When kids are communicating, parents should listen intensely and let the child know that they understand.

Some parents are better at empathy than others. Authoritarian parents have more challenges in this area. These parents want to make the final decision on all matters and don't believe children should have a voice. Authoritarian parents are the ones who respond to their children's request for an explanation with "Because I said so, that's why!" Authoritarian parents don't feel a need to give an explanation even though they may have a good reason. When kids ask why or why not, parents should be proactive and use the opportunity to explain how the requested privilege will impact the big picture or keeping the end in mind, the priorities, or keeping first things first. Some parents don't have a good reason for denying the child the requested privilege; they say no because they can! Parents must allow the child to state their case or position and then make the decision in the interest of the big picture (keeping the end in mind), putting first things first (prioritizing) and reaching consensus (win-win).

To demonstrate that the parent is willing to first understand and then be understood, parents could paraphrase what the child has communicated and reflect their feelings before passing judgment. Parents have all the authority anyway. It does not minimize that authority to communicate to a child that you have heard them, you understand their position, and in light of or in spite of his or her perspective, you are taking the following actions. Taking the child's position is easier for an adult because all adults have in fact been in the child's position; however, a child has never been in an adult's position, so honestly, a child can't think like an adult.

Lessons from the Field

While working as the superintendent at Camp Sweeney, a juvenile detention facility for boys fifteen to eighteen years old, I mediated many verbal and physical fights. Some of the fights were very intense and, of course, bloody. There was always a common theme to the fights. One of the combatants usually felt that the other had disrespected him. The disrespect was usually not physical; it often involved something that was said or even unsaid. Sometimes, the disrespect was identified as the way one boy looked at the other. The sender's look usually was perceived based on the receiver's schematic view or their perspective that had been developed over time by past experiences. After that look was received, the receiver would feel that a message of disrespect was sent and had to be answered. After reviewing and critiquing literally hundreds of these fights, I came to realize that these adolescents genuinely believed that the other person was sending a threatening message to the other. Unfortunately, the intended receiver of the perceived menacing message never sought to understand the other person's perspective. It was not until staff spoke to both combatants that we would all come to realize that the fight was the result of preconceptions, misconceptions, and sometimes even fear. By the end of the mediation, both would understand the other and could agree that they could both understand the other one's perspective. (I must add that it didn't mean that they were now friends and they would still bear watch; however, they understood each other.)

It is clear how someone who lacked this skill could end up in the criminal justice system. As indicated from the lessons from the field, people who don't seek to understand another person's perspective is subject to break the law. To seek first to be understood and then to be understood requires the willingness to communicate. Authentic communication requires two people to come together and talk. Authentic communication is difficult due to the increase in the use of technology. People just don't talk to one another anymore. Technological communication loses some of its meaning due to the inability to hear tone and intonation and see facial expressions and body language, which are all important parts of good communication. For parents to understand their children, they must abandon the "do it because I say so" attitude. I have witnessed hundreds of exchanges between parents and their children (some in my professional capacity and others in public because I am nosey), and it is clear that the parent is not remotely interested in hearing what the child has to say. In most of those cases, the parents have made up their mind prior to the end of the conversation. I have routinely directed parents that they should at least listen to their child before making a decision. The parent has nothing to lose except the time it takes to hear the child out. As I indicated above, even if the answer to a child's request is no, when parents listen, kids feel heard, validated, and respected. That respect is like currency and will be needed on the parent journey.

Habit Six

Synergize

Stephen Covey described synergy as the ability to get along with others and to celebrate diversity as opposed to merely tolerating differences. Most of my clients don't know how to synergize. In its simplest form, to synergize means to get along. In the words of the late Rodney King, "Can we all just get along?" I recall seeing a poster that read, "Everything I learned to be successful in life I learned in kindergarten." In the decades I have lived following kindergarten, I have come to realize that my kindergarten teacher, Ms. Forbbs, had in fact taught me everything I needed to know to synergize. At five years old, I was taught how to get along with other kids who did not always look like me and dress like me. Their hair may have been different; some of the other kids didn't live in a house like I did; instead they lived an apartment. Some of the kids in my kindergarten class were more aggressive than others, some were smarter and some of my kindergarten playmates took longer to understand the lesson. Some kids did not always smell good. Some of my five-year-old classmates didn't realize that they had to deposit their waste in the toilets. But in spite of our differences, Mrs. Forbbs insisted that if we "didn't have something good to say about a person, we should not say anything about them at all." I can honestly say that when I have not taken Mrs. Forbbs' advice and uttered things that were not nice, there have been negative consequences.

Mrs. Forbbs not only taught my classmates and me to be kind with our words, we also had to share and take turns. As kindergarteners, we helped each other and we respected each other's property. When new kids came to our school or classroom, we welcomed them and at least one of us were assigned as the buddy who would escort "our new friend" around the school. By the time I left kindergarten, I had learned how to synergize. Mrs. Forbbs did her part. It was my mother and all the other responsible adults in my life that helped to nurture and reinforce the skill. Parents must understand that they are "on" all the time. Whether they want to or not, parents are modeling their values regarding appropriate behavior at any given time. Parents are their kids' persistent and consistent instructor on how to behave. How parents get along with their neighbors is a good example of this. Some parents never speak to their neighbors or have had longstanding disputes with their neighbors. Some neighbor disagreements are intergenerational and no longer have anything to do with the actual neighbors. Parents just tell their kids, "We just don't like them." And if the child asks why they can't be friends with the nice child, the parent says, "Because I said so, that's why!" Children need to understand the reason they have to behave. It is not enough to say because you said so because, oftentimes, they see you misbehaving, but that is a conversation we will have in the chapter on *courageous conversations.*

Lessons from the Field

I recall being at a popular shopping mall on Christmas Eve. I was leaving work late and recalled that I needed to pick up another gift before the stores closed for the holiday. As I approached the crowded parking lot, I dreaded what I knew I would encounter inside the mall. When I arrived, the store was just as I had envisioned: chaos. There were many last-minute shoppers crowding the stores. There were so many people, I could only move very slowly through the stores. I had to constantly stop and let people pass. Consistently, I bumped someone as I squeezed by them. I had to keep saying "excuse me" time after time. During one of my brief pauses, I noticed a woman with a child who looked around three or four years old. Apparently someone had stepped on the boy's foot, to which he grimaced. The mother, obviously frustrated and tired of the crowd or life in general, *told the little boy, "The next time someone steps on your foot, yell @#$% [expletives]." The little boy looked at his mother in surprise and said, "But Mommy, that's a bad word!" The mother said, "That's okay, just say it!" Although the crowd in front of me had started to move, I stood there in shock—until I was nudged and someone said, "Excuse me!" [expletives]. Not only had that kid's mother encouraged aggressive behavior, she missed a teachable moment. She could have taught her son the value of being patient and tolerant. Mom could have explained to her son that crowds are expected in shopping malls on Christmas Eve and if he did not want to be in a crowd, he should do his shopping early when the stores had fewer guests. In other words, Mom could have taught proactivity and synergy!*

Habit Seven

Sharpen the Saw

The final habit that Covey offered, and that my experience has taught would keep people from ending up in the criminal justice system is that of sharpening the saw. Many probation kids had skills that lay dormant in their minds and body. They had talents that were waiting to be tapped into. Sharpening the saw requires that parents expose their child to things that will stimulate the five primary components of the personality, which include physical, social, emotional, mental, and spiritual. Each aspect of the personality must be stimulated in order for a person to have balance. One part of a person's personality may predominate during different life phases; however, each must be addressed at some point during development. As a matter of fact, throughout the lifespan, people must address all aspects of their personality at one time or another.

Even before social media came on the scene, parents have been inundated with research on the benefits of good nutrition and exercise. In addition, for a long time, it has been recognized that social connections are very important for children. Parents have been encouraged to enroll their children in school at an early age, not only for the educational benefits but also for socialization purposes. Kids don't need to be with their parents all the time. If only some kids knew what went on while they were at school, they would be shocked. My experience has taught me that it is truly a win-win that kids have to separate from their parents and go to school even if the parents are not employed, or more accurately, **especially** if the parents are not employed. In addition to socialization, kids are encouraged to have a spiritual connection with music, art, and even nature. Regrettably, these programs are the first to be cut from the school budget during the administrator's downsizing efforts. Accordingly, if children are to sharpen the saw based on Mr. Covey's teachings, parents and caretakers must continue to expose their children to experiences that will foster growth in all areas of their lives.

Parents are more diligent in assuring their children are physically, mentally, socially, and spiritually connected when they are young. During childhood, parents often overload their children with extracurricular activities, including music lessons, swimming every summer, and seasonal sports, and it is common for parents with small children to go on annual family vacations. Although schools provide many opportunities for physical growth through physical education—and to some degree socialization because schools are a social milieu, and even to a limited degree, art, music, and spiritual growth, the latter resulting from attending a religious school—parents are still responsible for assuring and advocating for their kids to be enrolled in these types of program and also for exposing their kids to extracurricular activities such as church, boys and girls clubs, community sports, and recreation programs. My many years of experience serving adolescents has taught me unequivocally that no matter what, kids will find some sort of recreation outlet and sometimes the social outlet is not good.

Beginning in the mid-1990s and continuing to date, probation departments became very committed to what's referred to as evidence-based practices. That meant that probation departments would only utilize programs and strategies that had been proven, by rigorous research, to work in reducing recidivism (returning to crime). One of the primary evidence-based practices involved the use of an assessment on offenders to determine what attitude or behavior was leading to offending behavior. Probation officers were trained to look for certain behavior or traits that had been proven to lead to community misconduct. To many probation officers' surprise, one of the primary factors that had been proven to lead to community misconduct for children was the absence of prosocial activities. Many of these kids were committing crimes because they were essentially bored. Many of the juvenile offenders' parents worked all day and the kids were left unsupervised so they would engage in fun and risky behavior that ended them up in the criminal justice system. Adults who don't have gainful employment are also at a higher risk of committing crimes for the same reason, boredom.

While I have your attention, allow me to offer a disclaimer. Making sure your children have social outlets to sharpen the saw does not mean that they should get involved with all the things you wanted to do as a child. Kids should be able to select their own saw, so to speak. Some parents try to live vicariously through their kids so they try and inspire their children to do all the things they never did. I really wanted all of my kids to play musical instruments because I was not able to. Once when I was trying very hard to convince one of my daughters to resume playing her flute that she had abandoned after high school, after bringing up the subject a few times, my daughter finally said, "Mom, why don't you play an instrument?" Although I wanted to say, "Just do as I say, not as I do," I said, "You are right. Maybe I should." The point is, if you don't read, don't expect your child to enjoy reading. If you never exercise, don't expect your child to want to get off the couch next to you, where you two have been watching television all day, to go outside and play. We would like our children to be hungry for knowledge, but some parents have not gone beyond the compulsory education of the twelfth grade. On one final note, parents can demonstrate their commitment to lifetime learning by not being afraid to learn some of the new things that go along with a growing society. For example, some adults refuse to use microwaves, automated teller machines (ATMs), cell phones, computers, or any form of social media. Parents must demonstrate a willingness to sharpen the saw. Some parents want their kids to socialize, but the parents are comfortable spending all of their free time inside the house without any hobbies. Remember, you must model, teach, and then nurture the habits before you can be considered an expert. Kids will find an outlet to avoid novelty and boredom and respond to their desire for excitement and fun. A parent's job is to understand this normal developmental phase and expose and nurture prosocial and positive outlets to constructive activities so the kids do not end up in the criminal justice system.

Lessons from the Field

When juvenile offenders are delivered to juvenile hall (juvie, detention center), the probation officer should immediately conduct a risk assessment to determine if the child poses a risk to themselves (suicidal, neglected, health or mental health needs) or is a danger to others in the community. The assessment consists of a battery of questions, the answers to which would be scored on a scale that determined no/low risk to high risk. In addition to questions regarding family and school status, the detention risk assessment scale included questions regarding the young person's extracurricular activities. The purpose for those questions was to determine whether the juvenile was engaged in prosocial activities. If the parent was able to demonstrate that the child was connected to the school via average or above average grades, participation on some sort of team, etc., the child would appear to pose less of an immediate risk of community misconduct. This makes sense because a person who is committed to community misconduct would likely not be in good standing in school or on a team. Later in the juvenile justice process, the probation officer will conduct a more comprehensive assessment, called a needs assessment, in which case the probation officer is looking at what factors may be leading to community misconduct and what is needed to prevent further misconduct.

There are specific factors that the research has determined may lead to delinquency or crime. In addition to substance abuse, problems in school, mental health issues, domestic violence in the home, and delinquent peers, the absence of prosocial activities have been found to result in delinquency during preadolescence and adolescence. This makes perfect sense because being engaged with peers and overall having fun with friends is the epitome of adolescence. Having fun stimulates an important part of the brain. Kids love it. There was a Cindy Lauper song entitled, "Kids Just Want to Have Fun." Later rapper Wiz Khalifa wrote a song describing all the things young people do because they are "young, wild, and free." The point that I am making is that regardless of whether parents steer their kids into prosocial recreation activities, kids will engage in some form of recreation. If a child can only get their leisure needs met by hanging out on a corner with a group of friends, hiding in a basement drinking alcohol, organizing or participating in a gang, ringing doorbells and running off, they will do it because adolescence is a developmental phase that is characterized by egocentrism, so everything that adolescents do is about themselves, and even more so than adults, children are driven by pleasure. Babies want to be fed and be soothed. School-age kids want things like toys and fast food, and playing in the park. Teens want all of the above and more. The only difference between a child's and an adult's drive for pleasure is the latter is able to control their urges and some of the urges are legal for adults. Adolescent crave amusement, and socializing with peers is a big part of their enjoyment. During the risk-and-needs-assessment phase of the juvenile justice process, I often learn that many of the kids had not participated in any extracurricular. I would ask, what do you do in your spare time? Most of the kids said, "Nothing." I would ask about hobbies. The teens would usually report they did not have any hobbies. It was not until the child was in custody, especially in the long-term Camp program, that we would learn that the kids had above-average skills in activities such as sports, oration, music, art, and writing. These skills or hobbies had not been pursued beyond elementary or even middle school lessons from the field.

Lessons from the Field

When I was a probation unit supervisor, one of the cases that I will never forget was that of group of middle-class private school boys who came into custody for armed robbery. The weapon used was a baseball bat. The case involved the boys taking a cell phone from the victim. According to the police report, five schoolmates were riding in a car and passed a boy playing basketball on the school yard. One of the boys got the idea that they would rob the young basketball player. Some of the boys got out of the car and ran over to the victim and asked him to "break himself," which was street vernacular for "You are being robbed. Hand over all of your valuables." One of the boys stood by holding a baseball bat. The other boys went through the victim's pockets and found the cell phone. When the boys were interviewed, they were asked what they were planning to do with the cell phone. One boy said "sell it," but the other ones said they didn't know. None of the boys had ever been arrested and all of them were in good standing in their private school. All the parents were shocked at the behavior since their sons had not caused any problems in the home or in the community. I would later learn that "breaking" victims was a trending behavior. The goal was not only to gain possessions but more for power, control, and overall fun.

Habit Eight

Delayed Gratification

The next two habits, delayed gratification and the ability to hear the word "no," are not part of Stephen Covey's seven habits, but I found them to be consistently missing from my clients' repertoire. These two habits could be added to the section of the book entitled "Courageous Conversations" because my experience working with kids, parents, and adult clients was that people are not comfortable with these skills and they were even more uncomfortable with my bringing the skills, or lack thereof, to their attention. Suffice it to say that I would get a lot of resistance when I introduced or reinforced the skills to my clients. Delayed gratification and the ability to deal with discomfort are also becoming increasingly challenging as technology is becoming more sophisticated, making acquiring desired goals more quickly. We don't have to wait for food to cook or heat, we can zap it in the microwave and have it in minutes. We don't have to wait for the bank to open, we have automated teller machines (ATMs) on almost every corner. We don't have to wait for our nail polish to dry, there are *superhot* drying machines that dries your nails in minutes, your nails won't even chip for weeks. You don't have to leave your home to purchase groceries or food, it comes right to your door. You don't have to wait until you get home to turn on your lights or heater, you can turn them on remotely so your home is warm by the time you arrive. You don't have to push a button to unlock your phone, just put it up to your face and it will recognize you. You don't have to drive your car, there are self-driving cars, or at the very least, there is no need to deal with the discomfort of trying to squeeze into a parking space; at the push of a button, the car will park itself. Some medications can be taken in one-day doses if you don't want to wait three to seven days for it to work. For males, you don't have wait to have a physical desire to be with another person sexually, you merely have to take a pill, and voila, you are ready to go!

Delayed gratification is the ability to resist the temptation for an immediate reward and wait for a later reward. Generally, delayed gratification is associated with resisting a smaller but more immediate reward in order to receive a larger or more enduring reward later. The opposite of delayed gratification is instant gratification. This mindset and resultant unproductive habit makes people strive to have things immediately. In many cases, instant gratification does not achieve the larger goal and often is the catalyst for ending up in the criminal justice system. The most often committed criminal offense is the unlawful taking of someone's personal property with the intent to deprive the owner of the property. These offenses include theft, larceny, burglary, and, the most serious, robbery due to the fact that robbery requires the offender to have a face-to-face encounter with victim. In the United States annually over ten million property offenses are reported; however, 60 percent of those offenses are simple theft, in which case someone is taking something from someone else because the thief is unwilling to delay gratification in order to acquire the desired object legally.

I have seen problems with delayed gratification while working with kids who wanted to keep up with the latest fads such as shoes and technology when their parents just did not have the means. I worked with adults who wanted to have a middle-class lifestyle on a lower-class budget. Therefore, these kids and adults will resort to committing crimes to get their desired goals as opposed to what appeared to be a long and lengthy process. I liked that my clients wanted nice things; however, my concern was that my clients could not wait until such time that they could achieve their goals. This inability to delay the gratification was what ended them up in the criminal justice system. Delaying gratification meant putting something off until such time that they could achieve their desired goals. Unfortunately, most of my clients saw delaying their goals as equivalent to their goals going into the abyss and never to be achieved; therefore, they went after their desires by any means necessary. Very often, the means in which they achieved their goals was what landed them in the criminal justice system.

Parents must begin modeling, teaching, and nurturing delayed gratification as soon as the baby comes out of the womb. Even if parents don't conscientiously model the appropriate behavior, at the very least, parents should be conscious of negatively modeling the desire for immediate gratification all the time. Parents model instant gratification all the time. They are impatient waiting in line; parents are impatient in traffic on and off the freeway. People have stopped preparing meals at home. By the time they arrive home, the food is being delivered, so they don't have to wait to eat. Some parents can't wait for their kids to finish a sentence. If the child is speaking too slow, the parent will finish the sentence. Delayed gratification is a developmental milestone during childhood development. During infancy a baby must learn to soothe themselves so allowing an infant to cry for incremental periods once all the immediate needs have been addressed (diaper changed, feeding, safe environment, appropriate clothing) will allow the child to soothe themselves independently. With a toddler who is crying to eat, or for a toy or other desired items, she can be told, "One moment, please . . . be patient. I am coming. It is not your turn. Let's allow the other kids to have it. Yes, I know you want that and I will get it in one moment."

Sometimes my one-year-old grandbaby will start crying as soon as I say the word "one" in "one moment, please," because she knows that means she has to wait. She is only one and understands the concept. Older school-age kids are taught to wait their turn, to celebrate others, like at birthday parties, and the big-ticket waiting item is Santa Claus. Kids wait several months for Santa to arrive. Similarly, parents can teach kids to count down the days until an event so they get used to delaying gratification. By the time a child reaches adolescence, they should have had a lot of experience delaying gratification. They have discovered that it was the parents that they were waiting on for Christmas presents, and during this phase, they are delaying even bigger desired goals such as driving, lunchtime, school to end, to be picked up, the results from an exam, letters from colleges, their turn on a team sport, and their turn to speak in class. More importantly, kids that learn to delay gratification and be patient will reduce the number of teen deaths per year, the majority of which are the result of traffic accidents. Fewer kids will run a red light in lieu of waiting the three minutes for the light to change again. Kids who learn delayed gratification will not race a train across the tracks, and kids will have the patience to wait for time to heal wounds instead of self-medicating or worst, taking their own life.

The kids that end up in the criminal justice system are not taught to delay gratification, so if they want a pair of tennis shoes that they don't have the money to pay for, they may just sneak into someone's school locker or home and take a pair. More aggressively, the person may confront their victim and tell them to "break down" and hand over everything. Just like babies wait to be soothed, parents must continue to nurture the skill to delay gratification.

Habit Nine

The Ability to Hear the Word "No"

The ability to hear the word "no" is similar to delayed gratification except there is a finality, a feeling of hopelessness that comes with "no." Hearing the word "no" is final because it means that the request is denied, rejected, inaccessible, or unavailable. To hear the word "no" means that it, whatever it is, is not going to happen. It's not only final, but there is a need to develop a different plan, direction, goal, move on, go to plan B, which is usually absent because there is no need for a plan B if the answer is always yes. Because some kids are used to getting what they desire, they are emotionally incapable of not securing their desired results. While working in juvenile hall, I have literally seen kids fall apart because they were told no. Some of these kids was not just spoiled; they were off balanced, experienced anxiety, and panicked because their request was denied. Society refers to kids whose wants are always accommodated as spoiled and spoiled rotten. I never really thought about the term "spoiled," which means to diminish or destroy the value or quality of. This is totally the outcome of spoiling a child. However, the psychological definition of spoiled, in reference to a child means to harm the character of (a child) by being too lenient or indulgent.

Kids learn the term "no" very early. As a matter of fact, "no" is one of the first words kids learn because it is monosyllabic and easy to pronounce. My grandbaby Nyla started saying "no" when she was just months old so young kids already knows what "no" means. But in most cases, it is the finality of denying a child's request that prevents parents from saying "no." In some cases, when parents have to provide that level of finality to a school-age child or an adolescent, it takes work. The parent has to explain, they have to be confronted with the look of disappointment on the child's face or the mean mug that some kids will put on their faces when denied their request. For some kids, the parents must engage in an argument with the child because the child feels as though "no" is just not an option. Arguments take a lot of time and effort. Some parents are already overwhelmed with responsibilities so they may find it easier to just say yes. This type of parenting is referred to as permissive parenting, which is the opposite of the aforementioned authoritarian parenting.

Permissive parents are very likely to overindulge their kids with lots of "yes" responses. This parenting style is characterized by low demands. Permissive parents tend to be very loving, yet provide few guidelines and rules. These parents do not expect mature behavior from their children and often seem more like a friend than a parental figure. Friends don't provide guidance, set limits, or have courageous conversations. This is unfortunate because that means the parent has missed many teachable moments and basically absolved themselves of their responsibility to raise their children in such a way that they do not end up in the criminal justice system. Kids will ultimately hear many "no's" in their lifetime, and since they learn best from those they love, it is important that parents are the ones who lovingly tell the child "no" when it is appropriate.

Lessons from the Field

I could write pages on scenarios where my client's inability to delay gratification or hear "no" resulted in them ending up in the criminal justice system. I think it would be fair to say that the majority of my clients committed their offenses because they could not delay the gratification until such a time that they could legally achieve their goals. I must say that in almost every case that I investigated and supervised during my tenure serving federal probation clients, the motivation was to achieve something quickly or to gain access to things that had been denied. One case in particular stands out for me. My client had defrauded a bank by getting various loans on properties in an effort to sell them for a profit. Initially my client purchased a home for income property. The market was at an all-time high, so he figured he could make even more money if he bought more property at higher prices. However, with the mortgage on his home, he was not able to get additional lines of credit. The client could not wait until he had the income, via the sale of the income property he had already purchased, so he decided to embellish his income. By the time the case had been referred to the federal probation department, my client had successfully purchased several homes and quickly sold them for a profit. He had made more money than he had imagined, but he continued to purchase more expensive homes. Unfortunately, in order to get the loan for the higher-priced properties, he had to say he had more income than he had. When filling out loan applications, he calculated his financial status based on the income he would have as a result of the sale before actually making the sale. As luck would have it, the housing market crashed and the million-dollar homes that he purchased would not sell for a profit. The bank had to foreclose on the property. The bank soon learned that my client had not secured the loan legally and pressed charges.

Parents most artfully model, teach, and encourage these nine habits. As I already indicated, people who possess the habits of proactivity, beginning with the end in mind, putting first things first, think about win/win situations, seek to understand or empathize, are able to get along and able to engage in positive social activities; able to delay gratification or accept the fact that the answer is "no" do not end up in the criminal justice system.

Chapter Four

THE PARENTS' INSTRUCTIONS MANUAL: A DISCLAIMER

Often, the parents of my probation clients would lament that they wished their child would have come with instructions. So for all those who have wished that their child had come with instructions, I say, request denied. In order to grant the plea, there would have to be a finite number of circumstances that could occur during the parenting journey. However, when raising children, there are too many variables involved. The families in which children are raised are not static; they are active, dynamic, and constantly changing. During a child's developmental path, there are a series of events, and the child's response to those events, that will contribute to defining the child's character. There are critical periods in a child's life, and some of those times have a bigger impact on their character than others. In fact, there are times in a child's life that will have a profound impact on his life. Most important, people come in and out of a child's life and those people will have a varying impact on the child. Because of the active nature of a child's life, parents must take an active role. Parents must begin proactively thinking of their role as soon as they become pregnant because it is the parental role and the resultant parent-child relationship that will determine how the child will develop.

Although this book is far from an instructions manual, this section and the corresponding information can be utilized as a reference guide for parents and caretakers raising children. There are three critical developmental stages that will be discussed: infant, childhood, and adolescence. By understanding each of these developmental stages, parents will be able to take advantage of timely and age-appropriate opportunities to nurture the relationship that will be crucial throughout the parenting journey. During each of the distinctive developmental stages, there are specific developmentally appropriate strategies that will provide the desired outcomes. Success during each of these stages is dependent on a parent's mode of engagement. For example, parents must never engage in a power struggle with an adolescent. When parents debate and argue with adolescents, it sends the message that there is equal power that is being debated. Parents always hold the power so there is no need to argue. This strategy is counterintuitive for most parents of adolescents. They feel that they have to prove themselves when, in fact, you only have to prove something that is in question. If parents remain in the parent mode, there is nothing to prove, children will recognize and respect the parents' status. Too often, parents get in trouble because they go out of character and oftentimes they lose the respect of the child. For example, sometimes children will say things in an effort to hurt the parent. They may say something like, "I don't like you." A parent's response should be adult and parental. The parent may say, "Really, that's how you feel? That's unfortunate because although your behavior is not loving, I love you anyway."

Parents must remain in the parent mode no matter what happens. No matter what happens. Departure from the parental role is a common mistake. Some parents take a break from parenting. I am not referring to respite, in which case you take a physical and proximate break from the kids. Those periodic and short time-outs are important for the mental and emotional stability of the parent and the child. However, the departure that I am referring to is more akin to a detour from their parental role. I am referring to when parents actually decide they don't want to parent for a time period. For example, some parents get so involved in their careers that they are not available for their children. Instead of attending back-to-school-night activities, some parents are at work. Instead of engaging with children after work, some parents bring work home. Instead of family vacations, parents refuse to take time off of the job for fear of losing seniority or promotional opportunities. Some parents may also take a break from parenting to pursue their personal interests. Instead of being at home baking cookies for their child's classroom party, the parent may be out on a date.

Some parents may not actually take a break from the parenting role physically, but although they are there, they fail to actually journey with their children. A parent that is not on the journey with their child is easily frustrated at their child's current situation. They are frustrated at the infant's constant crying and can't wait until she can toddle and at least verbalize what is wrong. The parent of the toddler is frustrated because the child embarrasses him because he does not share and every parent request is met with "no." The parent of the young school-age child is tired of helping with homework and becomes very frustrated when she has to help her child with the "new math" especially since the parent "didn't learn that way." The parent of the adolescent is tired of the mood swings and just wants the teenager to settle and be happy. For some parents the most exciting milestone is when their children no longer require constant supervision. Parents want to be able to leave their children at home for long periods of time. Parents want their children to have autonomy so that the parent can be autonomous. Some parents even think that when their children reach adolescence, they can ease up on the rings and be less involved. This is a huge mistake. Children are not old enough for autonomy until they are capable of thinking abstractly.

For those of you reading this book and your children are beyond infancy and perhaps even at adolescence, I say to you, it is never too late to begin using the right strategies and it is never too late to reconnect with children and establish a better relationship that yields better results. At any time during the parenting journey, parents can make a decision to establish a vision for their child, establish smart goals to achieve the vision, and then execute the plan accordingly. *It has been stated that "nobody can go back and start a new beginning, but anyone can start today and make a new ending."* I don't know who originally made that point, but it is very true.

Knowledge Is Power

In the sixteenth century, Sir Francis Bacon is believed to have coined the phrase "Knowledge is power." Throughout the centuries, many people have validated the axiom. My experience working with probation parents proved that the lack of knowledge resulted in weakened and broken relationships. Soon after starting my career as a juvenile probation officer, I realized that for many of the youth who ended up on my caseload, their problems had started many years prior to their arrest. For the majority of my clients, their problems could be traced back to their early childhood. What I found most interesting about the parents' reports was that with many of the behaviors that they found so challenging with their children, the conduct actually started out as age-appropriate behavior. Most of the parents simply did not have the knowledge, skills, and abilities to understand and manage these development phases to respond to their child appropriately. In many cases, not understanding the developmental level of the child prevented the parent from implementing the correct strategy to address the presenting problem. The parents' uninformed response often made the situation worse. We will examine three broad developmental phases of development in an effort to normalize the behaviors that parents can expect during these three phases.

What to Expect When Raising a Child

There are three critical stages of development in a child's life. It is important that parents recognize, understand, and most importantly parent their child in accordance with their phase of development. So far, I have spent a lot of time preparing you for the role of parent by giving some important knowledge that prepare parents for the role. I now want to discuss critical knowledge that will equip parents with the skills needed to raise their child to become productive and not end up in the criminal justice system. As I mentioned before, the most important thing about raising children is understanding your role at any given time. If you recall, one of the main premises of this book is that "parents do the best that they can at any given time with the resources they have at the time." Accordingly, it is important that parents have accurate information, in the moment, in order to do the best that they can to navigate the parent role in real time. I will identify three, broad, and distinctive, but equally important stages of development that require parents to execute a different strategy when engaging with their child. This section of the book is meant to be read and referenced. In other words, you will return to the applicable section at different times during the parenting journey. It will provide new information for some but a welcome refresher for others. You may even return to the stages when advising other parents, even your own children, who will raise your grandchildren. Advising your kids on raising *their* kids could be the topic of an entirely different book! However, suffice it to say, you are merely a consultant and should only consult when asked. But I digress, let's talk about the stages of development of the children you are responsible for raising and assuring that they do not end up in the criminal justice system. Prior to discussing the three phases of development, I would like to share an example of age-inappropriate parenting.

Lessons from the Field

Pulling far back in time for this lesson, I draw on my own experience. I recall that the mother of one of my elementary school classmates would walk her to and from school every day. When we matriculated to junior high school (now referred to as middle school), the mother continued to walk my classmate to and from school. By then, we were twelve years old! I never learned why the parent felt the need to treat her child like a preschooler; however, the mother's behavior was not appropriate parenting. She embarrassed her daughter, who obviously felt, like all the other 800 kids in the school, she could manage walking to and from school alone.

A more common example of inappropriate parenting is the "I will just do it myself" syndrome. Sometimes parents resist taking the time to teach their child how to do a task in exchange for doing it themselves. So often parents will get frustrated with the child's low learning curve so they will take over the task. Dishwashing is a good example. Instead of taking the time to teach a child how to clean the entire kitchen, including the table, countertops, cabinets, stove, and wash and dry the dishes, clean out the sink, sweep the floor, take out the garbage, they will do it themselves when they learn the child has done a poor job. I have learned from some of my probation kids that the reason they never learned basic skills is because their parents had completed their homework. My client would explain how sometimes he didn't understand the lesson and instead of the parent taking the time to explain, the parent would tell the child the answers. Of course, the child will do well on homework but fail the class due to poor classroom and test scores. I must admit that one of the most painful parenting tasks that I have experienced is teaching and supporting my children to read. Oh my gosh, they read each word soooo slowly and it takes forever to turn to the next page. I am so inclined to just read the words myself, but if I had, they would never have learned to read. I can now admit that, after the reading sessions, I would leave the room and go scream into a pillow.

Another example of inappropriate parenting, at the other extreme involves parents who treat their children as though they are older and more mature than warranted. Underparenting was a consistent theme with the families I served in probation. Very often, parents would allow their kids to have more freedom and responsibility than they could handle given their maturity level. Up to a certain point, children are concrete thinkers. They view the world literally based on the here and now. *Abstract thinking, which is a more mature level of processing the world, allows people to see things that are removed from sight or the present, like consequences. Abstract thinkers are able to anticipate outcomes because they understand the notion of cause and effect.* I have met parents who have no idea what is going on with their preadolescent. Children have come into custody, and their parents were not even aware that the child was out of the house. Probation officers have contacted parents to tell them that their child is in custody and the parent, initially in doubt, had to leave the phone to check the child's bedroom. I have worked with parents who had no idea that the school progress reports were issued. And still some parents were not aware that they could go online to check on their students' progress. These parents usually felt that their preadolescent was old enough to monitor and regulate themselves. When parents think that their kids are old enough to take care of themselves, that is the time when parents must become more vigilant, albeit sometimes secretly. During preadolescence, kids also think they are capable of making adult decisions. However, chronological age does not always equate to emotional maturity. For some people, their maturity level may not catch up to their chronological age until they are well into adulthood. I have encountered some very immature twenty-one-year-olds. However, I understand their lack of maturity because all learning comes from exposure, thus experience. Without practice of any skills, people will do the best they can in any situation with the resources they have. It is imperative that parents remain on the parenting job with their kids, highly engaged and cognizant of knowledge kids should have at each phase. Appropriate parenting means engaging with their children based on their maturity level, being careful not to under- or overparent.

Although it is impossible to develop a parent's manual that would cover all the knowledge, skills, and abilities parents must know, if parents are proactive and take the time to develop a plan for raising their child, parents will feel more empowered. My advice... know the developmental phase.

Chapter Five

Natural Child Development

In order to properly raise a child, parents must be able to communicate with and relate to the child as soon as the child leaves the womb. In order to communicate, parents should be aware of how children view and relate to the world. Appropriate communication and relationship with a child are parents' best parenting tools. Children's view of the world changes as they mature. Child psychologist, Jean Piaget provided the most comprehensive theory on intellectual development. His theory outlined how childhood plays a vital role in a person's development. In Piaget's cognitive development model, children *construct* an understanding of the world around them and experience discrepancies between what they already know and what they discover in their environment. In other words, children are products of their environment. That environment is the incubator for their development. Who children will ultimately become has some genetic basis; however, a child's experiences and how they come to understand those experiences is what they will use to construct knowledge. According to Piaget, children move through four broad levels of mental development; each level builds on the next. Cognition refers to thinking. Children progress from a very basic thinking level to a more complex-level thinking, Piaget referred to the thinking stages as operations.

The first cognitive stage is sensorimotor. This thinking begins at birth to approximately two years of age. During this time the children focus most on what they feel, see, and hear right in front of them. Once kids become toddlers until about seven years old, they progress to what Piaget referred to as the preoperational stage. During this time, kids are able to think about things symbolically. From about seven to eleven, kids' thinking become more egocentric and they are increasingly aware of external events. Most important, kids realize that their thoughts and feelings are unique and may not be shared by others. The final and more advanced stage of cognitive development is the formal operational stage. By adolescence, kids are able to logically use symbols and think abstractly. We will borrow from Piaget's developmental stage theory to identify and distinguish between four critical periods in which parents can have a big emotional and intellectual impact on their child's development. The theory will provide direction on how to efficiently engage children during the four stages. Parents will be given strategies to nurture the character in their child that is needed for children to become highly effective adults.

Birth to Three Years Old (Infancy): The Foundation

The fastest way to an infant's heart is through the stomach. Hold that thought. Most importantly, parents should know that how you begin to parent your child will have a big impact on the relationship you have with your child in succeeding years. Even if you are raising a child that is beyond infancy, this section may provide information that explains the status of your current relationship with an older child. The infancy stage is like the foundation of a house. Just like a building, infancy is likened to the lowest load-bearing part of a building; and if you lay a weak or shaky foundation, it will not provide the support necessary on which to build. The infancy stage is also the load-bearing period of the child's development because it establishes the relationship. Weak engagement, time, and attention will result in a weak relationship. During infancy, it will be determined if the relationship can withstand the load of childhood and the heavy load of adolescence. But for those of you reading this book after the infancy stage, there is still time to fortify or build the relationship. *Just like a house built on a shaky foundation, a contractor can undergird or even rebuild the foundation and make it strong. Parents of older children can also fortify or rebuild a weak relationship and make it strong.* But just like a builder, you will have to go back and revisit and tear down the old foundation (relationship) in order to rebuild. Let's look at the infancy stage of childhood development and what is needed to start the relationship off right. On your mark, get set . . . go!

Journey with Me . . .

As soon as you have a child, in that very instant, literally you go from being a single person who is only concerned with self-care to a parent responsible for someone else's needs. I really need that to sink in so take a moment to think about that fact and grieve your single status if you must. Now begin to reflect on the parent life in front of you. If you have a child, no matter whether you gave birth to the child or adopted the child, your status changes immediately. Your baby has just arrived into the [your] world. The baby is so small, soft, fragile, helpless, and cute (to you anyway). Side note: It was not until my children were grown that I looked back at their baby pictures and thought, "They were not as cute as I thought at the time!" I mean, they were all right as far as little underdeveloped humans go (little to no eyelashes, eyebrows missing, balding scalp hair, fat rolls), but to me they were the cutest babies ever born! I later learned that scientists believe that humans are hardwired to be attracted to babies so the caretaker will take on the responsibility to care for the baby. In other words, if babies were unattractive to their parents, there may be many abandoned babies. At the first sight of their baby, most parents are in awe. For many parents, having a baby is their biggest accomplishment up to that point. Parents feel like, "Wow, I made that?" "How could someone so imperfect like me make something so perfect?" It is a great feeling.

Very soon after the infant is born, parents are faced with another realization. In addition to being in awe of what they have made, parents are quickly confronted with the absoluteness of parenting; specifically, the infant is *truly* helpless and that all of the baby's needs are the parent's responsibility. And the biggest shock to the new parent's reality is as soon as the baby arrived, the parents' needs become secondary. Subjugating their needs is difficult for some parents. Prior to having a child, parents are egocentric for the most part so they put their own needs first. Once the baby is born, parents have to take a lot more into consideration even before leaving the house. Once the baby arrives, all of a sudden, the parent must pack a bag with diapers, extra clothes, possibly medication, prepare baby food, check the weather to see if there is a need to layer clothing, strap the baby in a twenty-pound carrier, grab toys, grab snacks, put the stroller in the trunk, which is not an easy task sometimes. Strollers are becoming increasingly more smart but harder to close.

Preparing to leave the house is not the only difficult chore that new parents have to contend with. Parents learn quickly that babies do a lot of crying, therefore all this packing and preparing may be occurring while the baby is crying! Baby's vocal chords are not developed, their voices are higher and make the crying louder and piercing. Prior to a parent having a baby, the only consistent noise a parent may have listened to is music and that was by choice. Music soothes or music can pick you up and put you in a good mood. I don't think new parents are packing bags and preparing to leave while rocking to the screams of their infant. I can't even count the number of times that after preparing to leave and hearing my baby cry, I just gave up and said, Forget it, I'd rather not go. I didn't say it that calmly either. One time, I couldn't get the stroller to close to put in the trunk of the car and became so upset, I threw it across the garage. It still didn't close!

Another new factor added to the parent life is a vast reduction in slumber time. Sleep deprivation is the first sign that parents must put one of their basic, and for some, most prized need aside. I see baby pajamas that read "My bedtime is negotiable." Even the most organized and consistent parents sometimes have to wait longer than desired to go to sleep. Babies set their schedules while in the womb. While in utero, babies may sleep during the day while they are riding around in the mother's warm and swooshy womb when mommy is most active. While mommy is sleeping and the world is quiet, babies may be awake in the womb. It kinda reminds me of my cat, which I can hear creeping around the house in the middle of the night. She literally sleeps all day and then when we are asleep, she gets up to roam around. Probably looking for flies or mice, which is okay, as long as the critters are gone by the time that I wake up. When the baby is born, often it will maintain the womb schedule until a new routine is established by the parent. Therefore, a new parent's first child-rearing job is the development of a structure for a child. Parents teach their infant, through modeling, that sleeping occurs at night, when it is dark outside and quiet inside, and arousal time is when the sun is out. There is traffic noise, the garbage trucks are in the neighborhood, delivery people come to the door, the vacuum and laundry machines are going, and of course, the television is on. Now, if parents are staying awake at all times of the night, then the child will not learn when to sleep. Some new parents put their kids to sleep and then get busy doing chores, washing clothes, watching television, getting on social media, and then they become angry when the child wakes up and will not return to sleep. *Kids, even infants, do what you do, not what you say.* The establishment of structure will be an ongoing responsibility throughout the child-raising process. However, during the first few years, establishment of a schedule is critical. The most important point is that during the infancy stage, parents have to discipline themselves in order to train their children. Parent discipline very often means that the parent will be inconvenienced.

Turn Off Electronics and Pay Attention

If I see another mother nursing or feeding a baby while texting or talking on the phone, I will be inclined to snatch the phone out of the parent's hands. Feeding, especially through nursing, is an extremely important time. It is a time of warmth and closeness, cuddling and cradling, intense affection and warmth. Unfortunately, many parents forego this time when the baby is content eating to get on their smartphone and scroll through pictures, go on social media, and even talk on the phone. The parents are so focused on the phone, they often neglect to even make eye contact with the child during feedings. Because infants are so helpless, parents must devote all of their attention to caring for them. Inattentiveness and distractedness are the antitheses to effective parenting. Kids are always on the emotional and physical move, so parents must stay ready. During the infancy developmental phase, children are constantly adjusting and adapting because of rapid brain growth. As the brain matures, one thing that happens is the pruning of the synapse. Synaptic pruning occurs based on how any one brain pathway is used. By cutting off unused pathways, the brain eventually settles into a structure that's most efficient for the owner of the brain, creating well-worn grooves for the pathways that person uses most. Synaptic pruning intensifies after rapid brain-cell proliferation during childhood. So what does all this science mean? You need to treat your child like a sponge and surround the child with plenty of water to sop up. The water I am referring to is information, knowledge, experiences, and opportunities to learn. Some parents limit the child's learning experience to what the parent believes is the child's ability to learn. That is a big mistake. The brain is growing rapidly during infancy; connections are being made that will be utilized for higher order learning later in the child's life. You ever wonder why babies get bored with toys so easily? It is because after a few seconds, the toy has lost its novelty. In other words, the baby feels like "been there, done that." The brain has already made the connections and recognizes the toy and the brain is ready to make new connections. That's why when you spend so much time unwrapping that gift that you were so proud to present to your child, they look at it for a minute and then look over at the tattered box that it came out of and think, "Hey, that looks interesting!" Because of the rapid brain development, parents must constantly expose their infants to new material to master. Parents should use new words, phrases, and objects to constantly engage their infants. Parents should talk to their infants as if they are young adults and can comprehend the conversation. An example of this is when babies are sitting in the kitchen while their parent is cooking. The parent can talk about what they are cooking. They can discuss the recipe and the fact that they need to add a cup of this and an ounce of that. If the parent burns the food, they can discuss that with the baby also and tell her that they should have been paying more attention or the fire was too high. Parents should just chat it up with their infant. Talk about anything. Count to one hundred, say the ABC's. Talk about how one plus one equal two. Talk about geography. Teach babies their left side of their bodies from their right. Show them the difference between up and down. Expose them to another language. Talk to them about the weather. Read the newspaper to them. Read aloud whatever you are reading (please use discretion as you don't want the first words to be an embarrassment). Teach your infant how to spell their name, yes, even with the hyphens and apostrophes because they are going to have to learn how to spell them anyway. Read this book to your child. I promise to use a variety of words to support brain development. Knowing that your child's brain is growing and making connections day by day and even minute by minute should inspire you to stay in teacher mode. While the parent is talking, the baby's brain is making all kinds of connections and soaking in all that information. Later, when language development begins, the infant will draw on all the vocabulary that is stored in the brain. Conversely, if the baby was only exposed to less-than-desirable vocabulary, or none at all, language development will be reflective of the limitation or delayed. Now you know how some kids end up getting high scores on vocabulary college entrance exams. They are just pulling out the information already stored in the brain.

Communicating with an Infant: Babies Cry

Now that you have turned off your electronic devices, you are ready to communicate with your baby. Piaget referred to the period between birth to two years old as the *sensorimotor stage*. During most of this stage, children are learning through their five senses: seeing, hearing, smelling, tasting, and feeling. To many parents' surprise, an infant's most keen sense is that of smell. Even when an infant can't see or hear the parent, they recognize them from their smell. However, infants initially understand the world based on how they feel and their comfort level. If a baby is wet, it cries because it feels uncomfortable. While in the womb, babies did not have to feel the discomfort of a wet diaper. If you have ever had to wear wet clothes, you know that it is uncomfortable. Because babies lack the ability to communicate and change their diapers, they cry when they get uncomfortable. When babies are hungry, they feel uncomfortable and they cry. Infancy begins at birth and extends to two years of age. The end of infancy usually corresponds with the acquisition of language. Accordingly, during the initial months of a child's life, they are unable to communicate verbally so they cry. Crying is the earliest form of communication for infants. How parents respond to their infant's cry for attention is critical in determining whether the infant is successful during this developmental milestone. When babies cry, the parent will assess what the child is communicating, and address the issue. Parents may feed the child, change the diaper, reposition the baby, put warm clothes on, take clothes off, adjust the room temperature, turn on or off the light, rock the baby back and forth to soothe, etc. Once the parent addresses the source of the discomfort, the baby is soothed and will no longer cry. When parents (or primary caretaker) is responsive to their child's needs, the baby will soon realize that the parent figure is a source of comfort. When the baby smells the source of comfort, they will expect to be soothed. The baby will associate the parent with comfort and emotionally attach to that figure. Some new parents and caretakers think that their infants love them. In reality, love is learned behavior that will not come until later in life, but early on, a child's attachment to their parents probably could be viewed more closely to appreciation as opposed to love. That is the reason that the way to a baby's heart is through food (and a clean diaper).

Late in infancy, babies are considered toddlers. The most famous toddler phase is often referred to as the terrible twos. When kids turn two, you can expect that they will be beginning to talk but they still cry a lot because it still works better than trying to articulate new and challenging ideas. Stringing together three- or four-word sentences in order to communicate a feeling is a challenge for a new talker. If you have ever communicated with a two-year-old, you know that very often, you have to ask him or her to repeat themselves. Two-year-olds have not perfected speech so sometimes what they say sounds like babbling. They may know two words and then use baby talk for the third word. Trying to communicate with a two- and even three-year-old can be frustrating and result in communication breakdown. Rather than try and communicate clearer, it's easier for the child to revert back to crying and the parent throwing their hands in the air in defeat. I have a two-year-old granddaughter; I don't understand her sometimes, but her four-year-old sister understands her very well. Very often when trying to understand my two-year old, I look at my four-year old and say, "What did she say?" She will then ask her baby sister, "What did you say, Marlee?" Marlee responds in the same broken sentences and my five-year-old translates accurately. I look at my two-year granddaughter, who is now relieved that I now understand her need.

Another important characteristic of two-year-olds is their newfound ability to act independent of the parent. Sometimes, that independence is manifested in terrible behavior (hence the name terrible twos). My third daughter's favorite phrase was "I do it." She wanted to push the stroller, open the garage door, open the refrigerator, pour beverages, cook, put her clothes on, put *my* shoes on. Two-year-olds begin to manipulate and throw things; they hide in the store—all of this is to get a reaction out of the caretaker because they now realize that when they do certain things, you react. Parents should understand that sometimes acting out behavior is merely a sign that the child is emerging into a new phase of development. Recently my two-year-old granddaughter took a toy from her four-year-old sister Milaya, who immediately protested. I responded with the same strategy I had used the month before by asking Marlee to tell me to whom did the toy belong. She pointed at her sister and I asked her, very politely, to give it back to Milaya. Marlee said "no." This was not a surprise because Marlee had started saying no a year before and she had not stopped. What was a surprise was Marlee's body language and the expression on her face. Instead of running away with the toy clenched in her little fist and crying, she looked me straight in the face and said, "No G Mommy." She wasn't sassy and she wasn't playing. She didn't yell or attempt to conceal the toy, but she had a look on her face that read, "I said no and what are going to do about it?" My first impulse was tower over her and make myself look as big as possible and then to take the toy from her and say, "Did you hear what I said?" However, I recalled in the moment that my little Marlee had come to realize that she could exercise some control over things and more importantly, she could control me, at least my moods as reflected in my facial expressions. Marlee could see that just by saying "no," the atmosphere changed as measured by the expression on my face. My face had gone from relaxed, soft, and kind to surprise and then stern with wrinkles in my brow. Like most two-year-olds that make the discovery that they can influence behavior, she was very pleased. I could tell she was enjoying her newfound sense of control. If I had related to her like an infant, in which case she was expected to be passive and do everything I desired, I would have taken the toy, watched her cry, and felt a sense of normalcy and satisfaction. However, Marlee was showing me that she had matured into a new phase in her development, one in which she realized she was separate from me, autonomous, and could manipulate me. What was more important was my realization that I would have to change my grandparenting strategy. We will discuss how to relate to a two-year-old later in the book; however, for the sake of finishing the Marlee story, let me conclude by saying that I simply reinforced the skill of sharing that Marlee's mother had already begun to teach. Although Marlee had already learned that skill, she had to learn to relate to me on that level. Most important, I didn't take Marlee's behavior personally. Telling me no was not about me; it was about her maturing into an individual. Some parents would refer to Marlee's behavior as bad, terrible twos, a sign that she is hardheaded or have a dreaded strong personality. The truth is, Marlee is developing normally.

Attachment

This is a critical concept so pay close attention. Attachment is a strong emotional and physical bond felt toward a specific person or caregiver who is perceived as providing a sense of security and well-being. Children are born with an innate knowledge that they are unable to keep themselves safe and the innate drive to get their needs met by a parent. Attachment is the biggest milestone during infancy. Going back to the building foundation analogy, the degree to which a child is attached is most likened to a strong or weak foundation as it may determine the outcome of the parent-child relationship throughout childhood. As indicated, the sensorimotor stage is characterized primarily by how one is feeling. Children progress from passive reflexive and instinctive action to the beginning of symbolic thought. Another critical developmental milestone in this stage is the development of object permanence. This occurs when children learn that an objective continues to exist even though it cannot be seen or heard. For object permanence to occur, the child develops a separate sense of self from the object. The reason why parents are so important in a child adapting object permanence is because parents are the primary object in a child's life. Children learn whether they can rely on parents to be stable in their life. Whether or not the infant feels that the parent is permanent will determine if the child will have an appropriate attachment to the parent. At the risk of overstating this fact, the attachment forms the foundation on which you will build your subsequent relationship. In childhood, the attachment figure is seen by the child as the source of protection from danger and the source of relief from bodily stress. A child's ability to successfully attach to at least one adult is critical in the healthy development of their sense of self, sense of security, and ability to learn. Attachment in children is characterized by seeking to be close with the attachment figure when upset or threatened. In parents, attachment is demonstrated by responding sensitively and appropriately to the child's needs. The most important attachment figure for a child is not who simply feeds the child; instead, it is who plays and communicates with him or her. It is the person who responds to the child's need for comforting.

Appropriate attachment results in moral, social, emotional, and intellectual development. A child that is appropriately attached to a caretaker develops trust in the caretaker and transfers that trust to other relationships. A healthy attached child becomes self-reliant, develops a conscience and moral development, and facilitates social development by becoming independent. Being appropriately attached supports the child in dealing with stress, frustration, fear, and anxiety, and teaches the child to think logically. The parent's response during infancy is simple. Parent must be prepared to answer to the child's needs. The diagram displays the sequence of events that result in appropriate attachment.

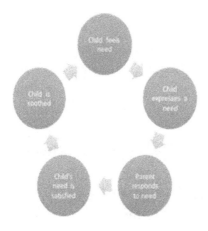

The Road to Secure Attachment

Children come out of childhood with one of four attachment outcomes: secure, anxious, avoidant, and ambivalent. The most favorable outcome is a child who is securely attached to the caretaker. A securely attached child becomes upset when a parent leaves but happy when the parent returns and is willing to re-engage. Securely attached children show signs of affection after separation. Children become anxiously attached to their parents if they are too preoccupied with their own situation and do not respond to their child's developmental needs. Parents of anxiously attached children are often over-punitive and harsh. The parent's behavior is unpredictable and the child develops a lack of trust. Ambivalently attached children will appear ambivalent when their parent returns. They may seem agitated and avoid direct eye contact with the parent when reunited. Avoidant attached parent-child relationships result when parents have repeated and prolonged separations. The child lacks trust in the reliable availability of the parent, and there is poor substitute care. The avoidant child will keep their physical and emotional distance from their parents. They do not seek physical proximity often. After separation they may acknowledge that the parent has returned, but they may walk away instead of greeting them. Avoidant attached children show a pattern of anger at the parent. The child may hit the parent, throw tantrums, and be defiant.

In summary, a few of the signs and symptoms of insecure attachment in infants are the child avoids eye contact, doesn't smile, doesn't reach out to be picked up, rejects the parent's efforts to calm, soothe, and connect, doesn't seem to notice or care when the parent leaves them alone, cries inconsolably, doesn't coo or make sounds, doesn't follow you with his or her eyes, isn't interested in playing games, and the child spends a lot of time comforting himself. Although the foundation for attachment is formed in the first three years of life, the child can recover by forming new relationships with responsive and permanent substitutes. The chances of recovery are best when the replacement caregiver is the new and improved *you*! The good news is that there are a few strategies parents can use to nurture or repair attachment issues.

Repairing the Weak Attachment Foundation

As indicated, weak attachment results from parents who fail to attune to their children for one reason or another. It is important to remember that children have an innate need to attach to a parent that is not diminished by the absence of an attachment figure. Also, children continue to desire attachment even if the parent is available but unwilling to engage; therefore, if a parent begins to attune to their child, he will respond favorably. Persistent engagement is a challenge for new parents because they are not used to having someone else for which to care. Additionally, there are many other things in a parent's world that are competing for attention like jobs, career, school, relationships, hobbies, unfinished business from childhood, and of course, technology and social media. Parents must make deliberate efforts to positively engage with the child and attune to their emotions. Parents who are sensitive to their child's emotions consistently assess whether a child is happy or sad, whether there has been a mood change, and seek to determine if the child is healthy. An attuned parent recognizes sudden mood changes in their child because the parent is purposely vigilant. I constantly see parents deeply engaged on their social media devices while the child trying to get the caretaker's attention. In addition to seeing mothers nursing their babies while staring at their cell phones, I've seen toddlers almost fall off chairs in public places because they manage to climb while their parents' attention is diverted. I have seen kids sneak away from their parents playing hide-and-go-seek and then the parent finally looks up and begin frantically calling the kid. When I see the panicked mother looking for their child, I usually give the parent an exasperated look and point in the direction of the hiding child. Of course, the kid hates me because I revealed their hiding place underneath the clothing racks. All that I am saying is that parents must be on active parent duty at all times when they are with their children. When parents are not physically or even emotionally able to attend to their children, they should secure a suitable substitute caregiver to provide relief.

Being engaged with a child can be exhaustive even for the most conscientious parent. It is important for parents to have respite. Time away from an infant benefits the parent and child! During separation, the parent gets relief and the child learns that the caretaker goes away *sometimes* but consistently returns after *brief* periods. Emphasis is being placed on the words *sometimes* and *brief* in the previous sentence. Prolonged and consistent absences during the infant stage has negative results. Think about any other job. If you took off for extended periods of time and often, you will likely lose the job. With prolonged absence from a job, not only will you not be able to demonstrate proficiency in the job, you will be considered unreliable. Similarly, absent parents are perceived as inefficient and unreliable. Recall the story of my client at the community day school who was raped by his father's friend who was often the day care provider for my client when the parents wanted to go out. My client felt anger toward his parents because he viewed them as inefficient and unreliable objects/parents. Overall, to repair attachment issues, parents must begin to and then consistently and appropriately respond to their children's behavior. Parents know their children best, so if there is a sudden change in personality, the parents should address the issue immediately.

During infancy, a parent's biggest challenge is to adapt to the role of parent so that the child will become securely attached to the parent. Parents begin this stage by making a conscious commitment to raise the child. When my juvenile clients would excitedly tell me that they were going to be a mother or a father, I would always say, "Ah, that's too bad." Of course they would look at me with surprise and say, "Why do you say that?" I say, "Because now you have to grow up and be an adult. Your carefree lifestyle is over. You now have to be responsible, and of course, right now, you are in custody so you are starting off wrong." Once I had my young now-deflated-mood client's attention, then I would bust out with, "Oh well, do you want to be a good parent?" They would always say, "Yes, I'm going to be a better mother or father than my parents." I would say, "Say it then and make a commitment to being a good parent." They would say, "I am." I would say, "No, say it!" When they would say that they were going to be a great parent, it was my hope that their brains would develop a good parent muscle and they would respond appropriately to parenting. Parents must recognize that parenting is an active process. Parents know that they have to be basically "tied to" the child and be the biggest positive influence. Infancy is a time when the parent's biggest responsibility is to quickly and consistently respond to the child's cry (figuratively and literally) for help. Parents who recognize that the infant brain is maturing and recording everything that the parent is doing understand their need to model and teach during the infancy stage. Parents must constantly talk to their child in an effort to engage the child and build future vocabulary. Parents should be mindful of the imprinting process. In order for a child to adapt the nine habits of people who do not end up in the criminal justice system, children must see these habits as soon as they leave the womb. Parents must use every opportunity to practice the skills while their children are young because during the child's next phase of development, parents will be required to model and teach the habits. Think of the infancy stage as a period, during which time parents plant the seeds of prosocial attitudes and behavior that will eventually sprout in their child when they reach adulthood. Parents must understand that although children are infants, they are highly impressionable during this phase of development.

Along with attunement, communication, and attachment, the need for discipline is another parental factor during the infancy stage, especially during the latter stages of infancy. In order to train their children, parents will have to engage in self-regulation. Potty training is a time when you realize the importance of parental discipline.

Lessons from the Field

My grandmother potty-trained my two oldest daughters while she cared for them during the time I was at work. My grandmother was so kind, patient, and just overall loving. As I look back, I realized that she literally regulated her life to care for my children as she took on all the roles of a parent during the day. My kids took a nap at the same time every day. My grandmother washed their hair at the same time each week. They had outside play at a certain time each day. My grandmother taught them to walk and made sure that she talked to them a lot so they could acquire language skills. My grandmother did not let anything get in the way of caring for my children. She loved it. Although she had retired from her job at a factory, raising my children became her job, and she approached it like the employee of the month. When I would drop them off in the morning, she greeted me with a big smile. As I pulled up to her home each morning to drop off my girls, my grandmother would be looking out of the window. If I was two minutes late, she would become worried. My grandmother was not obsessive-compulsive; she was just committed to taking care of the kids. So it is not surprising that both of my daughters were potty-trained by nine months! By the time I became pregnant with my third child, my grandmother was very ill. I recall telling her that she needed to get well because I would not know how to potty-train my new baby. My grandmother told me in a faint voice, "You need to train yourself." I figured it was the illness that had my precious grandma confused. It was two years later that I was training my baby. My baby was well over a year and approaching two years old (don't judge me) when I started the potty training. On one Saturday, my husband and I attended a major league baseball game. The seats were so high that we were as close to the sun as possible before incineration. After climbing what appeared to be two hundred stairs, we finally made it to our seats. I looked down from where we started and immediately began to dread the time when I had to walk back down the stairs. However, almost as soon as we sat down, my precious little two-year-old said, "Mommy, I have to go potty!" Lucky for me, I had put disposable panties on her, so I told her to go in her pants. She loudly protested, saying she had to go to the bathroom. It was at that moment that I recalled my grandmother's words: "You will have to discipline yourself." I didn't want to discipline myself; I wanted to force her to potty in her pants. But in order for the potty training regimen to move forward, I had to self-regulate and go down those stairs. It is imperative that parents discipline themselves to adhere to the structure they establish in order to parent their children.

Recently, my dentist bragged to me that he had potty-trained his toddler in three days! I would have preferred that he brag about discovering the first Novocain anesthesia that did not require a six-inch needle going who-knows-where once it goes in the gums, but since I am interested in supporting parents, I just kept my mouth shut (well, actually open while my dentist worked on my tooth) and listened. Prior to describing his foolproof, evidence-based potty training strategy, my dentist warned me that the method was not for the faint at heart as the system was highly involved, time-consuming, and required parental sacrifice. My dentist explained that to train in a short time span, there must be a specific start date and time, and there is no going back. In other words, once you take off the Pampers or pull-ups, there is no going back; it is panties and drawers all the way, until you go back to disposable diapers when you become incontinent again in old age. My dentist described a sort of pageantry for the disposing of the disposable Pampers, which starts by telling the child that it was time to get rid of the diapers/pull-ups. You must first get buy-in from the child. You can encourage them by buying cute underwear with their favorite character. Once they are verbally and physically prepared, the latter as evidenced by staying dry all night, asking to be changed, going to get the Pampers to be changed, or just flat-out saying, "Parent, I think my diaper needs to be changed," then you are ready for the work. According to my dentist, he put panties, or nothing at all, on this daughter, and for the next three days, he would engage his daughter every couple of hours to determine if she needed to use the restroom. Yes, he even had to get up in the middle of the night and take her to the restroom. My favorite part of the story was when he showed me a picture of his daughter in the backyard with no undies on after having urinated in several places in the backyard. According my dentist, his daughter appeared to feel empowered by her ability to pee outside. When I told my dentist how exhausting that sounded, he said that he was sleep-deprived but he enjoyed the experience of spending quality time with his daughter. As a dentist, he is away from home from long hours at a time, so those three days were quality time with his daughter.

In summary, I have tried to impress upon parents the importance of the infancy stage. During this phase of development, the parents lay the load-bearing foundation that will undergird not only the entire parent-and-child relationship but also future relationships. The biggest milestone during the infancy stage is attachment. Kids are naturally wired to attach to a parental figure, so be aware. If the parent is not the consistent attachment figure, the child is at risk of attaching to another figure. It is best that the child attaches to their parent if the parent is willing to be a consistent and appropriate role model. Children must come to rely on their parents to be consistent soothers, comforters, and providers. Parents must attune to their children at all times during this stage and must respond to their child's needs consistently. Although this stage is associated with much crying, parents must learn to communicate with their children and begin teaching the child how to verbalize their needs. Teaching verbal skills should occur as soon as the child comes out of the womb. Finally, parents' primary role during this stage is that of a role model. Parents are consistently modeling the behavior they want the child to acquire as they get older. Remember, the terrible twos period is actually a signal that the child is on-target developmentally. The phase is only referred to as a bad period because kids are no longer passive pieces of clay. They are now individuals and they know it!

Chapter Six

THREE TO SIX (CHILDHOOD)

For purposes of this book, I am defining *childhood* as the time that children are at preschool age until preadolescence. This is a broad age range, so I will discuss the period in two periods: three to six and then seven to eleven. Developmental periods are not perfect entities; they fluctuate, so some kids will demonstrate skills at earlier or later ages. Piaget refers to the stage as preoperational and describes symbols as the child's means of communicating to the world.

Whew, the infancy stage is finally over. You can sleep again! For most babies, by the time they are two, they are sleeping all night. Yahoo! And by the time that most children are three or four, parents are able to save money on disposable diapers, and even day care costs are reduced once the child is potty-trained. I haven't met one parent who said they missed having to clean adult-smelling poop off of their baby because by the end of the infancy stage, the baby's bowel movements are very smelly due to the introduction of a variety of foods. The money that is saved as babies go from infancy to toddlers can be saved and put into their college fund. In addition to saving money and sleeping all night, kids should now be out of those heavy infant cradles, and so parents don't have to lug around the baby seat. Some parents have actually injured themselves carrying that car seat with their forty-pound baby. Most impressive about the ending of the infancy stage is that most three-year-olds can walk fast enough to keep up with the parents' pace. As a matter of fact, most three-year-olds are running; at this point, parents don't have to carry them around everywhere. At three years old, potential babysitters start answering their phones again. As an extra bonus to ending to babies entering childhood, people will invite you over to their houses again because three-year-olds understand what "no" means. If you have raised an infant, you know that most of the challenges that come with the infancy stage result from the total dependence on the parents. Some parents describe the infancy stage as crippling or even a burden because during this stage, parents feel as though they are weighed down or carrying cargo. Parents are tied to the baby. Some mothers nurse for the first couple of years; some parents are very cautious about babysitters; some parents fear that something will happen to the baby, such as crib death or physical illness; and some parents take extended leave from work, so their finances are impacted. By the end of the infancy stage, some parents will return to their careers. Whatever the case, it is clear that the infancy stage has its challenges, and many parents welcome the time when their child is ready to go to preschool and later on to school.

Two of the milestones in childhood are the acquisition of symbolism and the development of intuitive thought. In other words, kids will need to be able take the symbols, organize them in some tangible fashion, and then provide some sort of order. It's one thing to know what a "ruff ruff" or dog is, but it is another thing to understand that dogs and people are different. As is the case in the infancy stage, it is important that parents are able to communicate with their children; therefore, understanding how the child processes the world is important so that the parents can journey with them. During childhood, the child will view the world through symbols. Symbolic thinking is a view in which characters or internal images are used to represent objects, persons, and events that are not present. Parents see examples of symbolic thinking when their child is engaging in pretend play, writing, drawing, and speaking. Symbolic play is connected to creativity and the ability to connect with others. When raising a child who is demonstrating symbolism, one of the things a parent will see *animism*. This is the belief that inanimate objects are capable of actions and have likable qualities (stars sparkle because they are happy; a child falls down because the ground is mad). *I recall when I was little and I would hurt myself, my mother and grandmother would discipline the thing that hurt me. So if I fell down, they would stomp on the floor and say, "Bad floor." I would be satisfied because their stumping meant that the mean old floor was being punished. My parents may have allowed me to stay in the symbolic stage too long. I still get mad if I bump my foot or stub my toe. I look at the abusive inanimate object with such disdain. I have almost fallen on the street and I look at the crack on the sidewalk (or nothing at all) and roll my eyes because, of course, it is the ground's fault that I almost fell and not my neglecting to be careful.*

At the risk of sounding too technical for what I planned for an easy-to-read parenting book, I want to further elaborate on the symbolic thought in childhood because it is very important that parents are clued into what they should begin seeing so that they know that the child is meeting developmental milestones. *Artificialism* is a form of symbolism that may be demonstrated by a child who believes that environmental characteristics can be attributed to human actions (it's windy because someone is blowing hard). *Transductive reasoning* is demonstrated when a child draws a relationship between two unrelated and separate events (a parent gets in a car accident, and a child gets in trouble at school). Another symbolic thinking style in young children is *intuitive thought,* which is demonstrated by inquisitiveness. Children during this phase are curious and ask many questions. They know a lot of information, but they don't really know why or how they know it. Intuitive thought comes across as sort of mystical. Parents may think, where did that come from, why are you even asking those questions? Don't forget that their brains are growing and making connections, so the child is trying to make sense of all this information. They have a vast amount of information, and they don't know where it came from and what to do with it. Your job, parents, is to provide answers. Children who, during early childhood, may believe that a baby came from the stork can later understand that babies are born from their mother's body. As is the case with symbolic thinking, children during this phase are just seeing codes, figures, and cryptograms, so intuitive thinking may appear to adults as unreasonable. Therefore, if they believe that it rained because they spilled the milk, that is their preoperational reality. If they believe that the cat food is human food, that is their reality. It is the parents' job to move kids from seeing symbols to understanding symbols.

Preoperational thinkers engage in *centration,* which means that they will focus attention on one aspect of a situation while disregarding others. If a parent were to give two preoperational thinkers the same amount of juice but used two different cups, the kids will think that the larger cup has more liquid. They are only looking at the big cup. Even if you showed the child that you are putting the same amount of liquid in each cup, they may only be able to focus on the size of the cup. If you asked two kids to organize a set of blocks and you gave each of the same blocks, but of different colors and materials, one child engaging in centration may organize the blocks based on colors and the other child may organize based on the material. Organization will be based on what the child chose to focus on.

I recall when my one of my nieces was very young. She could not have been more than three years old. We were standing in a store line, and I, just entering adolescence, was holding her. My niece was looking over my shoulder. By thirteen years old, I was already about five feet seven inches tall, so she was pretty high up in the air. My niece began to tap me on my shoulder and say, "Auntie, look at that . . . Auntie, look at that!" She became more desperate in her attempt to get my attention, so I finally turned around to look at what she was pointing at. There was a little person standing behind me. Although it was obvious that he was a grown man (facial hair, premature balding), it was also clear that he was very small. The top of his head was at my butt. This was confusing for my little three-year-old niece. The little person had been waiting for me to turn around, and when I did, I saw that he was already smiling. I said to my niece, "Yes, I see him," and I tried to turn her face around. My attempts were futile as she kept asking me to look, so after making my purchase, I hurried out the store embarrassed. I didn't have enough sense to explain to my niece that the person was an adult but small. My niece would eventually understand and appreciate that people come in all sizes, but that day, she left totally confused because all my niece was focusing on was either the person's small size, which means he was a kid, or his adult face, which meant he should have been bigger.

Another preoperational thought process is called *conservation*. Children engaged in this thinking are unaware that changing the substance does not change the basic principles. The best example I have of this is money; conservative thinkers are not going to understand if you take their twenty quarters and give them one measly five-dollar bill that they still have five dollars. And I have seen kids having tantrums in restaurants when their parents try and cut their pancakes or sandwiches into "little" bite-sized pieces for their little mouth. As far as the preoperational thinker is concerned, you made their food (symbol) smaller.

Irreversibility is another preoperational thinking mode. Children are unable to mentally reverse a sequence of events. For some children, even if you pasted that pancake back together again, it will not be the same. Finally, symbolic thinkers demonstrate *inclusion*. They are unable to understand that one category or class cannot contain several classes. So a child with this style of thinking will not understand that eight dogs and three cats are eleven animals. However, once the child begins to engage in *intuitive* reasoning, they will be able to tell you that there are more dogs than cats.

Now that you understand how kids process the world through symbols, the knowledge should minimize the amount of frustration parents experience at this age. Very often, because kids at this age can talk, parents expect that the child's conversation should be logical and make sense. Some parents will even get mad. *My husband tells the story of being a very young boy and traveling with his parents in a car. They passed a herd of cows, and my husband proudly proclaims, "Cow!" He said that his father became very upset with him and said, "Boy, you don't see the testicles on that bull? That's not a cow." My husband's ego was deflated because he tried to impress his dad by showing him that he could recognize the cows, only to be told he was wrong. My husband didn't understand why he was wrong until he was older and realized that bulls are male cows. But for years, he internalized the sadness he felt after being chastised by his father.*

It is the parents' responsibility to move the child from preoperational thought to operational thought. My husband's father missed an opportunity to discuss gender differences. But of course, he did the best he could in that given moment. My father-in-love didn't know anything about symbolic reasoning. Some parents also become concerned and even angry when the child appears to be engaging in fantasy play. However, rest assured, just like kids will ultimately be able to distinguish between cows and bulls, pretend play and imaginary friends are adaptive until the child is prepared to cognitively reason, which will occur later in childhood.

One day, while riding public transportation, I witnessed a mother and her two- or three-year-old son on public transportation. The little boy was sitting in a stroller and he was making noises assimilating a car engine. The mother, obviously embarrassed that the boy was making noises, kept angrily telling the boy to "shut up." As the behavior persisted, she moved to pinching him. Although his expression demonstrated that he was in pain, he continued to make noises until the mother's fingers turned red from pinching so hard. The little boy finally stopped making car engine noises and began to cry. Admittedly, the crying was not as loud as the engine noises, so mom was partially successful in stopping the behavior. The point is, making engine noises on a train is age-appropriate when you are two or three. Children are not concerned with social decorum. I was so sad looking at that little boy cry. I really wanted to go over and talk to the mother, or at least pinch her so she would start crying. But then I would have been arrested, lost my law enforcement job, and ended up in the criminal justice system.

Parents play a critical role in how soon children come out of pretend play. By journeying with them and gently reasoning with them, children soon learn that there is no papa, momma, or baby bear that will eat their leftover cereal.

Another milestone in childhood is the child's ability to adapt to the world. When kids are babies, parents adjust the baby's surroundings for them. As soon as infants are born, parents attempt to mimic the womb the best they can. Babies are swaddled during the first few weeks of life so that they can feel warm and secure. This helps the baby's temperature to remain stable until their own internal thermostat sufficiently keeps their bodies warm. Toddlers are given walkers and other toys to strengthen the legs until the child can walk. When babies are trying to sleep, parents may turn off electronics and even put their phones on silent mode so the child will not be interrupted. Some parents will soosh anyone talking too loud in the vicinity of their sleeping baby. However, at some point, the child will have to learn to soothe themselves. There are times when I am so tired, by the end of the day, I would love to have a big set of arms to rock me back and forth until I fall to sleep. But since that is not going to happen, I am glad that I learned early in my life how to settle myself in such a way that I can crawl (sometimes literally) in my bed and go to sleep.

LISA A. HILL, PH.D., LMFT

Some parents will go to great lengths to assure that a child is not hurt emotionally and physically (which they should). However, at some point during childhood, parents should be concerned with teaching their children to adapt to the outside world. Adaptation is defined as a change or the process of change by which an organism or species becomes better suited to its environment. When people talk about adaptation, they usually refer to it as discipline. Discipline is not just concerned with punishment; discipline is the practice of training people to obey rules or a code of behavior to synergize. Children need is to be suited for their environment. Being suited is similar to adjusting to the temperature. When it is cold outside, most people will suit themselves with a jacket as opposed to waiting for someone to come along and swaddle them in a blanket. What happens to people who do not behave or get along in society such as committing law violations? They end up in the criminal justice system. To avoid the pitfall of the system, parents need to train their kids to adjust to the changing variables in their lives.

In order for kids to adapt to society, parents will need to teach and model appropriate social skills. Although parents spend a lot of time teaching their kids during the childhood period of development, modeling continues to be an appropriate skill and teaching strategy during any phase. Parents can teach kids to say hello to people, say thank-you and please, and "excuse me" when they interrupt a conversation. Teach kids to be polite to other people. I have always enjoyed pushing my children in strollers. As soon as I received the okay from their pediatrician that it was safe for them to be outside and I was ready to exercise, I would take my kids on long stroller rides. I still take my grandbabies on stroller rides. Recently, I was strolling with my just-turned one-year-old granddaughter, Nyla. We walked around a lake. As we passed by other walkers and runners, I would smile, wave, or just say hello. Nyla, at one, was at the age and developmental stage that she liked to imitate behavior, so she started copying me. Every time someone would get close, she would quickly yell out, "Hi!" If she had her pacifier in her mouth, she would just wave. As a matter of fact, at some point during the ride, she fell asleep in the stroller, but until she went into a deep slumber, anytime she heard me greet someone, she would pop her head up and wave. I found it quite entertaining, but I must admit I was happy when she fell asleep as she was beginning to say hi over and over to the same people each time we passed them on the lake's path. The point is, it is never too early to begin teaching, especially through modeling appropriate social skills.

Sometimes, when kids socialize, that means the parents have to socialize. Parents don't always feel like socializing, and more importantly, other people don't feel like socializing with a kid that is a stranger. My soon-to-be three-year-old granddaughter has reached that stage that some parents dread—a time when kids want to talk to everyone and sometimes ask inappropriate questions. If you have modeled being social, your kids will reflect that trait at some point.

At two years and ten months, Marlee is very friendly. Her opening greeting to strangers is always, "Hi, what's your name . . . What is your mommy's and daddy's name? . . . Where are they?" She gets those questions out so quickly that I am often unable to stop her.

I have a lot of experience with this age group. I spent a lot of time babysitting my nieces and nephews, and after raising my own four children, one would think I would be used to what I refer to as "little kid chatter." In spite of my familiarity with little kids, these questions always catch me off guard. And at my advanced age, I am not as quick to redirect my little grandchildren's attention or to interject something like, "Please stop bothering the nice person." Sometimes when I realize that I am too late to stop the interruption, I just smile and let it happen. Luckily, most people are polite and just journey with new little communicators. Of course, I have had people ignore my kids and act like they don't hear them speak. My most memorable recent encounter was with a lady that was sitting in an airport. Our flight was delayed for five hours, so me, my husband, Marlee, and her five-year-old sister Milaya were sitting in a crowded airport. As soon as this particular woman sat down, Marlee began with her usual questions. I said, "Marlee, please don't bother the nice lady." The woman responded, "That's right, just wait for my husband. He loves talking to people; he will answer all of your questions." As soon as her husband arrived, they both moved. Personally, I didn't mind. I wanted to let my frustration from being in the airport five hours have its time, so I didn't want to play nice with strangers at that moment.

The childhood developmental phase is representative of a time that children will continue to experience rapid brain development, but because they can communicate, parents will actually see the fruits of learning. Parents are sometimes amazed at what their child will say at this stage. Actually, the child will manifest the words that were taught to them during infancy. By three years old, children are becoming more efficient at language skills, so they can begin communicating what they have heard and internalized during infancy. Understanding the axiom "garbage in, garbage out" is appropriate during this phase. Whatever has been communicated to the child will come out verbally and behaviorally. For some parents, they will spend a lot of time reteaching their child appropriate behavior. Think about it: if every time a parent became frustrated and used various expletives, the child will do the same thing. I have seen many embarrassed parents in public when their child used profanity out of frustration. The parent was understandably embarrassed because, in many cases, the foulmouthed child was too young to have learned the word by reading a book. Parents of toddlers need to talk, talk, talk. Not just so kids hear your words, but it is the content of your words that will make a difference. Parents of toddlers are consistently in the teacher mode. Every moment is a teachable moment, and no matter how old your child is, it is not too early to sneak a big word on them and grow their vocabulary.

Did you ever aspire to be a schoolteacher? Even if you did not, you will play the role of an educator during the childhood stage of development and through most of preadolescence. During childhood, parents will continue to build on the foundation (relationship) that they established during infancy. By three years old, it is believed that a child's brain is 80 percent developed. Children are now able to speak but do not have a full grasp of language. However, as they move through this phase, their language will become broader. Children's view of world is through not only recognizing symbols but also the manipulation of symbols. During childhood, there is an increase in pretend play. Children in this phase are not able to see things from different views; they only see things through their own perspective, and so they are very egocentric. In other words, children in this phase of development really don't care how other people feel. Preoperational thinkers are not only egocentric, but they also only see things in absolutes. "I want to eat now; I don't want to wait for the food to cook. I want to stay at the park, I don't care that it is raining. I want a horse; it doesn't matter how much it costs or that we live in an apartment. I want to climb that ten-foot tree; I don't care if the branches are very thin." It is the parents' job to move a concrete pre-operational thinker into abstract reasoning. Parents do this by explaining and broadening the child's view. Parents calmly advise that food cannot be eaten raw; in order for food to cook, there is a need to expose it to heat by way of cooking. Heating the food will take time. During that time, the child must wait. Parents explain that it is cold outside, and so they must leave the park, or parents can show their child a sign that lists the time that the park closes. Then the parents can say, "In following the posted rules, we must leave the park." In letting a concrete thinker know that branches are thin and cannot bear much weight, if the child climbs the tree and gets on the tree's fragile branches, he will surely fall. Falling from ten feet will cause an injury. I know, exhausting, but in order to not have a seven-year-old demand to eat, parents must support the child's cognitive development.

Lessons from the Field

Never Discipline Wearing Your Underwear

Now that you know that kids are egocentric, can sometimes only hold one image, or attend to one idea at a time, parents are cautioned that they should never discipline their child while only wearing underwear. And never, never, never discipline your kids coming out of the shower or bath naked. My kids like to tell stories about their childhood. My older two frequently compare their childhood to that of their younger siblings. Of course, my older children feel like they had it tougher than the younger ones. They are probably right because their dad and I are less intense, we are older, and well, we are older, tired, and slower. One day, they were telling stories about how many lectures I would give and how they dreaded getting "the talk" after they had done something wrong. My daughters went on, and through bursts of laughter, one of them reminded the other of the times I would lecture them in my underwear or worse, naked! My kids said they feared that they would get into more trouble because the entire time I talked, all they could think about was my body that they hoped they would never have or in looking at the underwear. They could only focus on why I would wear the type of bra or panties I had on. They both agreed that it was really difficult for them to attune to what I was saying because they were so overwhelmed by what they feared was to come in their lives. After they laughed wildly, one of my kids went on to say that it wasn't the body or my lack of attire—it was the fact that my anger and lack of clothes did not match, and they could not take me seriously. So parents, please put your clothes on before disciplining your kids.

Once Again, Get Off, Electronics

It is going to be even more important that parents get off of their smartphones and social media during the young childhood stage. As you probably have realized by now, this phase requires the in-your-face engagement that I discussed previously. During the young childhood phase of development, parents have to pay close attention to their child. Not only are kids more active and mobile during this time, but they are also beginning to be more autonomous. Not because they have earned independence, but because parents have welcomed the new freedom that comes with having kids that are fully potty-trained, sleeping all night, can play independently and with other children, and are in school all day. It is really the parents' autonomy from the child that may result in the parents being more drawn to their electronic devices. What makes electronic devices even more attractive to parents of young children is that kids at this age also love electronic devices. Three-year-olds love getting on YouTube and other websites to watch videos. If allowed, kids at this age will watch videos for hours alongside the parent. Television is another electronic device that must be monitored. According to recent Nielsen ratings, kids in this age group watch over twenty-four hours per week, and the number of hours increases as kids get older. Adults watch up to almost fifty hours. This does not include the added time on streamed television or watching videos on social media. The American Academy of Pediatrics (AAP) recommends that kids spend no more than an hour a day on any screen, which means limiting television, computers, and smart devices. I would imagine that the AAP recommendations are a shocker for some parents because their recommendation means that some parents will have to find another babysitter and additional playdates in order to comply with the AAP's recommendation. Okay, the bottom line is that during the young childhood stage of development, parents are the primary teachers, and unlike schoolteachers, parents are in teacher mode during all waking hours. So you can't just turn off the television and do nothing; you have to turn off electronics and then engage the child in some activity. If not, they will sneak back on their favorite entertainment. Remember my little friend who interrupted my quiet time in the hotel hot tub? That's the type of teaching and parenting that I am referring to. Even when kids are sleep, parents should be thinking of their lesson (parent) plans.

Lessons from the Field

One day, I had taken my oldest granddaughter Milaya to the park. She wanted to get on the dreaded tire swing. Having raised four children of my own, I had come to dread the time when they desired to get on the tire swing because it required a new and higher developmental ability. Usually, when a child first asks to ride the tire swing, they have not mastered the skills to actually take on the swing. To ride the tire swing, you must be able to balance yourself and hold on while the swing is moving around in circles and back and forth. I get goose bumps just thinking of that monstrous swing. In addition to the dual motion, there is a very big hole in the middle, and if the child does not have the dexterity to hold on while laughing wildly, swinging around, and back and forth, they will fall in or off the tire. Needless to say that each of my four children has fallen in and off. On the day that I took my granddaughter to the park, I was not emotionally ready to see Milaya fall. I am her grandmother. I am older; I didn't want to try and lift her up and dust her off. I didn't want to hear her crying. I just wanted to have fun at the park. Please don't judge me.

What makes the tire swing even more challenging is that it is not fun unless you are going fast and even faster! While I was cautiously allowing my four-year-old to try out the swing (eye roll), little six-year-old Brian runs over and motions me to stop the swing so he could get on. How did he motion, you ask? He stood dangerously close to the moving swing and stared at me with his runny nose. He then held his hand, demonstrating the universal stop sign. I was amused, to say the least, so I stopped the swing. The way Brian jumped on the tire swing, it was obvious that he had proven he had the dexterity to handle the tire swing and had demonstrated the skill so many times. I began to push the two little ones on the tire swing. Little Brian kept saying, "Push faster!" Brian then stood up, and so my grandbaby slowly stood up. Although I told Brian that standing didn't appear safe, he assured me that he had stood on the tire swing before and could handle it. I began to slowly push the two. Brian kept yelling, "Faster, faster." When I told him I didn't want to push him any faster for fear he could fall, he told me, "My mother pushes me fast." At that point, his mother walked up and joined the conversation. She said, "Brian, what did I tell you about being argumentative?" He lowered his head humbly. She said, "You should say thank you to the lady for pushing you on the swing." Little Brian complied but quickly added, "So, Mom, can you push me fast?" The mother had not only taught Brian to be polite, but she also had obviously taught him what it meant to be argumentative, and she was reinforcing the skill right there in the park. Brian had the vocabulary, but he was still preoperational so he didn't care about my feelings.

Overall, the childhood stage of development can be exhausting. Although childhood is viewed by many parents as less challenging than infancy, the childhood period of development has its own challenges. Childhood is a very active time period for parents and children. Instead of being reactive as in the infancy stage (responding to crying, changing the diaper after it gets soiled, sticking a pacifier in the mouth, etc.), parents of a school-age child must anticipate and be prepared to act. I am referring to parents waking up each morning and immediately being prepared to start talking, answering questions, instructing, directing, and overall teaching. There is no time to waste. The childhood stage of development is characterized by rapid learning and increased comprehension. Kids are beginning to maneuver all the symbols they encounter. Even if you did not aspire to be a schoolteacher, you will play the role of an educator during the childhood stage of development. Your primary role is to move the child forward as he makes the transition from concrete thinking (one cat plus one dog equals a cat and a dog, to one dog and one cat equals two animals) to abstract reasoning. Kids naturally develop these skills on their own if exposed to the skills under the right conditions. Finally, teaching social skills is also very important during the childhood phase. Parents not only model good social skills, but they actively teach the skills consistently as the child will learn through repetition. By the end of the childhood phase, some scientists believe that the personality is established, so parents should work really hard during this phase to assure that their kids have the attitudes, behaviors, and overall personality of people who do not end up in the criminal justice system.

Lessons from the Field

While walking in a park one day (yes, I spend a lot of time in the park observing childhood behavior; again, don't judge me), I met up with a little girl and what appeared to be her grandfather. I believe it was her grandfather, but I have learned through trial and mostly error that you should not assume that a mature person is the grandparent. One time, I was at an indoor play gym for toddlers. I saw an acquaintance that I had not seen in a few years. He was supervising two young children and was holding an infant. I confidently inquired about the age of his grandchildren. He smiled and said, "Don't let this gray beard fool you. These are my kids." I was embarrassed, and he was embarrassed that I was embarrassed, so we just talked about how cute his kids and my grandkids were. Anyway, I digress. On the day that I was in the park, when the man and little girl were within talking distance, the little girl loudly and confidently said to me, "Hi, I am Anyla and I am four years old!" I smiled and said, "Well, hello, Anyla. My name is Lisa and it is nice to meet you." Anyla smiled and ran off. When I passed by her grandfather, he said to me, "She can spot good people." I thanked him but could not help but to think that the little girl's communication skills, if developed appropriately, will be very useful as she gets older. Anyla was demonstrating good social skills and synergy. Although we have to teach our children to be very careful, we do want our kids to develop necessary skills that will facilitate interaction and communication with others.

Chapter Seven

Seven to Eleven Years (Preadolescence): The End of Santa Claus

Preadolescence is actually a continuation of childhood, but preadolescence comes with the ability for a higher level of thinking. Therefore, if your child is still insisting that Santa Claus exists, he may be "playing you." Preadolescents, sometimes referred to as tweens or even middle schoolers, come sooner with each generation. A few years ago, I would have identified preadolescence beginning at eleven. However, due to the maturation of society and the increased use of hormones in food, preadolescence can begin as early as seven. By seven years old, some kids have already begun to release hormones that result in the bodily changes of an adult. Piaget refers to the preadolescence as the concrete operational stage of cognitive development. According to Piaget, this time period is characterized by the development of logical thought processes. Kids who are in the concrete operational stage exercise thinking that is more mature and adult-like. By seven years old, kids continue to view the world through symbols, but they have a better understanding of those symbols. By the time your child is about seven years old, most of them have matured to a level where they can make concrete connections. The number two and another two makes four. Now you can put the same amount of fluid in different size glasses and a preadolescent will understand that the amount of liquid remains the same because they now understand the notion of conservation. That's good news for parents of multiple kids who argue over who has the most soda pop. Preadolescents demonstrate the beginning of inductive reasoning. In other words, they can make inferences from observations in order to make a generalization. However, preadolescents can't go from generalization and apply it to a specific outcome. For example, kids understand that if A is bigger than B and B is bigger than C, then A is bigger than B and C. Most preadolescents are able to see another person's perspective even if they don't agree. Children at this age can only solve problems that apply to actual and concrete objects, not hypothetical tasks and abstract concepts. When it is raining outside, a coat is needed. If you touch a hot stove, you will experience pain. If a table is really heavy, two people will be required to lift it.

One reason a school-age child may continue to go along with the reality of Santa Claus is that they have matured to an even higher level of cognitive thinking and they have learned the skill of manipulation. The preadolescent may have figured out that if they play along with the Santa game, toys and gifts will show up on Christmas morning! Still, in other situations, some kids are aware that Santa Claus is a myth at this age, but because the parents are unwilling to let go of the fantasy, the kids just play along. Again, this is evidence of higher-level thinking. The reason that kids naturally figure out that one obese man or woman cannot carry enough toys for every kid in the world in one night on a sled that is pulled by flying reindeer is that they have acquired the ability to think logically. By seven years old, children have been in school for a few years. Even if they have not been exposed to certain knowledge in their immediate environment, their new friends that they meet outside the home will surely let them know the truth. Many kids have found out the shocking truth about Santa Claus from one of their new little peers who may be further along cognitively. One of my daughters told me, once she was grown and she had received many toys from Santa, she found out that there was no Santa because she recognized her dad's handwriting on the thank-you note from Santa, who had taken a bite out of the cookies and left a half-consumed glass of milk. Because kids will naturally come to understand the myth of Santa Claus, I advise that parents understand the natural phases of childhood development, begin to journey with their kids, and teach them to think logically respectively.

By the time kids are seven, they have pretty much adapted to school. Many are in the first or second grade and attend school all day. At this age, kids spend more qualitative time in school than anywhere else. Think about it, what other system consumes that much of a child's time five days a week? Teachers and schoolmates play a huge role in a child's life. During this preadolescence period, kids usually have one teacher that they stay with all day. It is not until middle school and adolescence that a child will experience multiple teachers. Spending a lot of time with one teacher and playmates is important because this time also coincides with a desire to acquire knowledge. When kids are at school-age, they are learners, and they like to talk and ask a lot of questions. *A school-age child's brain is like a huge canvas, and although there is some writing on the canvas wall, there is so much more space on that canvas on which to make marks.* The canvas analogy does not give justice to the amount of information a child's brain can take in. A canvas has limitations; however, literally, the child's brain is limitless. There is ongoing research that keeps extending the age at which time the brain is making connections, growing, and acquiring knowledge. The only reason that researchers are gaining more knowledge is because their (the researcher's) brains are growing and they keep figuring stuff out. A parent's job is to keep flooding the child with information. Now, that does not mean that you should force-feed your child information. What I mean is making sure your child has plenty of learning *opportunities* in and outside of school.

Lessons from the Field

I recall when I supervised the Truancy Unit in probation, this sixteen-year-old girl was referred for truancy. When I met with the family, the mother indicated that her daughter was very smart but lazy. The daughter sat silent. The mother informed me that the child's laziness and lack of motivation had cost "them" a scholarship and admission into a private school. The mother was very disappointed in her daughter because her older child had attended the school and it had become a tradition, which my truant client was breaking. When I talked to the probationer alone, she told a slightly different story. She indicated that her mother was verbally abusive when she was younger. If the girl could not understand a new school concept, the mother would yell at her and make her work on homework late into the night. The girl said that her mother would stay up and berate her, calling her names like stupid, idiot, and crazy. As soon as the girl started high school, she had enough and decided to quit going to school all together. When I talked to the mother about what her daughter had disclosed, the mother admitted that she was "strict on her," but that she just wanted her to learn.

Parents are responsible for providing the resources needed to be successful. Resources could also include a tutor or merely another adult who has the patience and stamina to teach school concepts in a caring, appropriate way, without profanity, frustration, and degradation. In addition to providing opportunities for learning, I don't want to minimize the parent's teaching role during preadolescence. To put it plainly, during preadolescence, the parent must continue to be available to teach at all times. I know this sounds exhausting, which is the reason I am preparing you. If you have the benefit of reading this book while in the contemplation phase of becoming a parent, this information is very timely. For those of you who already have at least one child, I say, "Get in where you fit it." That means you will have to start teaching as soon as you put this book down. Although babies start out little, cute, and passive learners, preadolescents are active learners, and parents will be required to be a primary educational dispensary of information. A dispenser is someone who distributes. I think that is a wonderful analogy for parents. Parents distribute all kinds of things during the parenting process, most importantly, love, care, concern, money, money, and more money. However, a big part of what parents give out is information. During preadolescence, parents will continue to teach the lessons that they began during early childhood. Since preadolescents have a higher level of understanding and communication, parents will have the ability to not only teach higher learning, but also check for understanding. Taking from another is stealing; good hygiene is important for good health; be polite; being on time is important; be truthful; don't use profanity, etc. The teaching of this knowledge is not in vain. The reason parents must teach their children good manners, to adapt to society and engage in prosocial behavior, is to reach the ultimate goal of synergizing and sharpening the saw. And by now, you know that the decisive goal is to assure that the kids don't end up in the criminal justice system.

As previously stated and to emphasize the point even further, the teacher role is most important during the preadolescent phase of development; this time coincides with a child's unlimited capability to learn, a strong desire to acquire knowledge, and a time when the parent can still exercise a high degree of control over the child's life. Additionally, teaching and learning are easier by preadolescence because by this time, most kids are effective communicators, so barriers to two-way communication are removed. By preadolescence, kids can be trusted to bathe themselves (notwithstanding those kids who were never shown how to bathe appropriately or effectively), and they can feed themselves by preparing easy meals. Preadolescents can pick out their own clothes and even iron them. My nephew Michael was ironing by the time he was seven years old. My sister, his mother, hated to iron and loved to sleep, but she insisted on freshly ironed clothes, so she taught my nephew to iron very early. By the time my nephew was in middle school, he was ironing his mother's clothes. Michael is now grown with his own child, but he is still very meticulous about ironing.

Lessons from the Field

While serving at the probation department, I ran across many clients whose parents had neglected to capitalize on their concrete thinking status, so the child could not only avoid the criminal justice system but also impart the importance of good hygiene. While supervising the probation department's Family Preservation Unit, one of my line probation officers offered to give a class to clients on hygiene. She reported that she too had many clients who routinely neglect their hygiene needs. During one of the classes, the probation officer went over, in detail, how to clean the entire body. Initially, the young clients were embarrassed and laughing. But then many of them started paying close attention. It became increasingly apparent that some of the information the probation officer was providing on hygiene was novel information. She started at the head and ended by showing them how to clean in between their toes. I remember sitting there thinking about who had taught me how to clean my toes. I recalled my mother having this little song about toes and pulling on them, and perhaps that is how I learned, but I honestly could not recall. I was the youngest of five children, so perhaps I saw one of my siblings cleaning their bodies. In any event, it was clear that many of the kids in that room watching the probation officer perform a mock bath had not been introduced to purposefully cleaning in between all of their toes. Learning comes from exposure; therefore, if you are not taught to clean your toes, you will likely forget "to pull each toe apart and clean out the residue that forms from the toes being stuck together in sweaty shoes all day and the feet will stink." Parents, in addition to all the other things you have to teach your child, please teach them how to take care of their hygiene.

Parents have a newfound freedom with respect to assuring that children are meeting educational milestones in school. By preadolescence, most kids have a grasp on their school and homework, and if there are questions remaining, the child is usually articulate enough to inquire from their teacher the next school day. By preadolescence, parents usually don't have to plan out two to three hours a night to sit with the child and reteach the lessons that were taught during the school day. Recall that I said that I was always happy when my kids were about seven years old for all the reasons I stated above but for one reason in particular—they could read on their own. I seriously dreaded teaching reading because my undiagnosed attention deficit disorder would always kick in. When kids are learning to read, they read very, very, very slowly. They must enunciate each syllable to each word. With attention deficit disorder, you have to work really hard to focus and pay attention. Of course, when you are teaching a child to read, you have to be prepared to jump in at any time and help the child sound out a word. You also have to be prepared for questions along the way. Most importantly, you have to be excited for them because they are reading, so when they look at you after they have read a word, you have to be ready with a big smile and even a high five! You can't be caught with your eyes closed. Staying alert while my kids practice their early reading skills was difficult for me. Thank God for elder siblings. By the time my third and fourth kids were born, their older sisters were reading to the younger two.

Yes, there is newfound freedom when raising a preadolescent, but this is by no means a time when parents can back off. Parents must stay engaged because, along with schoolteachers, parents are on the first line to respond to all the questions that will constantly pop into children's heads. Kids wake up with questions, and they go to bed with questions. Right after school, after leaving their schoolteachers, kids continue to have questions. When confronted with a barrage of questions from the child after the school day has ended, some parents ask, why didn't they get all their questions answered from the teacher who is getting my tax dollars to teach my child? (This is not my position, but certainly I have heard many parents express this sentiment.) The answer to that question is because when they are in school, they are one of many students. The preadolescent stage of development is also a time when kids are comparing themselves with their age-mates. They need to make sure that they are just as capable as the next student. The last thing a preadolescent would want is to appear not as smart as another student; therefore, when kids come out of school, not only do they have less competition for learning, but they may also feel less self-conscious, so they freely unload additional questions onto the parents. Remember what Barbara Harrell Carson said, *"Students learn what they care about, from people they care about and who, they know, care about them."* Never forget that your child was your student before they were their teachers' students.

Too often, parents just don't want to be bothered with kids during the concrete operational preadolescent phase of development because the engagement is so intense. It is almost as involved as the infancy stage but in a different way. Some parents just want to turn it off! Parents have other "stuff" that gets in the way. They often tell the child to ask their teachers all those questions. Parents don't want to be teachers, so they just say anything to stop the barrage of questions. The kid may ask, why is the sky so blue, and the parent, who may have had it with the questions, blurts out, "Because if it were green, people would confuse it with grass!" What? Fast-forward a few years later when you forgot you told your child that skies don't want to be confused with grass. Now the child is no longer viewing the world through animism, so they clearly should understand that the grass and sky don't have a relationship like people do, so they don't get mad at each other. But just like they may have pretended to go along with Santa for a few extra years, they may share the grass-and-sky relationship with their teacher. The child's teacher sends an email home asking for a meeting. To avoid the embarrassment, my advice is that if you don't know the answer to the question, go Google it or have the child Google it. Don't try and explain it when you really don't know the correct answer. Some parents will spend a lot of time trying to appear smart when they don't know the answer. Albert Einstein gave good advice when he said, "If you can't explain it to a six-year-old, you don't understand it yourself." And for parents that just want to appear smart and know everything, distract the child for a few minutes while you go find the answer on one of your smart devices and then come back and appear to be a genius. If you just don't feel like answering questions because of "other stuff," just put your child in the hands of someone who wants to teach in the moment. This could mean a neighbor or a neighborhood kid that is slightly older. Yes, check the Megan's list first.

Dinnertime is a great platform for discussions. I know some parents are saying that people should not talk with their mouths full, so I teach my kids to be quiet when at the table. To those parents, I offer that the time in between bites at the dinner table and after eating when everyone is still milling around at the table is an opportune time to just check in with everyone. One of the biggest challenges for kids during the preadolescent stage of development is boredom and the mundane. Kids at this stage don't want novelty; they want new information and experiences. Their brains are just absorbing everything so fast, so they have a desire to keep learning. Parents of adolescents often complain that their child will say, "I'm bored, there is nothing to do." Parents immediately start throwing out all the activities that they can busy themselves with: "Go watch television; go see if your friends want to come outside; play video games; go practice your instrument or sport; read all those books you asked me to buy; go on your computer or smart device." But this is old stuff; preadolescents always want new adventures. Parents have to teach their kids, through modeling, how to be content with the ordinary. My main point is to make sure parents understand that preadolescents can't help wanting excitement as these emotions are innate. Unfortunately, many kids respond to monotony with nonsocial behavior such as smoking, drinking, drug use, and community misconduct. In many respects, the incorrigible behavior is an attempt to add a spark in their mundane day.

To avoid kids resorting to nonsocial means of excitement to escape boredom, parents should make sure that, beginning at birth, they introduce traditions into the family. These traditions should include things like game night. It doesn't matter what the traditions and games are; what is important is that kids get accustomed to spending time with the family that includes positive role models. Being connected to family will prevent kids from relying on friends, and sometimes negative peers, to have fun. During these family game times, parents are modeling prosocial attitudes and behaviors, and teaching by answering all kinds of questions that may come up. Please note that if you are a poor sport and do not behave maturely when playing games, please send your child to someone else's game night because your behavior could be traumatic. Is it becoming clearer that a parent's job is to teach, teach, teach?

I alluded to another feature of preadolescence—competition. Preadolescence is also a time when kids begin to measure their talents and abilities with those of others. When kids start attending school with other children, they begin to compare themselves with the other kids in their classrooms, on the playground, in the stores, and in extracurricular activities. If you have been around school-age kids, you have seen them checking each other out even at a young age. Their growing brains are saying something to them about differences. They notice that some kids are taller, shorter, faster, have different hair and skin color, shoe sizes, etc. This is the time when parents will explain that people are different. Yes, you can even talk about genes and genetic markers. It may not make sense initially, but the brain will develop a memory of this information, and ultimately the child will be able to assimilate and recall the information when they are engaging in higher learning. During preadolescence, it is also a good time to begin talking about cultures, ethnicities, disabilities, and sexuality. This is your chance to put a positive spin on these important topics before society puts forth a definition that may be unproductive. You can even define your family's values during this time.

Although remaining close is important during preadolescence, parents must balance their closeness with the child's need to individuate. During the latter half of preadolescence, kids will start to act like full-fledged adolescents. Acting like adolescents occurs earlier for some kids. No matter how soon kids start their adolescent journey, during preadolescence, parents should begin thinking about childhood individuation. In other words, parents should start thinking about allowing the child to have more autonomy. I know some of my readers are wondering if I am crazy; I just said that parents should remain close and ready to engage, and now I am talking about independence? The answer to those questions are no, I am not crazy, and yes, I am talking about balancing engaging with children with independence. By ten years old, you only have a few years before the child will begin making independent decisions. Do you know that by twelve years old, the doctors may ask you to excuse yourself from the room so they can talk to the child alone? Many doctors will want to talk to the preteen to find out if there is any domestic violence or to offer the child the opportunity to discuss reproductive issues, like sex. I recall with my oldest child, when the doctor said, "Mom, I am going to ask you to leave so I can talk to your daughter alone." I politely responded, "No, thank you, I'll stay." As soon as a child reaches puberty, they are able to plan or accidentally start a family. I know the idea of a ten- or eleven-year-old making decisions about starting a family sounds scary for some parents, but it is physically possible. Therefore, you cannot wait until the child reaches puberty to explain reproduction and family planning. Don't parents buy shoes for their kids before they can walk? You anticipate walking and you look for the best walking shoes. A child is capable of having a child very soon after reaching puberty. Therefore, parents need to be prepared to have the conversation about reproduction proactively. Recall that proactivity is a skill that successful people possess. Kids have to have information about reproduction already locked in and loaded in the brain to proactively prevent unwanted conception.

Parents should discuss intimate relationships and sex early enough to prevent reacting to the challenges that can arise from not knowing, like sexually transmitted diseases and unwanted pregnancies. Also, sexual relationships involved a certain level of emotional maturity that most preadolescents don't have. Family planning and sexually transmitted diseases are just two of many issues that kids need to know about. I bring up sex and reproduction because it can really have a big impact on the child's life if they are not aware of the potential consequences. Other important issues parents most address are: general health, nutrition, diet, drugs, alcohol, bullying, and sexual abuse. The parent is the most important person in the child's life, so who would be a better person to have serious conversations. Don't wait too long. Time goes very fast when raising kids. Before you know it, the parents' job is over, and the kids are going out the door for good. (Well, at least some leave for good.)

Allowing independence leads to a discussion on the fourth important premise to this book. Independence is important because, very quickly, kids will be living separately from you. Living separately may mean a summer camp program, sleepovers, boarding school, sports camps, college, or the big move out into their own home. Therefore, it is important that kids learn as much as they can while they are under your influence and control because they will ultimately have to grow up and be able to think for themselves and live independent of you. The fourth premise of this book is that parents need to understand and appreciate that *your children come through you, not to you. It is your job to raise them in such a way that they are capable of leaving home and living on their own responsibly and productively.* You will not be with them all the time, and they will not have you to act as a thesaurus, road map, or instruction manual.

Kids must ultimately be prepared to live autonomously. Autonomy is a developmental milestone that, as early as school-age, kids must master. Put simply, kids must learn to do some things on their own. However, many parents view autonomy negatively as a loss of parental control. Some parents struggle with the fact that children will need and rely on the parents less and less as they mature, so some parents will go in the other direction and apply more controls. Some parents who fear losing control over their kids will become more stern and nitpicky. The kid may feel like they can't do anything right. If the bed is not made as neat as the parent would make it, they will complain. The parent may criticize the choice in clothes, how the kid combs their hair, now that the parent is no longer doing the styling. When kids begin to wash dishes, the parent will come behind them and complain that the child is not cleaning adequately. Because a child will naturally want to become more autonomous and parents may not be prepared to allow them the level of independence desired, conflict will occur. The child and parent will no longer enjoy being around each other. The child complains that they can't do anything right, and the parent complains that the child doesn't do anything right. Both are right, but not for the right reason. Knowing that children need to be autonomous at a certain age will help parents accept and support this important developmental milestone called independence.

A word of caution regarding autonomy: as kids get older, especially once they hit the preadolescent stage, they may give off the vibe that they want to be left alone. However, parents must remain close enough to be able to observe, albeit at a distance, and ready to engage at any moment. Where parents of preadolescents make a mistake is that they "catch an attitude," because the youth normally does not want to be bothered, so the parent may throw their hands up and adopt a laissez-faire parenting style. This type of parenting style is overly permissive. This is not the time for that. A preadolescent's brain is not mature enough to handle that level of freedom. They are not prepared to make the type of decisions that they may be confronted with at this phase of development. Parents must continue to be attuned to their preadolescent.

Lessons from the Field

Too much freedom may result in loss of hair. Sometimes a child's acting out behavior is a clear message that they are not able to handle the amount of autonomy they have. I recall my eldest daughter was quite distraught when she discovered that her four-year-old daughter had not only cut her own hair but had also taken a huge plug out of her nineteen-month-old sister's hair. My daughter explained that her daughters were playing "quietly" in the room they shared, and when she went into the bedroom to check things out, she saw her four-year-old quickly throw something behind her dresser. She soon discovered it was a mixed wad of both daughters' hair. Their mother was quite angry. She felt that her older daughter should have known better. However, I reminded her that some kids cannot handle too much independence. Children will let you know how much supervision they need in one way or the other. Even teens continue to need active parenting. Many of the teen boys I served in probation would proudly disclose that they were sexually active and had been since preadolescence. With kids maturing so soon, I was not surprised. However, to my surprise, they would share that they were having sex with their multiple partners in either the boy's own home or the homes of their girlfriends. Sometimes, they would commit the forbidden act in the parents' bed because "it was bigger . . . the room was cleaner . . . and in some instances, there was easy access to the bathroom." What!? In either case, the unsuspecting parents would leave the child home for long periods of time. I recall explaining to one parent that perhaps her son could not handle the level of freedom that remaining home alone for long periods of time afforded. She shot back that she had to work and that her son was too old to have a babysitter. I said, well, is he old enough to hire a babysitter for his own baby, or will you pay for that while you work? Parents must be prepared to dig their heels in and consistently parent their children until they reach that proverbial finish line.

WARNING SIGNS

In addition to the changes in attitude that result from confronting adult issues such as drug use, becoming sexually active, and engaging in behavior that may be illegal, abrupt changes in temperament may signal emotional problems, such as anxiety and depression. A decade ago, I would not discuss this issue during preadolescence; however, children are maturing sooner and parents must be proactive by having the knowledge first and a strategy to deal with these issues if they arise. Parents often miss the signs of these emotional problems in their child because the symptoms can be counterintuitive. In adolescence, depression may manifest as solemnness or irritability. Therefore, the outward behavior of depressed teen is often perceived as contentious, incorrigible, aggressive, and most dreadfully, delinquent. Instead of understanding that something is wrong and the child needs help, the depressed child may be viewed as bad and in need of juvenile justice intervention, and even locked up in detention. Most often, depression and anxiety is overlooked, masking the fact that the child is in need of therapeutic intervention.

According to the most recent version of the Diagnostic and Statistical Manual (DSM-5) of Mental Disorders, depression in adolescence is described as not sleeping a lot, sleeping too much, appearing agitated so moving around a lot, moving slow, lacking energy, not being able to make a decision about things or not knowing what to do, bored, not being able to concentrate, jumping from one thing to the next, missing school, inability to concentrate in school, irritable, hostile, feeling worthless, weight loss, weight gain, alcohol use, drug use, and reckless behavior. If you have been around preteens and teens, you have seen almost all of these behaviors at some point. Instead of calling it depression, it is usually called teenager or adolescent syndrome. Because these symptoms are so common, parents may miss or dismiss them as normal adolescent behavior. In many cases, it is normal behavior. However, in order to determine if the behavior is indicative of depression, parents must take the extra step and engage their child. Is the behavior normal for the child? Did it come all of a sudden? Did the behavior change following some other event in the child's life? Most medical offices offer a depression assessment scale that they can give right in the office to determine if a referral to a therapist is warranted. The best way to find out if your child is suffering from depression is to ask the child if he or she is okay. Ask them, "How are you feeling? You seem sad or you seem agitated. Is there something bothering you? Is there something I can do to help? Is something happening at school?" If nothing else, by asking these questions you will validate the child by letting him or her know that you recognize that their behavior has changed and you want to help.

In addition to depression, anxiety disorder in preadolescence and adolescence is often undiagnosed, although it is easier to recognize. *Anxiety* refers to the brain's response to danger or stimuli that an organism will actively attempt to avoid. Worries and fears are a natural and adaptive part of childhood development. Anxiety and fear meet the criteria for a clinical anxiety disorder when the concerns are persistent and excessive, causing notable distress or impairment in day-to-day life. Anxiety disorders are the most common childhood-onset psychiatric disorders. Anxiety disorders in children (up to twelve years old) and adolescents (thirteen to eighteen years old) are associated with educational underachievement. The symptoms associated with anxiety disorder in children and adolescents are excessive apprehensive expectation of something bad happening. The excessive worry occurs more days than not but for at least six months. The worry is prevalent at home and school. In spite of his or her efforts, the child is unable to control the worry. The worry manifests as being keyed up, restless, mind going blank, muscle tension, unable to fall asleep, and unable to stay sleep. Similar to depression, anxiety disorder in preadolescents may appear to be part of the adolescent syndrome. Parents must rule out social problems and organic causes, and have the child examined by a professional if these symptoms are present.

Even if kids give off the vibe that they don't want to be bothered, continue to monitor, ask, and keep asking. Check with the child's teachers or other relatives, and ask if they believe the child is behaving differently. If there is someone that the child is more comfortable speaking to, even an older sibling, ask that person to inquire. Don't take it personally if your preadolescent does not respond kindly to your concern. Ask and exit. Your expression of concern could save your child's life.

Lessons from the Field

When I was a probation supervisor, I was assigned to a newly implemented Truancy Unit. In collaboration with the district attorney's office, the probation department was responsible for mediation with preadolescents and adolescents who had been identified as habitually truant in the school districts. These children had not responded to the school's efforts to address the truancy. As a result, the case was referred to the district attorney's office, who would have the option of filing a truancy petition against the minor, and ultimately the child could end up in a juvenile detention center for contempt of court. One of the unit's first cases was a young girl who had refused to go to school but would not disclose the reason. As the supervisor, I sat in on the initial meeting. In reading the girl's probation file, we determined that, although the girl had previously been a good student and in good academic standing, all of a sudden she began refusing to attend school. The young girl's objections were described by her mother as "out of nowhere." Since her mother did not understand what was happening with her daughter and had no knowledge of possible mental health issues, she initially responded out of fear. The mother started dragging her daughter out of bed each morning and into the car screaming. The girl would get out of the car in front of the school in tears with her hair and clothes in disarray. A couple of times, the mother dragged her to school in pajamas! On other occasions, the mother had a truancy officer come and pick the girl up and take her to school . . . Feeling defeated, the girl would concede to compulsory education and attend class as long as the truancy officer was in the building. However, as soon as the officer would leave, the girl would leave the classroom without even talking to the teacher or the other students.

When the truancy case was referred to my office for mediation, the girl looked at me and without hesitation said, "No matter what you do to me, I will never attend school." It was clear to me that the young lady was suffering from some kind of trauma. Because even though she emphatically refused to attend school, her eyes were conveying to me that she wanted help. I felt like she was saying, "Figure it out, help me." Of course, I was not put off by her attitude because I had experienced much worse, but more so because I am nosy by trade and design. I was now more curious than ever. What would make this honor student feel so strongly about not attending school? After asking her a few questions, I realized that she was experiencing deep fear. After ruling out bullying, it was determined that the girl had developed anxiety and experienced a few panic attacks in the classroom. Therefore, regardless to how irrational the girl's behavior was, the fear of suffocating and losing control in the classroom in front of her peers was very real to her. The threat of being held in juvenile hall for failure to attend school was less scary than risking having a panic attack in the classroom. We were able to get the young lady into therapy and on medication to control the anxiety, and she returned to school. When parents notice a change in their child's behavior, they must seek to understand and then be understood; this is one of the habits of successful adults.

In summary, the fact that preadolescents can now think more logically by making inferences and now thankfully can understand another person's perspective, parents must continue to nurture this thinking. Parents will continue to teach as they did in the previous stage of development, but now parents can apply a higher level of reasoning. Now that you know that the child is able to think logically, it is up to the parent to make sure they practice those skills. For example, during the previous stage, recall the child that wanted to climb the ten-foot tree with the fragile branches. In that stage, you may have explained this principle, but the child did not really grasp what you were saying. However, during preadolescence, the child truly understands that a seventy-pound kid on a thin branch means the kid is coming down. However, during adolescence, the child will understand that gravity is the reason that the kid is coming down off of that fragile tree limb.

Preadolescence is a time when parents actually enjoy spending time with their kids. Because kids are concrete thinkers and can use some logic, they can actually hold a real conversation that a parent can follow without having to go in and out of the fantasy realm. During the concrete stage, there is a balance of autonomy and dependence. During preadolescence, most kids will still want to engage with their parents and family members sometimes. Even if the kid does not want to fully engage, parents still exercise pretty much total control over the child. Preadolescents are still smaller than most parents, so the parents' governor status still result from a fear and dependency factor. However, parents are cautioned not to rely on power and fear to control the child's behavior. This skill is only useful for as long as the child actually physically or emotionally fears the parent. Once kids reach a certain degree of independence, the fear factor will not be effective because, even if the child cannot defend herself from the parent, by adolescence, they may have the ability to escape. Speaking of escaping, preadolescents don't drive legally, so they don't have the mobility of an older adolescent, but as I alluded to, driving and being able to put miles between themselves and the parents is a soon reality. For some parents, they view preadolescents as big kids. They still want to sit on your lap, but they may be too big and awkward. The best advice I have for parents of preadolescents is to journey back and forth with the child because during the next phase, adolescence, parents will have fewer opportunities to engage with their soon-to-be adult.

Preadolescence is the phase of development when parents are at most risk to under- or overparenting. Recall my story of the parent who walked her daughter to school throughout middle school. Parents who overparent may not be ready to let go of the total control they have over their children. Some parents fear that the child is not prepared for any level of independence. This may be true if the parent was not engaged in teaching, directing, and managing the behavior in the previous phase of development. However, if a child's cognitive age has not kept up with the chronological age, parents will have to get on the fast track and get the child caught up, but parents must start where the child is. I discuss this more under the chapter entitled "Courageous Conversations" in a section heading, Get in Where You Fit In. Conversely, some parents are all too ready to be free of their children during preadolescence, so they give their child too much freedom. These permissive parents may look at the child's large body and take into consideration the chronological age and not consider actual maturation. Many of these kids ended up in the juvenile justice system because they could not handle that level of freedom. During preadolescence, it is imperative that parents remain in position to teach, instruct, manage, and direct their kids balancing the child's (and parents) desire for autonomy. Remember, parents are on a mission to teach their kids all of the habits of successful people who do not end up in the criminal justice system.

Lessons from the Field

When kids under eleven are brought into the juvenile hall, the staff work very hard to get them out as quickly as possible. It is generally agreed among juvenile justice professionals that exposure to the juvenile hall is traumatic for children under the age of eleven. Unfortunately, preadolescents do get arrested and some for pretty serious crimes. When kids under eleven are arrested, there is more of an effort by childcare professionals to try and find out the cause of the community misconduct. Part of the reason that underlying reasons are always believed to be driving the early onset delinquency is that, it is believed that at this age, the parents continue to exercise a prerequisite amount of control over their children to a degree that kids will not get into trouble. Unfortunately, some kids get into trouble because their parents choose not to exercise the right amount of control. When I worked in juvenile hall as a corrections counselor, I recall this little boy who came into custody and then decided to sue his parents for neglect. We were all shocked by this disclosure because before that time, we had never heard of a ten-year-old boy taking legal action against their parent. The little boy, through his attorney, attributed his acting out behavior in the community as resulting from his parents' neglect. What I remember most about this little boy was how out of control his behavior was in the juvenile hall. He would constantly threaten staff, spit, yell, resist, plug up his toilet so his room would flood with water, and most egregiously, he would smear his feces on the viewing window. It was not until much later that I learned about the trauma this little boy was likely suffering. I later found that my young detainee was not the first to sue his parents. The first known case was filed in 1980 by a twelve-year-old boy named Gregory Kingsley in Denver, Colorado. Gregory alleged that his drug-abusing mother and alcoholic father had neglected to care for his needs. Even children recognize the parental responsibility to provide support for their children. It is imperative that parents remain in the parent role.

Chapter Eight

ELEVEN TO EIGHTEEN (ADOLESCENCE)
CALL ME BY MY FIRST NAME

Now we get to one of my favorite topics of conversation. I love talking about adolescents! I enjoy the other phases of development also, but adolescents offer a unique challenge and I enjoy a challenge. I realize that most people do not share my admiration of adolescence. Some people feel just the opposite and dread being around adolescents. There are some people that are genuinely afraid of adolescents also called teens. They become defensive and guarded when confronted with a teen. I have seen adults reposition themselves or their kids to avoid directly encountering a teen, especially a group of teens. I have seen adults treat a group of teens like a pack of rats fearing the rat-pack effect. Teens are aware that adults are afraid of them. Adolescents have reported to me that people will grab their purses or cross the street when they are approaching them. Some teens take offense and will capitalize on an adult's fear by "mean mugging" the adults. In other words, the kids will play into the potential victim's prophecy and act aggressively. One time, I asked a group of juvenile offenders what someone could do to prevent being robbed. One kid immediately said, "Nothing." But the rest of the group spoke up and said that there have been times that they were not even thinking about robbing anyone, but then the person would act very timidly and vulnerably, and when the young man sensed weakness, he took advantage of the opportunity.

The research has confirmed what that group of adolescents said about victimization. Command presence and confidence is a survival tool that law enforcement utilize all the time. Command presence is demonstrated by stature, tone of voice, and facial expression. It says, "I am in control." The opposite of command presence is demonstrating fear, uncertainty, and anxiety. Notice I said demonstrating these vulnerable traits. A person with command presence may possess fear; they just don't show it. What my group of young offenders was telling me was that I should not look weak. If you encounter a group of teens, look at them and maybe even speak so they know you see them and you are not afraid. I have used this strategy in many situations on and off the job. The fact that I am still alive and well to write about it attests to the validity of command presence because in my career, I have been in some really scary situations. Oh, by the way, regarding the young man in the above example who said there is nothing that I could do to prevent being robbed, it turned out that he was victimized several times, therefore traumatized, so he truly believed that victimization was inevitable.

In spite of my fearful brushes with adolescents, I love working with this age group. Although I am no longer working directly with probation youth, my clinical interest and focus is working with adolescents and their parents. Many people have asked why I enjoy working with kids at such a challenging age. I love this stage because

I really enjoyed being adolescent. I didn't know it at the time, but adolescence was potentially the best time of my life. I place emphasis on the word "potentially" because adolescence could have been great, but I had some issues that were not addressed properly. But hindsight allows me to see with perfect vision, so I appreciate the error of my ways. I also see the error of my mother's and father's ways. I see the error in my teachers' ways and all of the responsible adults in my life who did not act responsibly. More recently, I see the errors in my ways as a parent and, most importantly, I saw the error in the ways of thousands of parents I have had the pleasure of serving during my career as a community corrections professional and family therapist. Of course, there is no condemnation directed at any of the adults in my life nor at myself, because as you know very well by now and can easily say it with me: "People do the best they can at any given moment with the resources they have." When people know better, they have the option to do better.

I write this section of the book for all the parents that have or will raise adolescents or, as they are sometimes referred to, teenagers. Instead of looking back with that perfect vision affectionately known as hindsight, this book will give you a potential for adequate fore vision. You will do the best you can because of the knowledge and resources you have in the moment. For parents of adults that struggled during this stage of development, it is my hope that this section will provide validation to you once you understand how difficult this phase of development for children is to navigate. It is also my hope that you will become reliable historians for other parents who may struggle. On a brighter note, you will become a sound consultant if you have the pleasure of becoming a grandparent. Being a grandparent is also the time when you get emotional revenge on that wayward child who now has your beautiful grandchild, who may have some of those challenging traits and behaviors that caused you grief when raising your beautiful grandchild's parent.

During adolescence, the role of consultant will be the most prolific. As I indicated before, parents don't want to be consultants; they want to control, guide, direct, and just hang on tight, especially when their child is an adolescent and experimenting with life. I have heard parents of adolescents say that they wish it were legal to hold their teen hostage in a basement until they are mature enough to make good decisions. Unfortunately, some parents have actually resorted to kidnapping their own child physically and certainly emotionally during this time. Suffice it to say that when you are raising an adolescent, be prepared to have good, not so good, and overall bad days. Your relationship will be sporadic, unsteady, sometimes loving, and sometimes you will feel like you and your teen are mortal enemies. You will love them, but certainly there will be times you will not like their behavior. It's okay to feel that way. It is also okay to tell your child that you don't like their behavior in the moment. In my experience, I have seen or heard about adolescents who laugh, cry, engage, disengage, offer love and affection, offer scorn, and sometimes can be emotionally and even physically abusive. During adolescence, you may not get many nagging questions as in the previous developmental stage because, to most adolescents, parents are pretty lame, don't know the answers to contemporary questions, and to most adolescents, parents simply don't understand. When I was younger, my mother and grandmother loved responding to my needs with stories of their childhood. A common example was if I asked for a ride somewhere, my elders would talk about the several miles they had to walk each day to and from school. If I wanted a new pair of shoes, I was reminded that my parents only had two pairs of shoes all year: a school pair and a dress pair. And when the school pair wore out, they wore the dress shoes. When the dress shoes wore out, they would stuff newspaper in the holes and keep going. My parents would shame us by saying that they would not have dreamed of asking their parents to spend their hard-earned money on something like a new pair of shoes. Although I would feel a little ashamed, I could not help but wonder what the heck does their old-fashioned, horse-and-buggy life have to do with the fact that *today* I want a new pair of the most popular basketball player's tennis shoes? Don't judge me, I was preoperational.

Because adolescents don't think parents understand them, and to be honest, sometimes we cannot make sense of their reasoning, they just stop talking to their parents. Now don't mistake their quietness for not possessing any questions. During adolescence, there are more questions than ever! Since adolescents don't believe their parents have the answers, teenagers believe that they need different sources of information. They may seek out their friends for advice or even an adult that is closer to the teen's age. An adolescent may go to anyone that is not their parent. It is critical to understand adolescent emotions because this is a time when many parent-and-child relationships develop trouble. It is important that parents understand that adolescents are going through a huge transition, and they are attempting to manage the changes. One day, you may be babying them; the next day (or minute), you may have to treat them as an adult. But make no mistake, adolescents are now capable of thinking more maturely, and so they view the world from a more mature perspective.

The primary reason that adolescents start to "act funny" is because they are now able to view the world more logically; therefore, some of the things that they saw or experienced when they were younger and concrete thinkers, they are now able to see more clearly and realistically. This being the case, some parents of adolescents are confronted on some of the stories that they told their child when they were young. A perfect example of this is when parents tell their children that the screaming noises that are coming from the bedroom are heated conversations between the parents. There is a point when kids are able to use conjecture or make deductions and conclude that the yelling the night before and the congenial or even lovey-dovey behavior the morning after does not make sense. The adolescent is able to deduce that that morning afterglow does not come after a night of arguing. Parents of adolescents should understand that once an adolescent realizes that the screaming noises that are coming from the parents' room is the result of their parents engaging in the behavior that led to the child's conception, the child is now forced to view the parents as people and not just mom and dad. After the child gets over the grossed-out feeling that comes from realizing that their parents actually have sex, the adolescent is forced to see the parent differently. The adolescent may want to now call you by your first name! Or even worse, they may call you by your bedroom name like Notty Ned or Not-Too-Nice Nancy. The point is, when kids reach adolescence, they have a more mature view of the world and they know the real truth now. Adolescents are able to view the world more realistically because they are no longer in the concrete operational phase of development and they are not seeing things in black and white. To an adolescent, one plus one may be two, but to an egocentric adolescent, one thing plus another thing could be just one if they don't like the other plus one.

By the time that most kids reach adolescence, they enter what Piaget referred to as the formal operational stage of development. In the formal operational stage, intelligence is demonstrated through the logical use of symbols related to abstract concepts. Teens may demonstrate hypothetico-deductive reasoning. In other words, they become junior scientists in that they are able to consider possible outcomes and consequences of actions because they are able to hypothesize. When using their hypothetico-deductive reasoning skills, they can look at a set of facts scientifically and form an educated opinion. Clouds in the winter will likely bring rain. Having unprotected sex could result in pregnancy. Use a gun, go to jail. Adolescents are able to think about their thinking. They now can use trial and error to solve problems. Adolescents are able to draw specific conclusions from abstract concepts using logic.

Before some of you get too excited, let me add that *just because kids can engage in deductive reasoning, it does not mean that they will*. Or even if they do use deductions, it does not mean that they will listen to reason. And finally, just because an adolescent is able to engage in deductive reasoning, it doesn't mean that the sound advice that they could give themselves would be followed because, at the same time that adolescents are engaging in deductive reasoning, they are also very egocentric and they only think about their needs. Therefore, their needs will often overshadow their reason.

Lessons from the Field

Recently, social media was trending a story of a teenager who had decided to film himself driving recklessly on a highway traveling at very high speeds. Unfortunately, the end of the video showed him crashing and dying instantly. I am pretty sure the young man understood the dangers of speeding while distractedly filming. However, he didn't think that he would be killed. The young man was only focused on the thrill of getting an action-packed video for his followers. He probably knew that his behavior was dangerous, but his desire to shoot an exciting video overshadowed his reasoning.

Research has shown that the adolescent brain is not fully developed until late teens or even into the early twenties. The prefrontal cortex is the part of the brain that is responsible for insight, empathy, and abstract reasoning. Because the white matter (myelin) has not fully developed, the neurons in the brain don't move and connect to the other parts of the brain swiftly. So although chronologically adolescents have reached an age where higher level thinking is available, without the proper nurturing of this level of thought, you will have an adult-sized adolescent looking at you eye to eye but lacking insight, empathy, abstract reasoning, and demonstrating self-centeredness, rude, and selfish behavior. On another note, the adolescent brain is very "excitable" and is attuned to everything in the environment. This is the reason they learn so rapidly. Due to the swiftness of learning, adolescents are more prone to addiction, which is learned behavior.

Lessons from the Field

The fact that adolescents can hypothesize does not mean that their theories will be proven true. I met many juvenile offenders who had a foolproof plan on how to get what they wanted. Their foolproof plan was so simple that they really thought they had outsmarted their potential victim. I saw this failed hypothesis often in juvenile offenders who would steal merchandize out of a department store. In addition to going into the store prepared with a backpack to hide items, one of my favorite dialogues was with teens who would get caught stealing out of a shoe store. My little offender would try on a few pairs of shoes and at least one pair that they wanted to own. Then, my smart teen would send the unsuspecting store clerk to the back to get two or three pairs of shoes. In the time it would take to get the shoes, the little adolescent genius would grab the shoes they wanted and run out of the store. My now client would say that they thought (hypothesized) that they could run out of the store and out of the mall (because they ran track and could run really fast) before the clerk returned and could call for security or the police. It was a sound hypothesis, but the experiment often failed, and the hypothesis found not true because unlike an experienced researcher, my client failed to control for extraneous variables. At the very least, many of my clients missed one-third variable, which was the store security. They didn't consider two-way security mirrors, sensors on merchandize, undercover security, or even the fact that they could fall during their fast exit from the store (which was highly likely due to wearing the pants below the butt and having to hold them with one hand to walk and run). I always asked the same question: "What makes you think Mr. Macys or Ms. Footlocker didn't have security to protect their merchandise?" 99 percent of the time, my now bright-eyed client (bright-eyed because now a light has gone off) would say, "I don't know, I didn't think about that at the time." In research, we call the store's security feature a confounding variable. It is a variable that the researcher failed to control. To my clients, I would say, "Yes, there are shoes. Yes, there is an unsuspecting store clerk. Yes, my client is a track star. Yes, there is a bus stop and Uber waiting right outside the store." But that store security is a dependent variable that has to be addressed. My hope was that they would realize that trying to steal was futile. However, sometimes I would get the same kid coming back more than once. They would say, "Ms. Hill, I tried to control that third variable. I knocked out the security guard!"

Although parents are preparing to go into a consultant role, role modeling and teaching is still crucial during this phase. Unfortunately, you are not going to get the same response to these roles as in your child's previous stages of development. If you are modeling behavior that is inconsistent with your personality, an adolescent will be able to see it with their newfound means of viewing the world. Adolescents can see dichotomies and ambivalence. They are like computer hard drives—they will pick up contradictions like a good vacuum picks up lint off a carpet. Literally, when two conflicting symbols come into the picture, the adolescent brain is like, "Warning, warning, contradiction!" An adolescent is not going to tell you that you are contradicting yourself; they will perceive you as fake and inauthentic at best, and an all-out liar at worse. This will drive a wedge in your relationship. Some parents deal with their contradiction by saying, "I'm grown. Do what I say, not what I do." That does not help. Don't get me wrong; that works when they are young and under your control, but as soon as they are able to be autonomous, kids resort to what they have been exposed to. The best thing a parent can do when confronted with addressing behavior that is unproductive but the parent has been engaging in the same behavior is to acknowledge the poor choice the parent made, reinforce that the behavior is wrong, remind the child that as an adult, you are capable of addressing the behavior more maturely, and at the very least, an adult is capable of dealing with the consequences of unproductive behavior.

I feel like it is necessary to say more about the adolescent brain, so parents have a clear picture of what they are dealing with. For purposes of this discussion, suffice it to say that the recent research has revealed that the adolescent brain experiences a period of major development similar to that of early childhood. Unfortunately, it is the area of the brain that is not growing that is causing problems. The brain develops from the back to the front. The more primitive brain is in control for a long time. The oldest part of the brain is responsible for primitive actions such as breathing, sleeping, and emotions. Yes, we are glad our children breathe and sleep; it is the emotional part that we are more intolerant of when they get older. Who wants a 150-pound person throwing a temper tantrum. While working in probation, I saw a lot of out-of-control young and not-so-young adults. Although their bodies are as big as an adult, they behavior does not match. Many parents are confused and experience dissonance when they see their oversized kid acting immature. My mother and grandmother used to always tell me to act like we had some sense when my behavior did not match my chronological age. When kids get big, their parents want to see maturity.

Maturity will not fully manifest until the brain has developed. The part of the brain that is responsible for coordinating and adjusting complex behavior, impulse control and controlling emotions, focusing and organizing attention, and all those other things parents want from their big kid are all skills that may not be acquired until twenty-five years old. Remember how hungry school-age children were to learn, so they asked question after question? Well, adolescents are just as hungry for data, but not for academic learning. Adolescents want experiences, fun, and excitement. An adolescent's number one goal is how to avoid novelty. All that learning that went on in the previous stage of development did not go to waste; that knowledge serves as a reminder that they have "been there, done that." Adolescents want more of something else.

In addition to having an underdeveloped brain and being driven by a primitive brain similar to lower animals, adolescents are also experiencing a surge in chemicals called hormones, which cause them to act different. Between eight and fifteen years of age, the brain releases a special hormone that starts the body to change. I know, eight years old?! As you can see, this is a wide age span, so two friends can be on opposite ends of the spectrum as they proceed through puberty. This can cause problems in longtime relationships also, as one part of the friend dyad may decide that instead of focusing on their best friend for life (BFFL), they are now wanting an intimate relationship with a person that they are sexually attracted to. Oh my gosh, at eight? Yes. That hormone that causes so much trouble is called the gonadotropin-releasing hormone (GnRH), just in case you want to do more research. When that hormone reaches the pituitary gland, it releases two more puberty hormones: luteinizing hormone (LH) and follicle-stimulating hormone (FSH). Boys and girls have these hormones in their bodies but depending on your gender, those hormones impact different parts of the body. For a male, the hormones alert the testes to begin production of testosterone and sperm. For a female, GnRH and FSH pinpoint the ovaries, which contain the eggs that have been there since birth. The hormones stimulate the ovaries to begin producing another hormone called estrogen. Now, with these three hormones (GnRH, FSH, and estrogen), the girl's body is prepared for pregnancy.

In addition to the changes that are occurring emotionally, the addition of hormones results in observable changes that take place during adolescence. There is a significant weight gain in both sexes. Boys will become taller, their shoulders will grow wider, they will become more muscular, and their voice will begin to crack and finally will deepen. Boys are usually proud to notice that their penis will lengthen and get wider and their testes will become wider. I am just telling you this because adolescents like to showcase what they are most proud of. So be aware.

Girls' bodies will show more curves. They gain weight on their hips and their breasts begin to develop. Some girls are surprised to see that one breast is bigger than the other and continues to grow faster. This usually evens out. To some girls' dismay, they will begin to notice more body fat. Just like boys, girls want to showcase their most prized possession, so don't be surprised when all of a sudden, girls are wearing low-cut shirts and too-small pants. For boys and girls, hair will begin to grow under the arms and in their pubic areas. Boys will begin to see hair on their faces. On a darker or bumpier note, the additional hormones may trigger acne, which may continue throughout the teen years. Girls will begin to see a white mucus discharge, and boys begin having erections. Boys may experience nocturnal emission (commonly referred to as wet dreams). Because boys don't always recall their dreams, they wake up surprised to find their underwear or sheets wet. Parents may be surprised that their teen boy is all of a sudden willing to change the bedsheets and even put them in the washing machine. When asked, some boys will hide the truth and say, "I just want to help out."

This book is not intended to focus on biology or science as there are a number of very good books on the market that will provide every detail of puberty, even puberty for dummies. My purpose of offering this brief and basic description was in an effort to highlight some of physiological changes that occur during adolescence since I have your undivided attention. This information is news to some and a refresher for others. Most importantly, this information is provided to confirm for the parents that when they see these physical and emotional changes, puberty is progressing normally. For some parents, it's helpful to know that their child's acting-out behavior is actually a good thing.

Adolescence: The Preseason to Adulthood

Although having an adolescent in the home can create turbulent times for parents, it is a necessary phase of development that kids have to go through to get to adulthood. Adolescence is another metamorphosis similar to going from infancy to toddlerhood and then onto childhood. It requires work to get to the next phase. Infants had to learn how to regulate, toddlers had to learn how to use the toilet, children must learn how to be more independent, and adolescents must learn how to become adults. It is almost never the physical changes that are problematic and cause parents' grief during adolescence. Instead, it is the emotional changes that appear to happen overnight. Even without knowing what type of hormones are being released, you can imagine and appreciate how having all these different chemicals going on in the brain will cause a reaction. Think about it: even if an adult mixed two types of alcoholic substances, they may begin to act crazy. Have you ever had a Long Island iced tea? If you have had one, you may not even remember because that drink has, among other intoxicants, gin and vodka, which are both 40 percent alcohol! What about mixing two potent drugs? Depending on the substances, there is a potential to go crazy. Accordingly, the introduction of those all those new hormones into the adolescent bloodstream is the reason that adolescence is such a challenge, and sometimes parents think that their not-too-long-ago sweet child has gone crazy. However, parents have to patiently help navigate their child through this metamorphosis so that they will make it to adulthood. To put it in sports terms, adolescence is the preseason to adulthood. Therefore, although their minds are racing from all the chemicals, adolescents still must take on specific developmental tasks in order for them to successfully mature into productive and successful adults and not end up in the criminal justice system. Adolescents' behavior can seem so sporadic and erratic, a parent may want to begin to treat them like a child again, and at the very least, give them less responsibility. Unfortunately, adolescents need to grow up because society is going to expect more from them, ready or not. By the time an adolescent reaches sixteen years old, they can legally drive, which means they will be responsible for maneuvering over four thousand pounds. Now, that is a scary thought. The main point is that, yes, adolescence can be turbulent. Yes, teens act crazy, but this is not the time for parents to back off. They may even realize that their kid missed some milestones, and the parent may have to back up and reinforce learning and skills.

Lessons from the Field

I recall when my third child was sixteen years old, I did not want her to get her driver's license. It wasn't that she was less responsible than her elder siblings; she was equally as irresponsible as the other two siblings, but what was different was that her dad and I had learned from the first two and we were kind of shell-shocked! My older two kids both had car accidents during the first two years of getting a driver's license. Two cars were totaled by the time my third child started driving. I recall telling my daughter's driving instructor at the end of her driver's training course that I didn't think my daughter was ready to get a license. Her instructor said, "Go ahead and let her get her license; it is the time when she is supposed to drive . . . don't hold her back." The fact of the matter was that I was not ready for my daughter to drive. I was not ready for more financial responsibility that came with higher insurance and co-payments for claims to repair damage. It has been five years since my third child was licensed, and although she has not totaled a car, she has had two fender benders and two speeding tickets. I told my husband what the driver's instructor said with a twist, "It is just the time for paying car insurances and repairing cars." My husband had another theory, but this book is not the appropriate place to share his position. As of this writing, I have three down and one teen driver to go, and of course, she is chopping at the bits for her turn to drive.

The main point is that, although the adolescent brain is not fully developed, they can engage in higher-level thinking that could potentially lead to some good choices. However, the adolescent brain is also very excitable and is attuned to everything in their environment. This is why they can learn so rapidly, but this is also why they may focus on the wrong thing or pick up on a number of negative habits. Parents, teach your kids how to think about confounding variables. This is an easy skill that you can begin to teach when they are young. When you read a book, in the middle of a page or the book, ask what could happen next. When kids, even teens, ask to do something risky, ask what their plan is in case something happens. What if you only invite one of your friends to your party, how might the other one feel? If you choose not to wear a coat or take an umbrella, what will happen if it begins to rain, how will you take shelter? My favorite, what if you don't study your vocabulary, how will you do well on the exam?

Facts or Myths?

Before I leave the adolescent phase of development (I told you, I love talking about this age group!), I want to expel three myths that perhaps I even alluded to in the preceding pages.

Myth one: Experience will make a person wiser, so if you allow your youngster to make bad decisions to learn from them, he or she will be better off. In other words, sometimes hitting rock bottom is a valuable teaching tool. This is a myth at the very least and a failed experiment in most cases. Experience alone does not make a person knowledgeable; it's evaluated experience that makes you wiser. In other words, in order for an experience to be a teaching tool, there must be understanding of the error. That is the problem with jails and prisons. If the person does not understand what he or she is guilty of, or more egregiously, if the incarcerated person is innocent of the crime, the resultant custody could have a negative impact at worst, and at the very least, being in custody will not aid in rehabilitation.

Myth two: Since I know better, I will do better. There is no guarantee that knowing better gives you the ability, strength, power, resources, and motivation to do better. Before being surprised by an adolescent's behavior, ask yourself, was he or she provided with the knowledge or skills needed to do better? Did they have the tools to do better?

Lessons from the Field

When I was the case manager over the probation community day center school, there was a young man who was eleven months from turning eighteen. His mother was totally fed up with him. She reminded him constantly that when he turned eighteen years old, he would have to move out. She literally reminded him almost daily. During the time he was at the school, it was apparent that in addition to lacking academic skills (he could not read or write on grade level), he also lacked social skills in that he felt uncomfortable talking to people. What was most obvious is that in eleven months, he will not be prepared to take care of himself or a household. However, in spite of the young man's lack of maturity, his mother put him out on his eighteenth birthday. The young man spent time sleeping on the couch of various friends. One day, soon after turning eighteen, he came by his mother's house to shower and when he left, he was killed instantly after someone drove through a stop sign. The car accident was a tragedy, but what was equally catastrophic was the mother learned very late that, although her son reached the chronological age of adulthood, he did not have what it would take to live on his own.

Finally, myth three: Parents erroneously believe that it is usually their child's friends or associates that cause their kid to make wrong decisions. In other words, it is not my kid's fault, it is those other bad kids with whom he or she is hanging out. My response to parents who say this is usually, "That is what the other kid's parents said about your kid." Then I advise parents that, notwithstanding bullying, kids will hang around people that they are comfortable with. Just like birds of a feather who flock together, kids of the same mind will act in kind. Parents cannot pick their kid's friends; they must only work on changing with whom their kid is comfortable with.

Lessons from the Field

On September 14, 2016, the local newspaper reported on a sixteen-year-old teen who, on a dare from his teenage friends, climbed onto the field at a stadium during a national football game. He then led the police on a chase. The chase was captured by a sports commentator who gave blow-by-blow details of the chase until the young man was tackled by the police on the forty-yard line. The minor was ultimately arrested on misdemeanor charges, had to appear in front of a judge, and was given minor sanctions. However, the minor's picture was on the front page of the local newspaper, his antics were described by a couple of the football players as awesome and funny, and fans said that the minor's behavior was the most exciting thing that had happened in the boring game. I don't think the arrest was a deterrent. I think the reward of the prank outweighed any negative consequences.

13 Reasons Why: You Should Talk to Your Teen

At last, we come to the end of our discussion on adolescence. There is movie trending called *13 Reasons Why* based on the book by the same name and written by author Jay Asher. The story is about a high school girl who commits suicide after a number of unfortunate events at school, which some may define as extreme bullying. However, some of the offenses committed against the victim are more accurately defined as criminal acts. Prior to the suicide, the victim records narratives to thirteen people she believes is responsible for her decision to kill herself. I watched the series because many people were talking about it, hence the show was trending. The discussion about the show was controversial. Some people believed that the show depicted an accurate view of suicide, so the show could be used as a teaching tool. Some critics believe that the show glorifies suicide and could set off teens committing suicide. As a therapist and researcher, I wanted to form my own opinion because the fact remains that suicide is a leading cause of death in the United States. Research has shown that suicides may increase after a publicized suicide, especially if the suicide victim is a celebrity.

A copycat suicide is described as emulation of another suicide that the person attempting suicide knows about, either from local knowledge or due to depictions of the original suicide on television. A spike in copying suicides after a widely publicized suicide is known as the Werther effect. Suicide contagion results when a publicized suicide serves as a trigger, in the absence of protective factors, by the next suicide by a suggestible person. Suicide contagion usually spreads through a school system, which makes sense as school is the primary social milieu for children. Finally, suicide clusters are defined as several suicide incidents in a particular time and place, and have been linked to social learning from recent and nearby events.

I decided to watch the series along with my fourteen-year-old, who had already started watching it on her smartphone. After watching the first series (I have been told that there will be a second season), I was shocked by the depiction of the parents of the eventual victim as they were so engrossed in their own lives that they could not see their child was hurting. There was one scene where the parents had fallen to sleep on the couch and the daughter came to them late at night and indicated that she was going out for a walk. The mother mumbled something off about the weather outside and went back to sleep. The victim was gone for several hours and returned after being brutally raped. When she arrived back home, the parents were still sound asleep on the couch. Another character in the movie was depicted as having a history of emotional instability requiring medication, but the fact that he came home from school intoxicated on one occasion and with a black eye on another occasion did not move the parents to action. Although *13 Reasons* is a fictional television show, it inspired me to remind parents of the need for constant communication with their children once they reach adolescence.

Lessons from the Field:
Thirteen Reasons Why You Should T*alk*
to Your Adolescent

1. *Children always have something important to say.*
2. *Communication takes you into their life.*
3. *Children need someone to talk to and you may be the only one available.*
4. *Communication is the gateway to all positive relationships.*
5. *Communication signifies personal investment.*
6. *Communication is another way of saying "I love you."*
7. *Communication allows you to take part in your child's world (because of the World Wide Web, their world is expansive and growing).*
8. *Children are concrete thinkers and may need an abstract perspective to understand life.*
9. *Bullying is real and anyone can be the victim of bullying.*
10. *Your child could be suffering from some form of trauma.*
11. *Your child could need validating.*
12. *Teens may be considering taking their lives.*
13. *Because their life may depend on it.*

Chapter Nine

RAISING THE ADULT CHILD

Why did you come to this chapter? Were you looking for advice on how to raise your adult child? You do not raise an adult. Your time is up. You have had your chance to plant good seeds and all you can do is what the farmer does each season: wait. When you children are grown, you are consistently and persistently a consultant. Your time to raise your child is over once they reach the age of majority. For some children, the threshold is eighteen years old. However, certainly by twenty-one years old, you are no longer in an emotional or physical position to elevate your son or daughter; they must be internally motivated to live productive lives. If they end up in the criminal justice system, it will be the result of their own free will. Don't get me wrong, your adult son or daughter may reside with you, but you are not raising them. They should be contributing to the household either financially or by providing a service. Although the adult son or daughter is living in the same house and maybe even sleeping in their old bedroom, they are renting the room at this point. There is recent research regarding the emerging adult. Some have suggested that there should be another developmental phase of development between adolescence and adulthood because today's young adults are not ready to launch. I don't have an opinion whether there is validity to that argument; irrespective of whether there is a new developmental phase, the subsequent phase of development after adolescence should correspond with the parent behaving in a consulting role and allowing the child to live as autonomously as possible. Go back and review the section on consulting. Recall that a consultant gives expert advice based on experience. Emerging adults should not keep their laundry with the family's laundry. Emerging adults can either purchase their own food or offer to supplement the family grocery expenses. For some of you reading this book, the notion of no longer raising an adult child is a surprise. Some of you are taken aback, and even a few of you are less than happy. Well, somebody had to tell you, so I decided to courageously confront the issue. As a matter of fact, in the next chapter, I will confront a few issues that I have confronted during my tenure as a probation officer, manager, therapist, parent, and just being another human being who is interested in parenting practices, and overall, just nosey.

Chapter Ten

COURAGEOUS CONVERSATIONS

We have arrived at the chapter in the book that will separate this book from all the other parenting books on the market to date. I am hoping that this chapter will set a trend for future parenting books in that professionals honestly and boldly discuss and sometimes confront parenting issues. Parents should understand that there are *parenting choices* that may be counterproductive to a good parent-child relationship at the very least and traumatizing for the child at the worst. Recall that I have advised many probation officers and therapeutic clients that sometimes you have to have tough conversations. Courage is not the absence of fear; courage is moving forward with fear. What follows are a compilation of experiences I have encountered during the thirty years I spent serving clients in the criminal justice system and working with parents as a therapist. I also humbly add a few mistakes that I have made while raising my four children. Even if I didn't want to add some of my own parenting errors, not doing so would paint a picture of my hypocrisy in my children's eyes. What follows in this section are seeds of advice that are not in any order of importance. My goal was to put the information out there. Parents are asked to read each courageous conversation, and similar to a good piece of meat, eat the flesh and spit out the bones and marrow. To the parents that may become angry at what it is written, I will do something that my probation officers could not: I will hide behind the pages of this book. If by chance I see you, I will do as I advised my probation officers: I will run. So get ready, get set, here it goes . . .

Hurt People Hurt People

In addition to reading and learning what academia has to say about childhood development, it is strongly suggested that parents attempt to resolve their own childhood issues that may get in the way of parenting. Many parents could benefit from clinical counseling to address unresolved family of origin issues prior to becoming parents. Parenthood finds many adults still recovering from traumas from their own childhoods. Some of those events have been painful, so oftentimes when everyone is excited about and focused on the new baby, parents may be triggered by recovered memories. It is often said that "hurt people hurt people." In other words, if you are in pain, you may respond in such a way that you inflict pain. The pain can be emotional or physical. In Dr. Kenneth Hardy's epic book, *Teens Who Hurt*, he describes how there is an interplay between families that may result in adolescent violence; the violence may have originated from intergenerational pain and trauma. In either event, some parents are not emotionally prepared to be the consummate role model that good parenting requires. Unless parents are willing to take an honest look at their own childhood, perhaps through counseling, they may struggle emotionally while raising their children. As former governor of Minnesota Jesse Ventura said, "Learn from history or you're doomed to repeat it." Accordingly, parents must be willing to look at their childhood and reconcile the fact that some things did not go well when they were under someone else's care. As a matter of fact, some parents had absolutely traumatic childhoods. Childhood trauma can come from almost anywhere and manifest out of what appears to be nowhere. With some traumas, it is easy to pinpoint the origins, but most are complex; therefore, trauma can be triggered and appear to be unprompted.

Lessons from the Field

During the writing this book, there was a report in the local paper of a road rage shooting. Apparently, two drivers were in dispute and began arguing with each other out of their respective car windows. One of the drivers apparently called a friend to the location, and that person shot at the other driver, hitting the victim in the head. The wife of the victim, who was the front passenger in the vehicle, had to take over the control of the car from the passenger seat. She managed to get her husband to a nearby hospital; however, there was nothing that could have been done to save the victim. He had died upon arrival to the nearby hospital. What is most disturbing about this story is the fact that the victim's five-year-old and infant sons were in the vehicle. The five-year-old witnessed his father being brutally murdered in front of him. The five-year-old experienced the panic and overall pandemonium that surrounded the murder of his father. It is expected that the child will need ongoing emotional support to manage the experience for years to come. But this is where some, even well-meaning parents make a huge mistake. Some parents will make sure that the child receives support initially; however, they don't understand the need to get counseling throughout the developmental phases. Child therapy is great for young concrete thinkers. However, later when children mature and begin to think more abstractly, new images develop about the traumatic experience, so the older child needs a different type of intervention. So in the above road rage incident, even if the mother were to get her five-year-old-son counseling and he appears stable, it may not be until years later that the now fifteen- or even twenty-year-old may start to have symptoms. If he starts to exhibit a lot of aggressive behavior, his actions may appear to be spontaneous. Recall my young probationer who was molested as a child. As he matured, he began to associate his victimization to his dating and intimate relationships. My probationer needed abstract reasoning to make sense of the previous abuse. He needed answers to understand that he was the victim of rape, that his abuser's behavior was in fact criminal behavior. You would not explain rape to a five-year-old, but an adolescent needs clear and honest facts to make sense of what happened to him.

Children are not the only ones who may need a more mature explanation to childhood experiences. Parents must reckon with the fact that the bad things that happened to them as children was not their fault either, because as children, they could not choose their parents nor could they select the environments in which they were raised. Being a child is likened to being a passenger in a vehicle: you go where the car goes. If the car turns left, you are going in the direction on the left. If the car gets on the freeway, you as the passenger will be traveling on the freeway. However, if the driver gets a ticket, it is not the passenger's fault. If the driver crashes the car, unless the passenger obstructed or distracted the driver in some way, the passenger cannot be held responsible for the accident. In the same respect, kids cannot be held responsible for the bad things that their parents caused. The point that I am making is that adults cannot change the past, but they can launch from it. One of my favorite quotes is, "You can't change the past but you can start a new beginning." When children make it through a horrible childhood, it is a time of reflection. It is a time to look at the childhood and make some decisions about how they will use their experience to their benefit, to direct their lives now that they are all grown up. As an adult, you are in driver's seat and you now get to decide what direction to go. You decide if you will wreck the car, so to speak. Parents can model the ability to move on after adversity by being great parents in spite of their beginnings. Don't carry unresolved issues into your adulthood because hurt people hurt people.

Change the Story: Heal Your Childhood Trauma Through Laughter

Understanding that everyone may experience trauma and many adults survive the trauma and become parents, I want to offer some advice that has helped me through my childhood trauma. To the degree that it is possible, find a way to heal your childhood trauma prior to your parenting journey. I have provided therapeutic counseling to many people who were struggling with memories of bad childhoods. Through counseling, my clients have had the opportunity to gain an understanding of why they react to their children in the manner that they do. Some parents have even discovered that their dysfunctional childhoods have led to overall challenges in other relationships. Through the therapeutic process, I have helped parents discover that although they cannot change their past, they can change the narrative behind past events in their lives. Adults can develop new stories about their childhood by developing a description of events through a lens, which focuses on their ability to persevere, their resilience, and ultimately their success. My four siblings and I were raised by a single mother. Although my grandmother was a consistent financial and emotional resource, my mother often struggled in both areas. As a result, I learned how to persevere during hard times. For example, there were times when our electricity was turned off due to nonpayment. One of the things my siblings and I learned was that if we placed our pants in a creased position between the bed mattresses at night, by the next morning, there would be no wrinkles and our pants would have a pretty nice crease down the middle. Very often, my mother had to work late, and there were times when we didn't have a full-course meal. To this day, I don't feel slighted if I don't have a full meal because I am content with a sandwich. As a matter of fact, as I have gotten older, I would prefer a peanut butter and jelly sandwich over a full-course meal. Although I didn't like going without bare necessities when I was young, I have changed the narrative and found joy in knowing that my mother exposed me to a lifestyle that made me not only strong, but also thrifty and an overall survivor. My siblings and I often laugh at our childhood experiences, and the pants-under-the-mattress trick has saved me as an adult during power outages. That is just one of many poverty tricks. Thanks, Mom.

Another example of how I modified my childhood schematic view has to do with my absentee father. I used to tell people that if they looked up the phrase *deadbeat dad* in a thesaurus, they would find a picture of my father. My father did not come around enough for my sisters and me to form a relationship with him in which we would even call him dad or father. On the few times he would visit, we would just get in his face and start talking. I think if I thought long and hard enough, I could come up with the number of times I saw my father during childhood. Needless to say, my father was not part of my life in any significant way. I resented my father's absence. Again, although my grandmother was a consistent second parent, I felt slighted because I didn't get to be a daddy's princess nor did I get any of the other benefits that I perceived other girls received from their fathers. I later realized that, but of my father's lifestyle, there may have been even more unhappy memories coming out of my childhood if my dad had more influence in my life.

In spite of the fact that I didn't know my father as a daddy, I have come to appreciate the fact that, even in absentia, my father passed on some pretty good genes. My father was a handsome man, which is likely why my mom was attracted to him. My mother, by all accounts, was beautiful. But thankfully, my father kicked in some pretty nice features. My dad was a tall man; my mom was relatively short. I am tall, which has provided me with a command presence that came in handy as a probation officer, professor, and probably got me out of a few fights when I was young. Most importantly, my dad loved people, not really his kids, but he loved to socialize. Most useful for me, my father had a sense of humor. My mom kept her social circle pretty small, and by the end of her life, she mostly surrounded herself with family, whereas my dad literally had a party soon before he died. Most of my childhood friends would attest to the fact that I used humor a lot while growing up. I continue to appreciate humor and, lo and behold, I discovered that the research has proven that having a good chuckle has many health benefits. Laughter decreases stress hormones and increases immune cells and infection-fighting antibiotics, which improve resistance to disease. Snickering triggers the release of endorphins, which are the body's natural chemicals that make a person feel good. Research studies have also found that laughter reduces blood pressure and helps to tone your abdomen muscle. Inheriting my father's sense of humor may result in my living a long life with a six-pack abdomen. Okay, well, I guess after having four kids, one by cesarean section, I can forget about the six-pack, but it could have happened! Thank you, Daddy.

In summary, parents have the ability to not only change the narrative about their own childhood, but in the event that one of the parents is absent, the physical parent can help the child develop a story about their heritage that she can feel a sense of esteem even if one or both of the parents proved to be unfavorable role models. One more message to the physical parent: stop assassinating the absent parent, because in doing so, you are describing a great big part of your child. If you are describing one of the parents in a negative light, you are saying that your child is made up of some very bad material, and since you selected that person and are responsible for your egg that "hooked up" with that sperm for fertilization to make the child, you are saying something really bad about you. Don't try and convince your child that their other parent changed after conception, because as you will read in this book, the personality is pretty established before the ability to make a baby. Making the other child feel bad about the absent parent will send the message that the child is the product of two questionable people.

Have You Apologized Yet

For some parents that are reading this book, they are well on the parenting journey. Some may have children that are grown. You have read this book and realized some of the misinformed parenting decisions that you have made. Once you understand where things went wrong, parents can begin to make amends. In order to start a new relationship, some parents will have to do more than just acknowledge the past relationship and all the things that happened in the past. It is time to say "I am sorry" for the things you did or didn't do. An acknowledgment and apology for hurting someone is the foundation for forgiveness and transcending a harmful relationship. It does not matter whether your kids never appeared bothered by the past and your relationship appears to be good; kids are waiting for their parents to apologize for their mistakes. So why not initiate a discussion and get the giraffe out of the room. Why? Because giraffes are large and they take up a lot of room. Giraffes are beautiful animals with their long legs and necks, but they are a huge distraction. Even after seeing giraffes many times, I still look at them in awe. Harboring or repressing resentment for the past also takes up a lot of room in a relationship. Resentment takes up the emotional space where relationships should flourish based on good memories. Resentment is like a boulder in the path of a stream. The boulder slows the stream down. A common probation example could not illustrate this point more *Lessons from the Field.* Some of my parents had not been great role models when their children were very young. Some young parents acted immature when their children were young. Some parents loved to party, travel, get high, or they were just overall absent. Thankfully, these parents returned just in time to address their now teens' incorrigible and delinquent behavior. However, sometimes the absent parents' return was bittersweet. Kids are happy that their parents are showing concern; however, very often, the parent is playing a role that is new to the adolescent. The partying mom and dad have taken off their party clothes and inebriated demeanor in exchange for a stern look of compassion and control. The teen is looking at the parent as if to say, "Who are you?" My favorite example of this was one of my probation kids whose mother would have the kid's dad call him from prison to say he was going to severely punish him if he did not act right and obey his mother. The kids had not formed a relationship with their dad, and now he was doing twenty years. By the time the dad got out of prison, the kid would be a young adult. Unfortunately, that kid ended up doing time in the same prison as his dad. I guess since the father could not come to his son, the son went to the father. *Irony? No, kids do what you do, not what you say.*

In addition to apologizing to your kids, you must apologize to yourself. I have found in my practice that *many people suffer from what I refer to as madatme (pronounced as mad at me) syndrome.* Some feel guilty about how they have behaved in the past, and instead of apologizing and, more importantly, forgiving themselves, they carry around this guilt. Like all syndromes, there are symptoms associated with madatme: depression for no apparent current reason; anxiety due to worrying that the past will repeat itself; self-medication with drugs, alcohol, and over-the-counter drugs; excessive spending on the kids to alleviate guilt; being unusually hard on the kids as a distraction for self-flaws; and a series of poor relationships. Of course, this list is not exhaustive. My suggestion is that you go in a room with a mirror. There should be nobody in the room or within earshot. It would be better if you are home alone. Some people may decide to go stay in a hotel. It is most important that you are not in a position to feel self-conscious about someone else hearing you. Once in the room alone in the mirror, stare at yourself for several minutes. If you are wearing makeup, hat, wigs, or any other ornaments that you have applied to change your appearance, please remove it. Now continue to stare. I mean really look at every inch of your face. This may take several minutes.

After really looking at yourself, say this out loud: "I am who I am. I have made mistakes in my life, too many to remember, but I know I have made mistakes. That was the past and today is today. I can't do anything about the past. Today, I am in charge of my life. I will make conscious decisions from today forward. I am truly sorry about the past. I forgive myself for my behavior. I love myself today and from this day forward." The first time you recite this mantra, you should be alone; however, practice saying it every day until you really believe it and feel different about yourself. Now that you have a clean slate, there is nothing stopping you from being the parent of your child in such a way that he or she will not end up in the criminal justice system.

Learning from Mistakes

In addition to telling your child that you're sorry for past mistakes, don't be afraid to tell your kids that you are now wiser and as such, you are basing your current parenting decisions on your newfound wisdom. Parents don't have to keep making the same mistakes just so they don't have to acknowledge they were once wrong. *I have met many parents who believe that they are not able to correct their child's behavior because of the many mistakes the parents made in the past.* Parents who are hiding from their past usually have been absent in the child's life. For example, I mentioned that there was a serious drug epidemic in the '80s and '90s. Many parents neglected their kids because they were engaged in drug-seeking behavior. Thankfully, many of the parents managed to beat their drug addiction and return to their families. However, for some parents, many years had passed and the kids had grown up. Many of these kids did not respect the parents' authority because they were either angry at the parents' absence or the child had seen the parents in very compromising positions that were unmotherly or not fatherly. Parents who were hiding from their past feared that the child would challenge their authority and confront them on their past behavior, so the parent would just ignore the behavior. The parents' absenteeism did not only result from drug use, but some parents may have been in prison or had mental health issues. I met kids whose parents left one family and started another family, or even parents who were pursuing their careers to such a degree that they rarely spent time with their family. My response to parents who were reengaging in their child's life was always the same: "You are stronger and wiser now, and the parenting that you are currently providing comes from learning from your mistakes." I would also provide an example that they could use with their child: "If I had been given a ticket for accidently driving down a one-way street, should I allow my child to do the same thing? If I saw my child heading for that one-way street with the poorly visible one-way sign, would I not warn my child?" Parenting is an art, and sometimes you don't do the right thing. The goal is to learn from mistakes, avoid making the same mistakes, and then telling someone else about what you learned from your mistakes. Portia Nelson's poem, "There Is a Hole in My Sidewalk," is a good example of the power of parenting with experience.

There Is a Hole in My Sidewalk

By Portia Nelson

I walk down the street. There is a deep hole in the sidewalk. I fall in. I am lost . . . I am helpless. It isn't my fault. It takes forever to find a way out.

I walk down the same street. There is a deep hole in the sidewalk. I pretend I don't see it. I fall in again. I can't believe I am in the same place. But, it isn't my fault. It still takes me a long time to get out.

I walk down the same street. There is a deep hole in the sidewalk. I see it is there. I still fall in. It's a habit. My eyes are open. I know where I am. It is my fault. I get out immediately.

I walk down the same street. There is a deep hole in the sidewalk. I walk around it.

I walk down another street.

Raising Children vs. Having Children

Some people use *having children* and *raising children* interchangeably. You hear it all the time. People say, "I have three children." This implies that you merely possess something and there is no deed. You possess them like you have a car or you have a pair of shoes. Recall that one of the premises to this book is that kids come through you, not to you. Raising children is different and more involved than merely having children. *The term "raise" is defined as "lift or move to a higher position or level; increase the amount, level, or strength of."* Parenting can occur passively without much effort. However, raising a child means conscientiously putting forth effort to grow the child, to move them forward, higher in all respects, emotionally and physically.

Parents are responsible for raising their children. The term "to raise" is a verb, which signifies the need for an action. Raising children requires parents to consistently do something. Think about it: a baby can't stay the same size and maintain the same emotional level that is present at birth. He must move forward to a higher level of functioning. Can you imagine a seventeen-year-old teen falling out on the floor and crying every time he was hungry or had gas? Actually, I have seen a similar scene when working in juvenile hall and in my role as superintendent; however, my point is that children must be taught higher levels of behaving, and parents are the ones that must gear up, bear down, and actively raise their children. There are so many outside (the family) stimuli that could impact how a child develops physically and mentally. If parents fail to raise their kids, there are outside influences that will take the parents' place, and you may look up one day and your 150-pound sixteen-year-old son or daughter is flailing around on the floor because you would not allow them to drive your new car.

Parents: The First Mirror

Because I don't blame parents for what they do not know, this is an area that I preach every time I have a parent in front of me. This is a tough conversation because parents tend to get on the defensive when this subject comes up; however, please read this section with love. Parents have the first opportunity to ascribe positive meaning to their children's lives. As a result of parental feedback, children initially learn who and what they are. I have heard parents say, "She acts just like her dad . . . He thinks like his mother . . . All my kids do poor in school . . . Obesity runs in our family . . . We are all overweight . . . Her dad was in special education classes, so I don't expect her to excel . . . Her mother was depressed, so she is depressed." My favorite parent "poor excuse" is, "His dad was in jail, so it makes sense that he is in jail because he gets his criminal ways from his father!" These are just subtle insults that parents lobby against their kids. Of course, while working with some of my probation clients, I have seen them get right to the point. They will call the child stupid, fat, ugly, dumb, useless, etc. With respect to ascribing a parent's traits to their children, I am not saying that parents should not be proud of or even aspire to have their kids acquire parents' traits and behaviors. After all, It is inevitable that children will have some of their parents' traits through the transfer of the DNA. And for many parents, initially, it is delightful to see the manifestation of some of the genes passed from one generation to the next. For example, sharing the same eye or hair color of a parent or grandparent is nice and confirming of relatedness, especially in instances where the paternity is in question. Inheriting athleticism, verbosity, patience, temperance, artistic ability, and a high intelligence quotient (IQ) are all good traits to pass along.

However, unlike genes that manifest without warning, there are some behaviors that may have been ineffective for the parent, and passing those traits on to another generation would not be productive. Some examples of unnecessary behavior and attitude traits are being quick to anger, compulsiveness, impulsiveness, depression, anxiety, addiction, lying, cheating, stealing, apathy, overeating, undereating, lawlessness, unfriendliness, contentiousness, excessive risk-taking, and recklessness, to name just a few. Many of the people who ended up on my caseload in the criminal justice system demonstrated many of those characteristics, which is what landed them in the system in the first place. The parents' first step in preventing the passing down of unproductive attitudes is to first recognize that they are present, and then make a conscious effort to change. Remember, kids do what you do not what you say. Take a moment and think about it. Are there character traits that you have that have caused trouble? It does not have to be trouble that landed you on the wrong side of the law, but maybe interfered with relationships. This question is rhetorical, and you don't have to disclose your response to anyone except yourself.

Lessons from the Field

I recall a young female probationer whose last name clearly indicated at least part of her heritage. When I acknowledged what I thought safely identified her race, she quickly corrected me and claimed to be of another race. It was clear that the young lady did not share the race of which she was claiming. Initially, I thought she was playing. However, it became increasingly clear that she had totally internalized the hatred for her race and completely internalized the appeal of another race. It was later determined that her mother had denied her culture, and although she had a daughter who was of the very culture she was denying, the mother consistently denigrated her heritage. As a result, she hated her true self. Although my client resisted profusely, the young lady was referred to counseling. (You are right if you are thinking that her mother needed counseling too. However, we had no jurisdiction over the mother; therefore, no authority to direct her into counseling.) Parents ascribe meaning to their children, good or bad.

Be as Nice as My Dentist

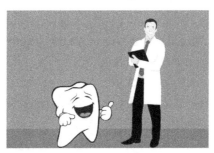

As I already indicated, parents are the first mirror through which children will view themselves. A few of the images that you want your child to see when looking at you is beauty, importance, smart, and unconditional love. Showing this type of benevolence is very easy when children are small and compliant. However, once their personalities become more challenging, showing unconditional positive regard is more of a challenge. I spend a lot of time overtly and covertly observing parents. I am always amazed at how agitated (to put it mildly) some parents are with their kids. Some parents are constantly yelling, directing, frowning, and threatening their kids. Sometimes, it is quite amusing to see a parent towering over this little child, and the parent has totally lost control. I have seen parents yelling with their hands flailing trying to direct this three-foot child. I know that parents have life issues that children do not know anything about, and so anxiety and irritability may be warranted in the moment. However, parents must learn to regulate and control their emotions. During a monologue, comedian Jim Gaffigan tells a funny story of how he could never understand why his father was so grumpy whenever they went on family vacation. It was not until Jim grew up and had to take his own kids on vacation and realized how expensive and overall uncomfortable the vacation was, that he could understand why his father behaved that way. Having spent several years vacationing with my own four kids, I get it. Kids have a lot of energy, they are free from worry about expenses, and everything has been taken care of for them. By the time the vacation rolls around, parents are broke, exhausted from planning, scheduling, packing, budgeting, making sure there is coverage at work, cancelling the mail delivery, boarding the pets, shopping for clothes, getting the car serviced, etc., etc., etc., that they are not too happy on the day of the trip. In spite of this, the trip must go on, so I would suggest directing the irritability to a more suitable source, such as running track or an exercise machine at a local gym. Even when families are not on vacation, parents sometimes must make a conscious effort to show love to the sometimes unlovable acting child in the moment. During those times when kids don't act lovable, I would suggest that parents practice being as nice as my dentist.

Lessons from the Field

Not long ago, I was having some major work done on my teeth. The work was more emotionally painful than physically. I had to keep my mouth open for long periods of time, turn my head from one side to the other, wait for the Novocain to take effect, rinse my mouth, and after all of that, I had to show up on time for the next visit. Do you know how hard it is to return to a place of pain? Because my dentist was super nice, my experience was more manageable. Throughout the time I was in the chair, he said things like, "Can I get you to turn your head this way please. . . Can you lean back please. . . Can I get you to close your mouth just a bit. . . " And after each request, he always said thank you. While doing the procedure, he kept saying, "You are doing so well . . . Perfect. . . Okay, because you are doing so well, we may finish quickly." My dentist always greeted me and sent me away with a smile on his face. My dentist would tell me stories to keep me entertained while my mouth was open, although I could not respond. The nicest thing about my dental experience was that the dental assistants rubbed my shoulders or patted me while I was getting the Novocain shot. Wow, I was not expecting that. Of course, the patting was to distract me from the huge needle going into my little gums, but the thought was nice. Since I couldn't talk, my mind started to wander, and I thought about how nice my dentist was as I stared into his eye through my protection goggles. Then it occurred to me, if all parents were this nice to their kids, they would model and teach benevolence, while sending the message that the child is worthy of being treated kindly. Aren't your kids more important than a dentist's patient?

One final note on being nice to your kids . . . Can you please smile? I often see parents with their kids, and the entire time the parents are frowning. Your expression on your face says much more than what you say because actions speak louder than words. And stop rushing and pushing your kids. I also see parents constantly saying, "Hurry up . . . Move . . . Go that way . . . Let's go." Okay, I said one last thing about being nice, but this issue is so important that I can't leave it without feeling like I have given you everything I have based on my experience. One negative experience with another adult could undo all the good work parents have achieved. One thing that I recently discovered while dropping my grandkids off at day care: if you work hard at being nice to your kids, which we all agree sometimes is tough, don't you think that other people who don't have to be with them all the time should be nice? What about people you pay to care for your kids? Shouldn't they be nice to their *clients*? Since I was a probation officer and worked with many kinds of offenders, I probably was more vigilant when it came to the people who cared for my kids. As a law enforcement officer, I was privy to the full Megan's list (a national list of all sexual predators), so of course I checked the list for names of adults associated with my kids. I also had access to criminal information networks that contained the list of criminal offenders. But even though I was careful, my experience taught me that it is not always apparent who will abuse kids. This fact is proven over and over on the hit television series, *American's Most Wanted*. In watching that show, I was always amazed at how surprised the victims or families of the victims were. My favorite episodes were the shows that depicted the potential victims finding out that their mates were offenders by watching *American's Most Wanted*.

Lessons from the Field

Three of my kids are all grown up and two have children of their own. Sometimes, I have the privilege of taking or picking up my grandkids from day care or school. Just recently, when I dropped off my one-year-old granddaughter at her day care, I noticed how sad and depressed some of the childcare providers were. They said good morning, but there was no happiness in their voice. I entered into a school room, and the teachers didn't smile or say good morning. I understand that they are not happy to see me. However, is it unrealistic to expect them to appear happy to see the kids? I've even caught childcare providers yelling at kids. One time, I heard a day care provider tell a little boy, "You are getting on my last nerve." I thought, it is only 8:00 in the morning, you have already used all but one of your nerves? I have asked a few teachers and childcare providers if they were okay or if they were feeling okay. These questions, at the very least, signal the teacher that they appear to have a problem. Although parents, or day care providers don't get paid the amount of a dentist, kids still deserve the same level of respect and adoration as the dental patient.

Stop Complaining

Along the same lines as being nice, I would like to encourage parents to stop complaining. Some parents spend so much time in a grumpy mood, precipitated by things that they cannot change. Recall that you are a role model whether you want to be or not. You are on at all times. When the traffic is heavy, parents complain. When public transportation is late, parents complain. When it is hot outside, parents complain. When it is cold, parents complain. When parents don't get a promotion, they complain. When the store doesn't have the right shoe size, parents complain. When they have to wait in line longer than expected, they complain. When their kids don't make the school team, they complain. I am not saying that parents should not ever show disappointment, but pick your battles. Make sure your kids know when complaining is really warranted. But instead of complaining, model and teach kids to just experience disappointment and move on. Remember that one of your primary goals is to raise kids who can adapt to society. One of the best strategies for adjusting to society is realizing that sometimes, things will not go well. There will be tough days and easy days. Life will not feel fair . . . As superintendent over the detention camp, very often the residents would appeal to me, the highest authority, on the poor manner in which they were treated by staff. Although we had a very efficient grievance procedure that ultimately went to a board, in most cases the allegation would come down to what the resident said and the staff member denying the allegations. Very early on in the complaint process, I would ask whether anyone had witnessed the allegations. If the young man said no, I would ask him if he believed the staff member would confess to the misbehavior, sometimes behavior that could lead to immediate termination. When the resident would say no, I would say, "So how should we handle it?" In most cases, the young man would say, "I don't know." That's when I would happily give my speech on the fact that sometimes bad things happen to good people, how sometimes people behave poorly, and how sometimes hurt people hurt people. I would tell them that although they had made a mistake, and in most cases there was a victim, sometimes life is not fair and that they had to accept that sometimes life "sucks." (That is not my choice of words, but sometimes you have to use the message receiver's vernacular in order to get the point across.) People who do not end up in the criminal justice system are acclimated to the constant changes in life, and they ultimately come to understand that sometimes, life is just not fair. For those of you who are wondering, sooner or later abusive staff members would be caught due to extra vigilance.

Lessons from the Field

Reinhold Niebuhr says it best: God grant me the serenity to accept the things I cannot change, courage to change the things I can, and wisdom to know the difference.

What Is in a Name?

I am going to switch to a subject that is sometimes difficult to discuss with parents, so I am going drop it in right quick. I want to gingerly and lovingly approach the topic of naming children. More specifically, I want to discuss the importance of selecting an appropriate and effective title for children. The reason I say that this is a sore subject is because I have found that people get on the defensive when you question the naming of their children. Even in my family, I have been, gingerly and without much love, told off after suggesting that a family member reconsider the name they selected for their child. In spite of the difficulty of the conversation, I am going to ask the question, "What are you naming your child?"

Researchers have proven that a person's name bears something about their class, education, and of course, ethnicity. Initially, these traits are reflective of the parents. However, very early on, the name becomes the child's designation. A name is a title. Before the baby arrives, parents should conscientiously decide what they will name their child as their name will become their label to the world. Very often, a person's title (name) precedes the physical introduction, so that in many cases, even before someone meets another person, they will form an opinion based on the name. Sometimes the belief is based on the title and the initial impression that the title bears, the title holder will not be considered any further. Think about it, if you are scheduled to meet someone named Jesus, you more than likely visualize a Latino. If you are planning to meet Ja'kwon, you likely picture an African American male. However, if someone tells you that you will be meeting with someone named Mary, you can be reasonably confident that you will be shaking hands with a female. There is absolutely nothing wrong with any of these names. As a matter of fact, they are beautiful names. My point is that these names, as well as many others, are met with preconceived impressions. People believe that first impressions are lasting; however, having a negative impression can be lasting and damaging. We form impressions based on titles all the time without knowing it. When we consider seeing a movie, our initial impression is based on the title. If we are in the mood for a love story, a movie entitled *When All the Zombies Came Out of Hiding* would likely not attract our attention. Similarly, if someone wants information on medicine, contacting someone with an MD designation will likely be desirable.

In addition to making assumptions, albeit sometimes false, about people based on their names and titles, opportunities may be tied to a name. Résumés with traditionally African American names such as Ja'kwon Jackson will not get as much consideration as Mary Beth Johnson. Some people may take offense by this comment. My response to the person who takes exception to the rules of child naming is, "Don't kill the messenger because the message is not acceptable." Information on names has been researched extensively. The research has also revealed that people are naturally drawn to people that have names that are easy to pronounce. And when making decisions about people in authority, such as political figures, people ascribe more confidence to easily pronounced names. Another study found that people are drawn to people, places, and things that sound like their name. Psychologists refer to this self-love as *implicit egotism,* which refers to the idea that we naturally gravitate toward people, places, and things that resemble our self. Because of implicit egotism, people prefer letters that are in their name and numbers that are contained in their birthdates. Accordingly, I would be drawn to *L*s, *I*s, *S*s, and *A*s and the numbers 3 and 15. Actually, my favorite number is in fact 3. We have all had the experience of meeting people with our same name and feeling a sense of closeness due to the commonality. And don't let us find out that someone shares our birthday. We will take that person home and add them to the family. It is not only the inherent name that can be problematic, but naming kids after particular nouns could also be problematic. Parents should be careful when naming their kids after inanimate objects such as alcohol and assigning nicknames after drugs. While working for probation, I served many Hennessey's, Brandys, Buds, Coronas, and Ensaynes (pronounced as Insane). While working in juvenile hall, I recall three brothers in custody that were named after three Hebrew boys from the bible named Shadrach, Meshach, and Abednego. According to the Bible, these boys were thrown in the furnace as punishment for not worshiping an idol. When the king's men returned to the furnace, expecting the brothers to be burned to a crisp, he found them unharmed. That's an awesome story and a privilege to bear the name. However, when I asked the boys about their names, they could tell me about their namesakes. The most surprising nickname I came across was a little boy whose nickname was "Coochie Digger!" Again, these names are the child's title, and because the object's meaning predates the child, the impression has already been established. A person with the name of Lunatic will have a hard time modeling any other behavior except craziness.

For parents who really want to stay away from common names and offer unique titles to their children, it is advisable that parents be prepared to at least offer the meaning or spirit behind the name they chose for their child. I have also met hundreds of children with very exotic names with equally interesting spelling. In addition to the fact that these kids are the last ones in their class to learn to spell their names, they learn during English class that their names are spelled grammatically incorrect. For example, the apostrophe is a punctuation mark that is only used for two reasons: to indicate possession (e.g., Lisa's book, the dogs' bed) or the omission of letters or numbers (e.g., he's, can't, '16). Therefore, if you name your child Bec'kyl or Ke'nyon, your child will soon learn that his or her name is not punctuated correctly. And some brilliant kid may question whether you were as serious about your education as he or she is since you didn't know how to properly punctuate. (Sorry, that may be a bit harsh. That's why I started this section with love.) If the parent chooses the name of a famous athlete, please be prepared to say why you liked the athlete. But keep in mind that if your child fails to meet your athletic standard as exemplified by his namesake, it could negatively impact the child's self-esteem.

Parents should also consider if they want to name a child a junior version of an adult. In most cases, boys are named after an adult male figure, usually the father. I have met girls who are named after their mothers and many that are named after a matriarchal figure. When a child is named after the adult, very often, the child is referred to as little so-and-so, or Junior so-and-so. As the name Junior implies, the child is given the title of a smaller version of the senior adult and all of his or her glory or lack thereof. Even the namesake proudly proclaims that the child is a smaller version of them. However, in the interest of assuring that children have an opportunity to forge their own positive identities, parents should reflect on what it means to name their child after an adult. *Parents must first ponder whether becoming a duplicate of the namesake would be in the best interest of the child in current generation and time.* Parents should ask whether there is a positive legacy that follows the namesake. I always ask kids what their names mean, especially if it is unique. So often, the child will respond, "I am not sure" or simply "I don't know where my name came from." I always tell them to ask their mother or father.

The famous boxer George Foreman reportedly had five sons. All of them were named George Foreman numbers one through five. So theoretically, there are five junior versions of George Foreman in the world instead of the famous boxer and several other potential famous men. I am not sure whether any of George's son went on to become boxers; however, I am sure that being named after their famous dad had an impact on how they viewed themselves and how the world reacted to them. I can only imagine that anytime someone met one of the five Georges, people would ask if they were the son of the famous boxer. The next question is probably, which one are you? Being the son of a famous boxer ascribes meaning. The point that I am making is that parents should be very careful that they are not stereotyping their children, ascribing a permanent and harmful image to the child. Instead of ascribing outdated, unproductive, or dysfunctional traits to your child, parents may use practical labels. Instead of calling the child little so-and-so, refer to your child as your little planner, your handsome winner, your pretty patient one, your social bunny. If you want to compare your child to a parent or another adult, refer to good qualities of even an absent parent and say things like, "Wow, you are just like your daddy or mommy who was a great runner!" The kid may not know you really mean that he or she played around or ran in the streets a lot. To the child, you just mean that you saw the parent move fast!

Lessons from the Field

My own daughter does not like her name. She will actually tell you she hates her name and would change it if it she didn't have to go through so much bother. My third daughter's name is Chellsee (pronounced Chelsea). When I was pregnant with her and on vacation, I saw the name "Chelsea" on a souvenir refrigerator magnet. When I saw that name, I immediately fell in love. I was late in my pregnancy, so I already had a name picked out. However, I guess you could say that I fell in love with the name Chelsea at first sight. I was excited to share the name with my husband. He liked the name; however, since he was an educator, he wanted her name to be spelled phonetically. I was pleased, he was pleased. However, I would later learn that

Chellsee was not so pleased. During a conversation on the subject of naming children, Chellsee, now a young adult, advised me that she "hated" her name because she always thought it was "too long." She also thought it was boring. To emphasize her point, she said her name, "Chell-see," dragging out the name and emphasizing the first and second syllable longer than necessary. She acted like, by saying it slowly, a light would go off, and I would agree I had made a big mistake by giving her such a ghastly name. My response? I said, "Oh, okay, well you can change it now if you like." Of course, I would never call her anything else.

This same daughter was in a graduate school class and the subject came up about names. Each student was asked to look up their name for meaning. My daughter called me and told me how disappointed she was to learn that her name had no meaning at all with the exception of a location. I asked her, did it matter that her name meant something to me and her dad? She said, no, it did not. I'm waiting to see what title she gives her children.

I had the opportunity to meet with a superintendent of a contracting firm. He had a unique name, even after asking him to provide the spelling, I could not pronounce his name. I then asked him if the name had a special meaning, and he told me he was named after an important river in his native country. He went on to describe the river with pride. I am positive that understanding the significance of the river and the fact that his parents wanted to give him that title had something to do with his success in life. I also met a woman in a Bible study with a unique name. She proudly proclaimed that the name meant "original Israelite." Since she was committed to Christianity, she was so pleased with her name and boldly proclaimed its meaning. Remember, the name you give your child becomes their initial title. It is the first thing people know about the child, and it could be the only thing they know because names are the first and sometimes final impression. First impressions are lasting, and sometimes people will not go beyond the first impression. Therefore, if someone is turned off or even biased toward a particular name, they may not go any further to get to know the person. The name you give a child could prematurely ascribe erroneous meaning.

Do You Really Live the Sins of Your Mother or Father?

I have heard it said that a child will live the sins of their parents. My interpretation of this adage is that you can be negatively impacted by how your parents live their lives. I don't think kids have to repeat parental mistakes to learn a lesson. The only benefit of repeating parents' mistakes is that you discover that two generations can engage in the same behavior. I am not sure how much that is worth. The consultant's primary role is to provide enough information and direction that the child does not have to repeat the parents' mistakes as I suggested before, if I get a ticket for driving down a one-way street, and a day or even ten years later, my daughter starts to turn down the same street, should I tell her not to turn that way or let her experience getting a ticket? Once she gets the ticket, what do you think she will feel about me when I say, "I got a ticket on this same street. I knew it was only one way." Instead of risking negative consequences, I would consult with my daughter and tell her that she is heading down a one-way street. Parents who have an appropriate relationship with their children are comfortable offering advice. The consultant realizes and appreciates that they have laid a strong foundation, modeled appropriate behavior, and spent much time and energy teaching. Consultants are waiting for their work to pay off. Recall that I said that children don't have to repeat their parents' mistakes. But children must be permitted to make choices. The consultant gives expert advice but leaves the door open for the child to choose. So with respect to the one-way street, a child may respond,

"It's okay that it is a one-way street. There are no police around," and head down that one-way street. They may or may not get a ticket. What is important is that the parent consulted with the child by passing down valuable information.

For some parents, the reason that consulting is so difficult is because they don't readily see their child as capable of making good decisions on their own when they reach adulthood. Like puberty, kids reach adult maturity at different times. For some parents, their young adult may be very mature at sixteen years old, whereas some kids take until they are twenty-one. For the late bloomer, parents get worried because they want to see the fruits of their hard teaching labor on their child's eighteenth birthday. When the parents perceives that maturity is lacking in their child that is now bigger than they are, out of desperation, the parents sometimes want to revert back to teaching. I have worked with parents who are still trying to teach an adult child how to talk to authority figures, how to clean, how to dress, how to apply for jobs, or parents who are directing their adult child's personal life, telling them how to manage their relationships, telling their adult child where to live, who to marry, etc. Of more concern is the parent who now wants to be a role model and expects the child to do what they do just because the parent is doing it. Once children reach adulthood, it is too late to model behavior that you hope your child will imitate. In most cases, adult children are not interested in being taught or told what to do, even if the information is correct. They want to be an adult; being told and directed is associated with being a child. Don't mistake it being too late to model and teach with parents being told not to provide constructive instruction. I am not saying that; what I am saying is that, once children reach adulthood, parents' instruction should be upon invitation from the child.

There Are No Do-Overs; the Time is Now

Parents must raise their children beginning on the day that they are born and don't stop until they are young adults and able to efficiently care for themselves. Parents of adult children will often say that time moves in light speed when you raise children. They grow up very fast. Of course, realizing how fast kids grow up can only be viewed in hindsight, because when you are in the midst of raising kids, time appears to move at a snail's pace. I have met parents who regret the fact that they didn't do a good job at parenting. Most have remorse over the little time they spent positively engaging with their kids and just having fun. Some parents are nostalgic over the past. They realize that it is too late to go back. They are right, you can't go back and there are no do-overs when raising kids. It is too late to begin breastfeeding a two-year-old. It is too late to push your twelve-year-old on the swing. It is too late to go on elementary school field trips with a high school sophomore. But it is never too late to begin a new relationship with your child based on the current developmental phase. If you have a teenage child, it is not too late to begin fishing, going to the hairdressers, shopping, golfing, jogging, going to car shows, having a mani-pedi, teaching him or her how to drive, going to the movies, playing video games, and other fun activities.

Prior to beginning a new relationship with a child, there needs to be a clear ending to the old relationship. The parent and the child must see a distinct line between the previous means of relating and the new, improved relationship. Before starting that new relationship, what needs to happen first is an acknowledgment on the parents' part that there is a desire to begin a new relationship. Parents must admit that they missed opportunities to connect in the past and they want to make up and start new. This is an important step. A conversation between a parent and adolescent may go like this:

Parent: Reagan, I was thinking about our relationship and I realize that we have not spent a lot of time together. I realize that it was my fault. I spent most of your middle school years working and competing for job promotions. I really miss that time. I know we can't get it back, but I would like to work on spending more time together. I know you have lots of friends and hobbies, but maybe we could schedule time together. What do you think about that?

The teen may have a variety of reactions. He or she may become sarcastic, laugh, become angry or, ideally, agree. The most important thing is that parents acknowledge that the goal is to initiate a new relationship. Parents should not be put off by the teen's response if it is not favorable.

Lessons from the Field

Soon after my third child was born, I started pursuing management positions in probation. Once I was promoted to management, I spent an inordinate amount of time working. Instead working a typical 8-to-5 shift, I started my workday early and ended late. Even when I was not at work, I was thinking about how to improve the units under my purview. As I look back on that time, I realize that my biggest priority was not my children. Yes, I took great care of them and attended to their needs, took them to social events, checked on their grades, etc.; however, I was not fully engaged.

My memories of my third child's middle school years are a blur. During that time, I had been promoted to an executive manager, and with the position came big responsibilities and very long hours. Although I recall my older two children's teachers by name, I can't recall the names of many of my third child's teachers. Although, my daughter jokes about the little time I spent with her and the absence of many shared memories, it became apparent that she felt slighted. One day, she shared how she had almost fallen out of a tree. She talked about how scared she was and that she had called for help to no avail. I told her that I didn't know anything about that, and she offhandedly said, "Ah, Mom, you were probably at work. You were never around." Although my daughter had made reference to how much time I spent at work when she was younger, this time I could see hurt in her eyes. Soon after that conversation, I went to her and apologized. I told her that I couldn't give her the time back, but I was willing to make it up to her by giving her more time now. My daughter was eighteen years old by then. Her response was "Uh, okay."

The Means of Conception Does Not Have to Justify the End

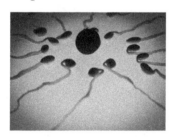

How a parent raises a child must not depend on how the child was conceived. Becoming pregnant could have occurred after several years of planning or the result of poor planning. The most important fact is that babies don't schedule their birthdates. As my second oldest daughter reminds me every time I am resistant to granting her requests, "I didn't ask to be born!" Although my daughter provides a good example of parental manipulation, she actually makes a good point. It is only because of her dad and I that she was born. In spite of all the medical and fertility advances that have occurred throughout the ages, the fact remains that conception can only occur after a male sperm and female egg unite and fertilization occurs. The owners of that sperm and egg are physically accountable for the birth of the child. I would be remiss if I didn't acknowledge that there are circumstances that can occur that would result in forced conception. In those instances, the most responsible person carrying the sperm or the egg must make the best decision for the child. If the decision is made to raise the child, there must be a commitment to take full responsibility for raising the child.

One of the clearest messages I learned during the three decades I served in the criminal justice system was that accountability and responsibility are not the same. To be accountable means that based on a certain fact (parentage), there is an obligation similar to a legal contract. Contracts are binding because people chose to enter into an agreement to be responsible for something. Some parents raise their kids because it is the thing to do to avoid being charged with neglect or suffer other emotional and financial liability. In some cases, obligatory parenting is enough in that it is better than no parenting at all. However, in all cases, children will do better with conscientious responsible parenting.

Lessons from the Field

One of the worst expression of regret that I heard during my tenure serving probation clients was a mother who said that her biggest regret was that she had not closed her legs shut as her son was leaving the womb, so he would have suffocated. Mind you, I had not solicited information on regrets. She offered this solution through frustration. Her son had been in a lot of trouble during his older years. As with any other parent, although I was taken aback by her comment, I did not judge her as a parent. Her regret made me judge her level of parenting strategies. This parent had lost hope of her son ever developing into the person she wanted him to be, so the only remedy the mother had was to erase her son's birth. Parents do the best they can at any given moment with the resources they have.

There is No Exchange Nor Can You Get Your Money Back

In addition to the few parents that I encountered who wanted to erase their kid's birthday, I have encountered more parents who had given up and wanted the juvenile justice system to take over raising their child. The parents would say, I did my best, now you take over. To be honest, most often it was the single mother who had raised their son without their father who had figuratively and literally dropped their kids off at the juvenile hall door feeling defeated. On a few occasions, we found those fathers and dropped them back off with the dad who claimed not to know the status of their kids. I recall one occasion when a young man had been released to return home, only to come back a few days later, rang the detention bell, and said he wanted to come back.

More common, parents who felt they had lost the ability to raise their child understood the principles of parents patriae, and they were happy to take advantage of the state's right to take over in the raising of an at-risk child. Over the past thirty years that I have worked with families inside and outside of the criminal justice system, parents have repeatedly asked for advice and direction in raising their children. Unfortunately, the cry for help often came after the child had been exposed to the traumatic experiences that are inherent in the juvenile justice system and after parents had engaged in many failed efforts to effectively relate to their child. In some cases, the parents found my guidance helpful but too late. These parents were either not willing or didn't feel capable of renegotiating their current dysfunctional relationship with their son or daughter. If you recall, reestablishing a relationship requires the acknowledgment of past wrongs, taking responsibility, apologizing, making amends, and distinctively and decisively beginning a new relationship. These steps are often very painful for the person attempting to make amends. But, parents must avoid the juvenile justice system at all costs. The juvenile justice system is not a recycling bin for children. As I have pointed out in some of the lessons in the field, a child's acting-out behavior has an etiology that can be addressed and thwarted if parents choose to stay on the parent path and advocate for their child. When kids begin to have problems, that is not the time for parents to give their kids to the system.

Lessons from the Field

When I was a probation officer assigned to provide casework to at-risk students at a community day school, one of the families I worked with was a single mother and her teenage son. The young man had been expelled from his comprehensive high school due to ongoing fighting. In the initial intake meeting with the minor's mother, she reported that her son had started challenging her authority at home. It was not long before the young man began exhibiting the same aggressive behavior that he was demonstrating with his mother at the community day school. He started challenging the classroom teachers and probation staff on campus. Although we began to see small but incremental improvement in the minor's behavior, his aggressive behavior at home continued. During one of the many meetings I had with the mother and her son, she became noticeably exasperated with my conversation. All of my suggestions to address her son's incorrigible behavior was met with "Yes, but . . . I know but . . . And you are right but . . ." At last, the mother stopped me from talking midsentence by putting her hand in the air and she said, "Ms. Hill, I really appreciate all your help, but I just need you to tell me where I can take him back to." After an awkward few moments of silence and noticing the look of bewilderment on my face, the mother further told me that she had adopted her son at birth, and although things had gone very well for the first several years, her son had started to act out in the last couple of years. Initially, it appeared to be mere adolescent behavior, including neglecting house chores and occasionally talking back to her. However, in the past two years, her previously compliant son had become incorrigible by staying out past curfew, truant from school, and most disturbing to the mom, he had become verbally disrespectful to her. After several meetings with the school personnel and now faced with having to collaborate with a probation officer, the mother decided that she no longer wanted to be her son's parent and she wanted to "take him back." When the young man heard his mother's feelings, he immediately retorted, "Good, I want to go back also . . . You have been threatening to send me back for a long time, so now I am finally ready to go also!" Again, I asked the two of them to where would the young man return? The mother said she wanted to return him to the adoption agency. To both of their surprise, I informed them that there was no adoption return facility and that adoptions are permanent. To emphasize my point, I told the mother that her son was as much her child as my birth children were my kids. Both of them looked at me with a look of surprise. However, after a few more awkward moments, I could actually feel the tension leave the room. Although there wasn't an immediate and drastic change in the young man's behavior, over time, his communication and overall relationship with his mother improved. No longer did the youth feel the pressure of believing his mother would inevitably abandon him at any moment. The mother realized that her son was her responsibility and there was no "out clause" for her. Therefore, she made a renewed and conscientious effort to raise her son.

Electronics Addiction

Let's talk about something less emotional and more contemporary. Is your child addicted to social media? Since kids do what you do and not what you say, are you addicted to your smart devices? Recall that I told you to turn off your electronics? Recall that I told you that kids will do what you do and not what you say? Do you abuse electronic devices, including television, smartphones, and laptops? Are you constantly on social media? If you are, chances are that your children will be addicted also because (say it with me) kids do what you do and not what you say. It is not too late to redirect the child's behavior; however, the parents will have to fully engage and fill the void left by the exciting electronic devices.

Lessons from the Field

I see young and old people who are so tied to their electronics that they will walk and not look where they are going. Their faces are glued to the device, and they never take the time to look up and survey their environment for the danger of oncoming traffic or an opportunistic offender. I have heard of many car accidents involving people being run over by trains. In many instances, it is because the driver is not cognizant of the train approaching because they never looked up from their devices to see the flashing rails descending. People who are tied to their electronic devices slow down foot traffic; they just get in the way. I have seen people almost get hit by oncoming traffic because they don't realize that the light has changed to red and they start walking against traffic. Like any addiction, in order to stop the habit, the muscle memory tied to the behavior has to be eliminated or at least minimized. Some addictions begin out of boredom, and the use of the substance adds excitement. The use of electronics and social media serves the same purpose. People use electronic devices to fill a void of boredom. While waiting in line, instead of not doing anything, people will pull out their phones and play games, go on online gambling sites, or they get on social media. Kids who have watched their parents do this will do the same. Also, while parents are not ceasing upon opportunities to spend with their child during down times, the kids are left to their own devices, and they learn to fill the voids using other means. The other addictive process to being tied to social media or electronic devices in general is the inability to turn the brain off. Some people are always in vigilance mode, in which case they are receiving information via news flashes, social media updates, and advertisements. Since the brain never shuts down, hyperactivity and hypervigilance can ultimately lead to mental health issues like chronic exhaustion, stress, anxiety, and even depression from the burden that comes from being inundated with bad news. The point is, make sure your child is not overusing or abusing electronics, and that they are balanced in that they are using their electronic devices to keep up with technology but still socializing and taking care of other life issues, like homework, spending time outdoors exercising, and engaging in family traditions and celebrations.

If She Loves It, She Won't Want to Lose It

Having warned parents against potential social media addiction, I want to keep in perspective the fact that, as a society, we are well immersed in a technological age and there is no turning back. People will never resort back to going in the bank when they can go to an automated teller machine (ATM). No one wants to pull out and unfold a paper map when they can get directions on their phone or even in their car's Global Positioning System (GPS). And my personal favorite, why wait forty-five minutes to heat food when I can cook it in the microwave for three minutes. That's a no-brainer. And of course, the medical breakthroughs from computer technology can't be undone. If there is a tumor growing in my body, I can get a quick CAT scan instead of waiting for the tumor to grow large and lethal enough for an X-ray to detect the image. Electronics are thankfully here to stay; however, as a society, we will have to learn how to balance our use of our devices so that they don't take the place of our ability to relate to one another and also assure that electronics don't intrude on a child so much that they cannot address their needs, such as hygiene, health, schoolwork, chores, and employment when they are older. I want to close this section on a positive note for parents. Electronics, at the very least, are a means of reinforcement for parents if they need more power, I mean, leverage with their children.

Lessons from the Field

My fourteen-year-old daughter loves her smartphone. She rarely talks on it, but she loves using her phone to chat online, play games, look at pictures, listen to music, watch YouTube videos, and anything else the phone has to offer. When she has free time, she is glued to her phone. Some parents are bothered by the close relationship their kids have with their phones because it takes too much of their kids' attention. I have heard parents complain that the kid would rather spend more time with the phone than with family. I often remind parents that the phones are the new-generation friends. Kids don't have to go outside or anywhere else to socialize. They have virtual friends at the tips of their fingers. Years ago, parents had the same concern about their kids spending too much time with their friends. But it's not that kids prefer or love the phone more than their family; it is just that the phone has more to offer in the moment. When a kid is watching an exciting video, they are entertained to a degree that parents cannot offer. One evening, I told my daughter that she could get on her phone for twenty more minutes before going to bed. Before I realized it, she had been on an additional hour. My initial response was that she purposefully defied me and had not honored her commitment to get off the phone in the allotted time. However, she humbly responded that she had merely forgotten the time. I took the phone anyway, but I understood and was spared the anger and negative feelings that came with the thought of being defied. You see, my daughter did not set out to defy me; she was actually a pretty compliant child. But she was caught up in the moment of enjoyment. Understanding that my daughter did not intentionally disobey me did not mean that she did not need consequences. Consequences provide an opportunity for teachable moments. The ramifications of disobedience will get a person's attention and will ultimately deter further disobedience. Removing a desired object gets a person's attention, especially in the case of an egocentric kid. Although I have to remain vigilant to assure that my daughter does not abuse her smartphone and other social media, I happen to love the fact that my daughter has found a "thing" that she loves because it is that very "thing" that I can take from her if she does not comply with my directions. My daughter dreads giving up her phone, so she will do whatever I ask at the risk of losing her beloved phone friend.

I Brought You in This World; I Will Take You Out

I think it is clear by now that parents need the knowledge, skills, and abilities to maintain their parental role and assure that their kids become productive adults. Parents learn really soon that they cannot bully their will onto their children. The old adage that parents bring their children into the world and can take them out is lost when the child reaches a certain age and there is a "showdown," and parents realize that pure deference to their authority has been lost and verbal commands are ineffective in gaining compliance. Parents understand society's expectations that children act a certain way and, sometimes out of desperation, parents may resort to ineffective strategies to bring children into compliance. Sometimes, when all else fails, parents resort to corporal punishment. This tactic may have worked well when the child was small and the parent looked like a giant from the child's three-foot vantage point. However, by late adolescence, many children are at least as big as their parents and able to look at their parents eye to eye. Additionally, during adolescence, children may be at the peak of physical health. Conversely, by the time a child reaches adolescence, most parents are approaching middle age and may be over the hill of their physical and mental crescendo. Therefore, by adolescence, children may be physically and mentally able to compete with their parents. To put it bluntly, by adolescence, children can very likely offer the parents a beatdown, and even if they can't physically win a battle, their brains are still growing and they may be able to outwit their parents. Finally, if all else fails, adolescents can outrun their parents so they can escape corporal punishment. Therefore, the use of physical threats and domination are no longer effective parental tools to control adolescent behavior. Now, during my mother's generation of parenting, there was a popular saying that is still used today: "I brought you into this word and I can take you out." It is more likely that the child would take out the parents.

In the absence of physical power, parents may reach out to the juvenile justice system for support. By the time children arrive at the detention center, some parents have asked, begged, pleaded, cried, and definitely threatened their child in an effort to bring them under control. Some parents have even checked out! During my tenure as a probation officer, I have witnessed occasions when the intake probation officer has attempted to make the initial contact with the parent to report the custody status of their child, and the number has been changed. Absent being able to contact the parent by phone, the probation officer is forced to conduct a residence verification based on the address provided by the detained youth. It is at that time that it is determined that the parent has moved with no forwarding address. Parents who leave their children usually are leaving the relationship. They have lost hope in having a parent-child relationship and are hopeful that "the system" will take over.

My Child Better Respect Me

Respect is a feeling of deep admiration for someone or something elicited by the object of the admirable's abilities, actions, or achievements. Respect is earned. Initially, a child's apparent respect for her parents can be passively achieved. In other words, it does not matter how the parents treat the child; there is a bond. When children are young, they revere their parents because in their concrete minds, they do not know any better. As a result of this unearned respect, young children will do what it takes to please their parents. However, reverence is attributed to the child's early attachment and dependence on the parents. It is not until children are older and are able to think abstractly that they may realize that the parental behavior is not worthy of respect. Once children are no longer concrete thinkers, parents' behavior becomes more comprehensible and clear. At some point, children are able to engage in abstract reasoning, so they begin to have a more authentic relationship with their parents. In other words, they see the parents for who they really are. For some kids, they come to realize that their parents may not have treated them appropriately. Recall my probationer who was molested. It was not until he became an abstract thinker that he was able to attribute his molestation to his parents' desire to transfer their responsibility to their friend, so that they could "go out." When my young probationer became an abstract thinker, he began to reason, albeit erroneously, that his parents were responsible for his abuse. Once kids advance into abstract reasoning, they may realize that some of the things that parents did or even didn't do was not right, unfair, or even harmful. One of the reasons that adolescents are so often described as angry by their parents is because they see the parents differently, that is why acknowledgment, taking responsibility, and then apologizing for past mistakes is so important. The main point is that respect is earned, and in order for parents to earn their kids respect, they have to consistently carry themselves in a respectful manner even when they don't think the child is paying attention or that she is old enough to understand, because it is inevitable that kids will, at some point, see the parents for who they are and maybe even begin to call the parent by their first name. Recall the discussion on the relationship account. During adolescence, parents may want to make a withdrawal from the currency in their relationship account. That currency was earned from being there for the child, complimenting, advocating, and providing for the child. In the absence of currency and respect, parents must work to earn currency that leads to respect. As I have mentioned before, there must be an acknowledgment, the taking of responsibility, and an apology. Ouch, this may hurt.

I Don't Like the Person My Child Has Become

I have met parents who love their kids but they don't like them. Some parents have reported this to me in shame. Sometimes, the disclosure of not liking the child has come after many discussions, and then finally, they will conclude that they don't like the child. Some parents have demonstrated relief from acknowledging that they do not like their kids, but they quickly add that they love them. Many parents are surprised that I am not surprised by their admission. I often validate the parents' feelings by pointing out that the behavior that they describe that the child is exhibiting is not likable. It is important that parents distinguish their dislike for the child's behavior versus the character of the child. However, if it is in fact the character of the child that the parents do not like, they must seek counseling to address their feelings as they may stem from deeper issues. Sometimes, the parents see too much of the traits that they don't like either themselves or another person in the child, so they transfer those negative feelings unto the child.

The courageous part of my conversation with parents comes when I have to confront the parents on the etiology of the behavior that the parents find unlikable. For example, when parents complain that their kids are ungrateful and spoiled, I ask whether or not the child has been overindulged. In most cases, the parents will admit that when the child was younger, they were given pretty much whatever the child wanted. When the child was younger, providing them with "gifts" was easier. However, as the child aged, the standard of the gifts became bigger. I have met parents who have purchased luxury cars for their children as soon as they start driving. Overindulging a child is contrary to one of the habits of people who do not end up in the criminal justice system. Children must be able to delay gratification. In respect to purchasing a luxury car for a new driver, kids could begin with a preowned car and earn a new car by having a good driving record. On the other extreme, some parents don't like the traits that they see in the child as it reminds them of traits they don't like in themselves or even the other parent. It always amazes me that when I ask parents, where do they think the child learned the behavior, the parent always says the absent parent. Still, in other cases, because the child resembles one of the parents, the other parent will resent the child. In most cases the resentment is unconscious and discovered during therapy. When parents find that their child has developed traits that are counterproductive and the behavior stems from how the parent related to the child (such as spoiling the child), a new relationship must be initiated. As is the case with starting all new relationships, parents must acknowledge overindulging the child, take responsibility, apologize, and then move forward.

Lessons from the Field

When I was a probation first line supervisor, I managed a field supervision unit. My unit was responsible for supervising youth offenders who had been placed on probation. The unit was also responsible for responding to youth who had been cited and released for minor behavior. The unit would receive dozens of these nonserious cases each month. In lieu of assigning these cases onto my already overworked probation officers, I would send letters to the family and ask them to come into the office for a group meeting. During the meeting, I would assess whether the case needed a referral to the probation officer or community-based program, such as counseling, to address their behavior. One case was a young man who had been cited for pulling a weapon on his mother. I met with the two individually. The young man was tall and muscular, and his mother was of average height and weight. The minor admitted that he had kept a knife with him at all times when he was home because his mother had threatened to kill him. When the young man made this comment, I was more surprised that the mother didn't change her expression and further did not deny her son's accusation. When I asked her, she admitted that she wanted to kill him. When I asked why, she said that he was too much like his father's people. She said that her ex-husband and all of "his people" were evil, and not only did her son look like his dad, but she believed her son had more of his father's blood in him. The young man was biracial, and the mother believed that her son was hopeless because he was more like "them." I asked whether her son had ever attempted to hurt her or acted aggressively toward her. She conceded that he had not, but it was only a matter of time before his "genes took over." The young man was a good student and was in his last year of high school. We arranged for him to live with a neighbor while he finished his senior year. The mother needed individual counseling; however, she was unwilling to participate.

Be the Duck You Hope Your Chick Will Become

One of the reasons that parents don't like the end product of their parenting efforts is because they did not model the behavior that they hoped their child would emulate. In other words, they didn't behave like the duck that they wanted their chicks to become. Parents must start the parenting journey with a vision of their child becoming a productive, self-sufficient, law-abiding adult. The blueprint to making that vision a reality is in the parent or primary caretaker. The parent is the primary catalyst for their children's success. The parents' ability to adopt and model the habits of highly successful people will determine if the children will internalize the habits. By adopting the productive habits, parents will automatically model the behavior for their children. The parent, who is usually the first and the most consistent person in the child's life, becomes the model for behavior. As I mentioned before but I think it warrants saying again, children will imitate the parent's behavior similar to how birds imprint on their parent or whoever becomes the most consistent person in the child's life. The best-known form of imprinting is *filial imprinting*, which occurs when a young animal acquires several of its behavioral characteristics from its parents. It is most obvious in birds, because the imprinting process manifests by the young birds following their parents around. Although the manifestation of human imprinting cannot be readily observed, children also begin to take on the behavioral and character traits of their parents at birth. Those traits develop incrementally as children mature and acquire new skills, such as walking and talking. Because of the imprinting process, parents must take inventory of the behavior and character traits they possess, discarding the ones that they do not wish to pass on to their children and developing the traits that will result in their child's success. Honest self-reflection will require discipline and honesty on the parents' part. In order for parents to positively influence their children, parents must first commit to being a positive role model. For some parents, this is a challenge because parenting is a selfless act. Therefore, if at all possible, before making the decision to have children, parents must understand one fundamental fact: *Children do what their parents do and not just what they say.* As the cliché goes, actions speak louder than words. Think about it: if you arrived at a friend's house and was invited in, but the host did not smile or appear happy to accept you. Upon seeing the displeasure, you ask if it was a good time to visit. Again, with a stern face, the potential host confirms that you can enter her home and turns to lead you into the house. How likely is it that you would feel welcomed? Based on the host's nonverbal clues of frustration, you would likely feel uninvited. That is because actions always trump words. This truism is most accurate when it comes to the messages that parents' behavior communicates to their children. When children are born, they will adapt to the environment in which they are born. Therefore, if you cuss out people when you get angry, you may find that your child to respond in kind.

Lessons from the Field

My mother used to ask me and my siblings to light her cigarette if she was in another room from where the cigarettes were. My siblings and I, all under the legal age of smoking, would happily run off and find the cigarettes and, with pride, fire it up! Sometimes, by the time we brought the lighted cigarette to my mother, it would have burned down, alerting my mother to fact that we had taken a few extra puffs off the cigarette. If my mother paid attention and noticed the near-cigarette butt we were bringing her, she would become angry and tell us that we were not allowed to ever smoke because it is a horrible habit. It is probably no surprise that I as well as all of my siblings started smoking cigarettes. This is no surprise to the reader because by now, you are well aware that kids do what you do and not what you say. Why would I initially think that smoking was a horrible habit when my mother, who was the queen of my universe and the smartest person in the entire world, was a smoker? My mother had impressed upon me that "mothers know best." My mother was my role model, and I wanted to act just like her. My mother was beautiful, and she looked really impressive puffing on that cigarette. Yes, I wanted to look impressive. The only reason I did not maintain the habit is I could never get past the nausea that came from being a novice smoker. I would become sick every time I tried to smoke. That didn't look like my momma. So I settled for combing my hair like she did and put the cigarettes away. Sadly, my mother died of lung cancer at a relatively young age. She had been smoking for sixty years when she died. She was right: smoking is a horrible habit. Thankfully, all of my siblings ultimately mustered the strength to suffer through the pain of withdrawing off of nicotine.

Prosocial Family Traditions

Ideally, prior to having kids, think about who you are and what traditions accompany you. Now think about your partner and the traditions that will be carried forth. Even if you already have kids, stop for a moment and think about what family traditions you want to carry forth into the next generation. If the traditions have been ineffective and nonproductive in previous generations, they probably won't be any good in succeeding generations. Maybe there were some traditions that were lost in recent generations that you may want to recapture. Traditions are customs, values, or beliefs that are passed on from generation to generation. Perhaps there have never been any traditions, but you want to start something positive. These traditions will be a foundation for kids as they face consistently changing and sometimes conflicting trends. Having traditions simplify and anchor the life of the child because they will not be subjected to the multitude of messages that are coming in literally every second due to the World Wide Web. Parents should begin to immediately discuss "the family's traditions," prefacing conversations with "the way our family handles this situation is by. . ." "The Kim family's manner of dealing with this condition is to . . . The Duplessises don't drink and drive. The Soo family are fisherman/fisherwoman. The Parkers all attend college. During Christmas time, the Torrences enjoy watching movies. The Singh family enjoys feeding the homeless one time each month. The Gonzalezes are a board game family; they play games every Friday. The Tuis are health conscious. The Grissoms don't smoke. The Joneses are philanthropists." Parents want to create a sense of togetherness in the family, so that kids don't have to create their own family unit. People have a natural desire to be involved in a community. The family is the first and most important community group.

Let's Talk About Differences

I would like to drop this topic in what appears to be out of nowhere. A discussion on difference is never timely. People get uncomfortable when you talk about race, religion, sexual orientation, and gender because they understand that these things still define a person, and in most cases, illogically and erroneously. Part of the reason that a definition on one of the above categories is problematic is because defining someone based on one characteristic is so limiting. A person's race is defined as a shared ancestry, which is manifested by things such as hair texture, skin tone, facial features, stature, and eye color. Unfortunately, that definition does not take into consideration experiences, social exposures, and most importantly, learning. However, because ancestry has an obvious physical manifestation, sometimes just looking at a person from another race may result in preconceived ideas. So think about it, does it make sense to solely base your impression someone on one single characteristic?

Ethnicity is another predominant determinant on which people base their opinion on another person. Ethnicity looks more at social mores and values because ethnicity usually is equated with a person's cultural group. Although people behave more in accordance with their ethnicity as opposed to race, it is still only one part of their being and ethnicity can only be implied. Until you get to know the person, you don't know what part, if at all, they subscribe to their prescribed ethic group. With respect to gender, usually a person's gender allows someone to define the limits on the person. You can't do certain things if you are assigned to a certain gender. My question is, what if the person can, in spite of their gender? The point that I am making is that you more than likely will miss all the other characteristics that may have a bigger impact on the person's being if you focus on just one part of who they are. But today, we have to talk about differences because distinctions are still a very big defining part of who we are as a society. Differences are a topic of discussion that transcends each generation to date. No matter how technologically advanced our society becomes, we just can't design something that would result in social equality for all people regardless of race, religion, gender, creed, or sexual orientation. Therefore, I must courageously add a section on differences in this parenting book. Perhaps, in writing this section, this may be the last generation that will have to address this issue.

Previously, I shared with you one of Barbara Harrell Carson's famous quotes that basically told us that kids learn their values from people they care about. This could not be truer than when it comes to how people feel about people that are different from them. Have you noticed that when kids are very young, they have a variety of friends? Young children don't always select their friends based on whether the kid is the same gender, ethnicity, religion or creed, culture, or if they prescribe by their actions, to their gender. Kids select their friends based on whether they feel good around them. If you play with dolls and I like dolls, we are friends. If you like to catch bugs and I like to catch bugs, that's all that matters. It is not until kids get to a certain age that they begin to make distinctions. Sometimes, it appears out of nowhere. More often than not, kids begin to act in accordance with their role models. In all cases, bias is learned. Although in time, experience may result in positive or negative bias, it's the behavior that is learned through important models in a child's life that will result in what I refer to as "early onset prejudice."

Lessons from the Field

Recently, I was listening to someone having a conversation with someone on their cell phone (in public). The person appeared to be having trouble communicating with the person on the other end because her voice continued to raise until she was almost yelling. It wasn't until she took the phone away from her face and said, "Oh my gosh, I can't stand foreigners" that I realized that the person on the other end of the line was not hard of hearing, but probably had an accent. However, I focused on how the exasperated person had modeled her displeasure with people who do not speak English. I couldn't help but wonder whether the person voiced her displeasure with non-English speakers in front of impressionable kids. In that brief conversation, if I was an impressionable child, I would have learned that people that do not speak English are frustrating, suffer from hearing loss because you mustn't just yell at them, and they are people to be hated. I don't think that this attitude is unique to English speakers. I could imagine the same exchange between a non-English speaker in a foreign country trying to communicate with an English speaker saying, "I hate these English-speaking foreigners." My point is that kids are very impressionable, and that racism, sexism, ageism, homophobia, and xenophobia are learned behavior. Even if you are very comfortable in your biases, I would suggest you permit your child to develop their own prejudices, or better yet, maybe you can allow your child not to be prejudiced.

Shame on You, Not Me!

Shame is never an effective teaching tool. Shame is defined as "a painful feeling of humiliation or distress caused by the consciousness of wrong or foolish behavior." I know there are some parents who believe that pain is a deterrent, but to a concrete-thinking child who only sees things in black and white, pain and humiliation is just that: painful. Think about it: if you did something that you regretted, in other words something stupid, would it help to have someone say that not only was the behavior stupid (and I mean literally without intelligence), but you are stupid also? Recall that your end goal is that your children will grow into confident, productive, and happy adults and will not end up in the criminal justice system. Recall one of the habits of people who do not enter that system is that they start with the end in mind. How do you think it will end if a child is constantly humiliated? Perhaps a visual would help. Every time a parent, who is the idol and role model to the child, says something humiliating about their person (not behavior), it is likened to taking a hammer and hitting a nail on the head. It is not only the pain of the hammer (the words), but it is also the fact that with each blow, the child is sinking lower and lower with respect to their self-esteem and confidence. Recall that parents are the first mirrors.

Lessons from the Field

Recently, someone sent me a video of a mother who was angry at her daughter because of something she had posted on Facebook. The teen had posted a picture and video that had not shown her in the same light that her mother viewed the teen. As a result, the mother forced the daughter to post a new video. In the video, the teen had to confess to lying on the earlier video. You could see the mother in the background saying, "Tell the truth and confess to being not only a liar but also a teen who was not part of the 'cool culture." You could see a look of humiliation on the teen's face as she painfully repeated her mother's demands. You could also see a look of power on the mother's face. In another video, a parent forced his son to post a video on Facebook saying that he was not the drug dealer that he was posturing to be, but in fact a scared boy. In both cases, the parent was in the background verbally abusing the child on the video. The message that was sent was that, not only is the kid a loser for pretending to be something he/she is not, but he is really a loser because even his or her parents don't like him. As a parent, I understood what the parents were hoping to accomplish. They wanted to deter the child from the behavior. Deterrence is discouraging an action or even instilling doubt or fear of the consequences. However, for deterrence to be effective, the deterree [sic] must be able to connect the consequences to the behavior that resulted in the punishment. So, unless the child truly understood that their behavior was wrong and that is why they were punished, deterrence will not be effective. If an offender feels like they were punished because they were not savvy or sneaky enough or that the punishment only resulted because the parent is unknowing or lame (as the teen will most likely say), then deterrence will not have occurred. What will result is resentment and bitterness toward the punisher. At more risk is that the punished person will not have respect for the punisher. A lack of respect, for the parent, is often the case with offenders who come through the criminal justice system. Sometimes, the experience is so traumatic that the lesson is lost.

Another Lesson from the Field

*A good example of a lost lesson was illustrated by one of my
probationers. I supervised a young man who had been sent away
to placement for his first offense. The kid had never been in trouble
with the law and was actually a good student from a decent family.
His arrest was the result of a bad decision. One summer, when he
was visiting his cousin, who had been in contact with the juvenile
justice system, the two went to visit the cousin's "girlfriend." The
cousin ended up in bed with the girlfriend in another room. When
the girlfriend's father returned home unexpectedly, the girlfriend
panicked and told the boyfriend that he needed to jump out of the
window because the dad would be (obviously) furious when he
learned that she was having sex at fifteen with a sixteen-year-old
boy. The cousin complied and jumped out the window, forgetting
about his cousin who was sitting in the other room. Unfortunately,
the boyfriend couldn't get out the window before the father saw him.
In order for the daughter to save face with her dad, she told him that
she had been forced into sex with the boyfriend. My client, who had
been waiting in the living room, was charged with accessory to rape,
although the girlfriend reported that he did not participate.*

*Although my client maintained his innocence, he was adjudicated
as a delinquent and sent to a placement for sex offenders in another
state. I met my client when he was returning home after two years.
In reviewing his placement release file, I learned that he was forced
to remain in placement for more than a year longer than expected
because he would not admit to being a sex offender. The program
case manager delayed his release because it was believed that my
client was not accepting responsibility for his actions by admitting
to being a sex offender. I supervised my client for several months
after his release to make sure that he was adjusting to returning to
his home community. The young man did very well and did not suffer
any probation violations or new offenses. I would call him a model
client. As with all of my juvenile clients, at the end of the supervision*

period, I met with him to discuss his upcoming court date. I advised him that he had met all the conditions of supervision and earned the recommendation for dismissal at the upcoming court hearing. He looked perplexed, so I reminded him that upon dismissal, he would not have to worry about me coming to his school and home. When that still did not get a smile, I asked him whether he was happy. He said, "I guess so," but sort of sadly. So I asked him what he would do now that I would not be in his life. He humped his shoulders. I started to ask if he had a girlfriend, but before I could get the G out, he said NO emphatically. He went on to say that he "hated girls and didn't want to have anything to do with them." I tried to assuage his fears of contact with girls and my client was respectful in listening to me, but I could see that all I was doing was planting seeds that I hoped would someday sprout because at that moment, my client's mind was made up. He was not deterred from criminal behavior because he did not connect his actions with the consequences. My client had connected his consequences to the inability of girls to tell the truth. My client was resentful and bitter, much like the children who are shamed by their parents in hopes that the child will learn a lesson and not repeat undesirable behavior. Shaming never works. It only makes the child feel like something is wrong with them and not the behavior.

Get the Help Your Kids Need!

I spend a lot of time visiting libraries. Not only does the library provide a relatively quiet environment to write, but I have also found that the library also offers the opportunity to see many parents in action. I see good and bad parenting. It is a therapists' playground! The greatest thing I see is parents who have hired tutors or taken advantage of free tutoring services for their children. School does not come easy for all students. There are many reasons why this is the case. However, in most cases, poor academic outcomes is because of lack of exposure. Kids' brains are like sponges, and the brain will soak up all the liquid (knowledge) with which it comes into contact.

Accelerated brain development occurs at different times; however, if a child is not in the most conducive environment to learn, another child in a highly conducive environment will surpass the former child. What that looks like is some kids do better in school than others. Think about it: if one student missed a lot of school during the early years due to illness, he or she may not have learned basic phonics and therefore may not be able to read by third grade. No matter what third-grade reading assignments you give that student, he will not be able to do it without remediation. Some parents are good about getting the help their child needs. If parents do not have the wisdom or fortitude to provide the remediation, they must get their child the help.

School help is not the only support a child may need. Some kids are in need of medical attention. There are some conditions that are completely curable today even more so than when I was in school. Genu varum and genu valgum, which are bowleg and knock-knee, respectively. Strabismus, which is the condition known as cross-eye, can all be addressed if treated early. Some kids enter into adolescence with these issues because they did not get the care needed to address the problems early on. The condition are not a few of the conditions that result in kids being targets for ridicule. Physical ailments are not the only issues that should be addressed early. As indicated previously, there are kids who are suffering from emotional disturbances that go unaddressed. If a child has a sudden behavior change or the parents begin to see erratic behavior, the child should be taken to a medical doctor to rule out any organicity. Once it is determined that there is nothing physically wrong that is impacting the child's behavior, a referral to a mental health specialist can be made.

Get the Help **You** Need

I eluded to this issue preciously. Raising kids is a challenging job, to put it mildly. Parents must be on all the time and during that time engaged in multiple tasks. I often tell young parents that they will never rest the way they did prior to having kids because parenting is a twenty-four-hour job. Whether you are a worrier, part-caretaker, or just appropriately invested in your child's happiness, you can never turn off. Even parents who write their kids off never have the same peace because there is energy put into remaining estranged. The courageous part of this conversation is that many parents enter parenthood already overwhelmed by physical or emotional problems. Mental or physical illnesses do not go away after having children. In most cases, existing illnesses are exacerbated by the increase in hormones and overall stress on the body from having a child. My appeal to parents who already have preexisting conditions is to get the help that you need, if for no other reason than it will free up emotional and physical energy to effectively parent your children.

Lessons from the Field

While working for the probation department, I worked with a parent who was raising two children: a teenage boy and girl. The girl had been arrested for a minor offense and then cited and released to her mother's custody. When they came into my office, the girl purposely moved to avoid sitting next to her mother. The mother immediately exclaimed, "Did you see what she did?!" I had noticed that the girl moved as soon as her mother sat next to her, but that was not the first time I had witnessed that exchange between a parent and a teen, so I just took a mental note. The mother went on to say, "That little [expletive] hates me after all that I have done." The mother told how she has put off her career to care for her kids and how she cooks for them daily, and cleans and washes all their [expletive] laundry. Every time the girl would try to speak, the mother would tell her to shut the [expletive] up. Finally, the mother got up, looked at me, and as she started approaching her daughter, she said, "I guess you are going to have to arrest me today because I am going to beat her [expletive]." To be honest, my initial thought was that I was obviously going home late because this case that looked minor on the surface was obviously more serious. I directed the mother to return to her seat and sit down, and asked the young lady to wait in the lobby. I returned to the office, prepared to have a very courageous conversation with the mother, but as soon as I arrived back to my office, I found the mother crying inconsolably. Through tears, she said that she had tried her best to protect her children so they have a better life than she had. She disclosed that her mother had made her engage in prostitution in order to pay for her mother's drug habit. She felt that her children, although they didn't know about their mother's childhood, should appreciate her more. The mother of my client was obviously suffering from childhood trauma. I encouraged her to seek counseling. Unfortunately, the daughter had to be removed temporarily until the parent could get the help that she needed and the safety of the daughter could be assured. Because of mandatory reporting laws and the paperwork involved with filing a child protective services report, I didn't get home until very late. This case demonstrated that, hurt people will hurt people, even their children.

Kids Want Your Presence, Not Your Presents

Some of the fondest memories I have is just lying around with my mother and grandparents doing absolutely nothing. I would just sit back and take in all of their "stuff." I watched their mannerisms, listened to their complaints, joys, fears, expectations, etc. When I was around my grown-up relatives, I would look as though I was watching a tennis match with my head volleying back and forth. My time with the adults in my life served as the epitome of "he said, she said." But when I was growing up, many parents subscribed to the adage, "Kids can be seen but not heard." Therefore, we could remain in the room only if we kept quiet. We were not permitted to comment on the conversation, grimace, or even laugh. During those quiet present moments, culture, values, and morals were passed down. We learned how to handle things, but most importantly, we learned that we were part of a community. Our family was our tribe and home base to which we could return when the world was rough. When I became an adult with my own family, I still would go to my grandmother's home in the middle of the day. There, I would find my retired mother, grandparents, and sometimes at least one of my siblings. We would just go there to have lunch or maybe just to check in. I enjoyed spending time with them. Some parents do all they can not to spend time with their kids. Social media, even multiple televisions with a gazillion channels, in every room is taking the place of family time. Some families live in large homes with family rooms, dayrooms, each child has their own room, and maybe even a game room. One family could be in the house and never see each other for a week. Families are the incubators where children grow and thrive. However, parents must spend time with the children, especially during critical stages of development.

Lessons from the Field

It is Christmas evening or the night of a kid's most anticipated birthday. You spent a lot of time and money making sure that the event was memorable. You even managed to get the most expensive, requested gift. It set you back for a couple of months, but you were not worried about overindulging your child in that moment. Earlier that morning, upon opening the gift, the child screams because she is happy that she received what was requested. They understood that it was a big request, but because they are egocentric, they also didn't care and hoped you would come through as usual. You scream because you are happy to see your beautiful child happy and also because you recall how much you spent, but it's okay, they are happy and you are happy. Fast-forward to 6:30 pm. You are tired and feeling satisfied, so you want some alone time to read a book entitled Keeping Kids In the Home and Out of the System. *It's a good book, so you get in your favorite spot and begin to read. Here comes that happy child that you spent all that money on and he wants to talk. He's sitting close to you so you can't move your arm to reposition the book. He is not even talking about the toy you bought. He wants to know what you are reading, why you have to wear glasses, how long you have worn glasses, what is that scar on your left knee, how did you get it, what are you drinking that smells like rubbing alcohol, and why is your hair turning white. "Oh my gosh," you exclaim, "where is that expensive gift I just gave you? How come you are not playing with it?" He responds, "I already did . . . I'll just hang out with you." Kids sometimes want your presence, not your presents.*

Kids Are Different Because You Are Different

Many of my parents are surprised that their children are so different. In most cases, when parents are complaining about the diversity in their family, it is after an older child has done well and has been productive, and then comes a child that is more challenging. When parents ask why their children are so different, I respond with "It is because you are probably different." Parent dynamics change over time.

Life situations change from one period to the next. Children are born into different seasons of life. Your life circumstance when you parent your first child may be drastically different when raising your fourth child and even your second child. Circumstances change quickly. For some parents, there is a full generation between their children.

Parents and families go through different seasons. And just like the weather seasons, some periods are characterized by storms and others are sunny and bright. Some kids may be born when the family has many resources, and by the time the subsequent child is born, the family's financial situation could be totally different. Some children are born when the parents' relationship is intact. However, by the time the next child is born, the relationship could have dissolved. Scientists say that some people divide life into pre- and post-. In other words, their lives may change drastically prior to a certain event or after an event has occurred. The pre- and post- lifestyle could not be more prevalent than when a death occurs. Some people live a different life once they lose a loved one. Sometimes, it is merely a wake-up call to their own mortality, which results in a lifestyle change. Sometimes, after a major event, depression sets in and changes the person's life. Still, other times a loss of a loved one puts the person in a different role, which forces the change. The oldest sibling may have to care for an aging parent.

Lessons from the Field

In my family, the pre- and post- was with the death of my maternal grandmother, who for several years was the matriarch of the family. My grandmother's home was the meeting ground for all of the family. Overall, my grandmother was such a validating person, and she was able to develop an independent, unconditional love and relationship with each of us. After my grandmother passed away, there were fewer family gatherings. My grandmother's sudden passing left a void in all of our lives, some larger than others. As a result, people changed. In my life, my grandmother was the caretaker to my oldest two children until they were of school-age. By the time I had my third child, my grandmother had passed away. Since I worked full time, and by that time, I was a manager on my job, my third child spent time in day care with strangers. Although I researched and found what I thought was a loving day care provider, the program could not match the unconditional loving home my two elder children spent time in while away from me and their dad. In addition, I was a different person. My grandmother passed away while I was pregnant with my third child. By the time my child was born, I was still grieving the loss of my beloved grandmother. Normal grief can last a few years. In my case, I mourned the death of my grandmother for about five years. Therefore, in addition to my third child going to a day care provider, she would not receive the unconditional love from my grandmother that my first two received, and she was being raised by a mother who was, at least in part, distracted by mourning the loss of a loved one. Therefore, my third child had a different experience than my first two. I have had to apologize to my third child. I acknowledged that I was different, I take full responsibility for being less than attentive, and I apologize. I could write another book on how different my youngest child's life differed from her three siblings. Not only was her dad and I older, but also my fourth child was born over two months early and required special care. Because of her fragile beginnings, her life was and is different.

There have been studies on the impact of birth order and some findings that suggest that a child's personality is determined by when a child she is born into the family; in other words, eldest children have distinct personality types as well as middle children and youngest children. However, some studies have shown that birth order is meaningless. In addition to birth order, I believe that it is the birth season in the family life cycle that has a big impact on the personality development of the child.

Take Off Your Party Shoes and Put on Tennis Shoes

Although most expectant parents understand that having children results in lifestyle changes, some parents don't understand the need to fully refocus their energy, attention, and priorities until after the child is born, at which time, some parents meet this reality with frustration and even disdain. Learning what to expect when raising children will help prepare parents for what is to come. However, parents must be motivated and committed to become good parents. At the very least, parents must make a conscientious decision to refocus their attention and energy to the needs of the child first and secondarily on themselves. The realignment of priorities is sometimes a challenge for new (and seasoned) parents. Some parents have children and carry on like status quo. When you have a child, it is no longer life as usual; lifestyles must change. Just like the body of a pregnant woman changes, the parents must change cognitively and socially. Some parents fail to make the shift from single-minded to responsible-minded. Parents can no longer spend an inordinate amount of money on their wardrobes because, now that they have a child, parents must allocate funds to clothe and feed the child. Sometimes, the parents may have to put off buying their annual pair of high-profile athlete's tennis shoes and buy walking shoes for the baby. Parents may have to miss the annual trip to the mountains to ski because the conditions may not be conducive to having a nursing infant. Instead of buying a two-seater sports car, it may be time for a minivan. Even when not buying a sports car, parents may not be able to afford expensive cars because they are now faced with high and rising day care costs and must put away money for college that is right around the corner.

Lessons from the Field

When I served as the superintendent of a camp detention facility, I would often spend time watching parents interact with their detained children. Some parents came to the visiting hour on their way out to the club. These parents would be dressed very expensively, and some of them were dressed in clothes that were not usually worn by parents. There were also times when the parents would have their son's or daughter's clothes on, but that is another story. Some of the parents would not act very maternal or paternal; they related to the child more like friends. I am not suggesting that parents must never have fun; I am suggesting that when parents interact with their children, they should relate to the child as a role model, teacher, or consultant. When not engaging with their children, they can take on whatever persona they desire.

If You Love Me, Let Me Go

Recall that one of the premises of this book is that children come through you, not to you. We must raise our kids in such a way that they are not only prepared, but want to leave us when they become an adult. We must proactively begin with that end in mind on the day of their birth, so that we fashion our parenting strategies in such a way that the child will be emotionally, intellectually, mentally, and financially prepared to leave home when they reach the age of majority. My father-in-love (law) was born in 1922 in Alabama. He had a sixth grade education. However, he was a gifted carpenter. He could develop plans and ultimately build beautiful buildings, but he could not spell well enough to write a contract. In spite of his limited education, my father-in-love had a vast amount of wisdom that came from sheer curiosity. My father-in-law had a hunger for knowledge; therefore, he would strike up a conversation with anyone. His favorite television channel was the *Animal Planet* because he believed you could learn a lot by watching animals in their habitats, where they are untrained or scathed by man. One day, we were sitting around, and he, in his own Southern manner of speaking, started a conversation about raising my children. I was a little hesitant to take advice from someone who obviously had not read the literature or any book on parenting, but I loved him and really enjoyed listening to him talk about anything. My father-in-love told me to always support my children but teach them to be independent. He then started talking to me about birds. He told me that when birds get to a certain age, the mother bird will push them out of the nest so they will fly. He said that parents should copy the behavior modeled by birds. He went on to say that there is a time when kids need to grow up and "get their own nests." My father-in-love said that if you don't encourage your kids to fly, they will never leave the nest. Well, of course, I was a college graduate at the time and I only trusted real research, not folklore. So just for the fun of it, I researched it and found that my father-in-love was absolutely right! Birds do push their young out the nest when they know they are ready to fly. If birds have enough sense and trust to encourage their kids to leave the nest, I think humans should follow suit.

Although birds don't actually engage in forward thinking, the ultimate goal of all parents should be to raise their kids in such a way that they eventually leave home with the knowledge, skills, and abilities to live independent of their parents. Accordingly, new parents should immediately adopt the view that their children come through them not to parents. It is never too late to make the cognitive shift and adopt this appropriate parental stance. Society does not intend for children stay with their parents forever. Children must forge their own lives in order to make their individual contribution to the world. Parents must understand their role in their child's life as one of making sure their children make their mark on the world. More importantly, children are not responsible for fulfilling their parents' deferred dreams. Parents don't get a second chance by living vicariously through their children's lives. When children are born, it is the beginning of a new path for the child. On that path, there are critical periods in which parents must engage with their children in such a way that it does not inhibit them from developing the skills necessary to become independent adults. Not inhibiting children from progressing is not only physical; parenting without borders also means ensuring the child is in a nurturing environment free from constant chaos and especially violence. Reflecting back on our earlier discussion on parenting requiring self-discipline, it is apparent that parents may have to regulate themselves. In a given situation, parents may have to refrain from arguing, control the urges, or refrain from undesirable behavior. Parents may have to parent themselves first.

Lessons from the Field

The best example of parents who refuse to let their children grow and go are those who refuse to allow them to go off to college. Some parents claim they can't afford it; however, some parents just are not ready to let go. I have met parents who follow their children to college. They relocate along with the child. You will never see a bird push their child out the nest and then jump down and catch them with the nest. You will also never see a bird push their little bird out the nest and then proceed to follow them for the rest of their lives.

Jump in Where You Fit in

Infancy, childhood, and adolescence are very distinctive life stages and require a different parenting strategy. Although each stage is interconnected and builds upon the next, there is autonomy during each stage, which requires that parents engage with their child based on his current developmental stage. It is important that parents not only have a basic knowledge of childhood development, but they should be able to focus on the current development phase, being mindful of the milestones that were met in the preceding stage while anticipating the succeeding stage. Talk about multitasking! Perhaps an example would be useful. When children are entering adolescence, the body does not always wait for the brain to catch up. Therefore, you may be looking at a very big baby. During adolescence, kids will automatically begin to pull away from the parents. As a matter of fact, some kids and parents will find it a bit uncomfortable for a child who is larger than the parent to sleep in the same bed. However, some kids continue to want to experience the closeness and intimacy that comes with cuddling in the same bed. If children are not emotionally prepared to push away but it may be physically necessary, because a queen-sized bed will not accommodate three people weighing in excess of five hundred pounds, parents may have to make a pallet on the floor to allow for the extra cuddle time. Understanding that kids may not have received "good-enough parenting" and nurturing during childhood is important to acknowledge, especially for parents who, for one reason or another, was not fully available to the child. Some parents missed childhood milestones because they were busy climbing the career ladder; some parents were physically, mentally, or emotionally ill; and some parents have been in custody or absent due to substance abuse. Therefore, they may have to revisit the previous developmental stage and wait for that big-bodied baby to catch up emotionally. Returning to previous stages of development may not be necessary in all cases, but parents must be mindful.

Recognizing that some kids didn't get good-enough parenting is very important for secondary caretakers, such as foster parents and adoptive parents, and people who work with adolescents, such as juvenile probation officers and social workers. They come into a child's life at various stages; therefore, the caretaker may have to jump in where they fit in. Very often, new caretakers to older children expect the chronological age to match the emotional age. This is rarely the case, especially for system-involved kids. Because of the likely trauma that has occurred in the family of origin, foster care and probation-involved youth are highly likely suffering from delayed development in one or more areas. Having to revisit a previous stage of development with your child is not always because of the parents' absence or even lack of exposure to certain skills. Sometimes, kids just don't get it. Sometimes, we take for granted that kids know how to do certain tasks before we find out that they cannot do the task. I learned the hard way that my adolescent daughter could not clean the kitchen. She would take the liquid soap, add a dab to each dish, then turn the water on, and rinse it. Once she finished all the dishes and wasted gallons of water and dishwashing soap, she would ball up the dish towel and proceed to some other activity, likely social media. She likely felt that she had earned a break since she had "cleaned the kitchen." By now, you know that there are many things missing from this picture. She didn't wipe the countertops, stove, dry the dishes, sweep the floor, and take out the garbage. When I would say, "How come you didn't clean the kitchen," she would say, "I did, I washed the dishes." Needless to say, I had to demonstrate what I mean when I say clean the kitchen. I allowed her to watch me model what I expected from her.

Lessons from the Field

Many system-involved youth have at some point stopped developing to focus on their current hierarchy of needs, which may have been to survive. A kid who has stopped developing at some point may not have learned the value of saying thank you and please. They may not fold their laundry. When I worked as a superintendent of a juvenile facility, it was common for the adolescent boys to hoard food to assure rations for the next day, in spite of the consistent daily availability of food. Many of the young men would arrive at the facility and resisted to taking off their shoes to sleep. They felt like they had to be "flight-ready." Caretakers of these kids could not understand the probation youths' need to stay prepared to flee. Very often, foster parents and probation workers would lament, "I am not picking up behind . . . babying . . . coddling this big @#$ young man or woman . . . I didn't do that for my own kids, so I am certainly not doing it for these kids!" I would have to remind them that they didn't have to do it for their own kids because they raised their kids "good enough." We cannot take for granted that system-involved kids learned to address their hygiene, how to speak, how to go to the bathroom, how not to steal, how to chew with their mouths closed, how to cut their fingernails, how to dress, how to not sexualize every relationship, etc.

Caretakers of children who are suffering from delayed development may have to go back and address the preceding stage prior to focusing on the skills of the current developmental phase while at the same time understanding what stage is next and begin preparing. If the child is not ready for adolescent responsibilities because they missed the preceding stage, parents must still prepare the child. In other words, while the parent is cuddling with the big baby, the child must still understand responsibilities such as chores. Adolescents must still develop abstract reasoning in preparation for the next big developmental milestone: separation/emancipation. Parents cannot continue to cuddle, literally and figuratively, apologizing for being absent; parents must acknowledge their absence, apologize, and move forward. I think that is worthy of repeating: if a parent has been absent, they must acknowledge, apologize, and move forward.

Lessons from the Field

With each of my children, I would learn that they had missed some developmental milestone. In most cases, it was around school. Most recently, I learned that my two younger children did not have a clue about how to calculate fractions. My youngest daughter had earned money for babysitting the neighbor's cats. Of course, she couldn't wait to spend some of her earnings, so within a couple of weeks, we headed to the mall. She had selected something to purchase and wanted to make sure she had enough money to cover the cost. I said to make sure to add 8 percent sales tax. She said, "How much is that?" Irrespective of how that deficit in knowledge would impact their ability to compete in school, I was concerned about not understanding fractions of numbers would impact their life skills ability. In spite of the fact that my youngest daughter was fourteen years old, I had to teach her how to calculate fractions and percentages, so at the very least, she would be able to calculate discounts and taxes. It did not matter that she was beyond the age when this skill should be mastered in school. I couldn't spend time wondering what happened and why my child missed the lesson. I had to jump in where she was and get her caught up. I was using websites for elementary school kids. After a few review sessions, my daughter fully understood fractions, and now she was prepared to go into a store and budget how much she will spend, including discounts and taxes. What good would it have been for me to say, "What, you don't know fractions!" I responded the same way I did when I found out one of my kids were running a fever. I would say, "Uh-oh, I need to get fluids in you and get ready to offer medication if needed." When I learned that my daughter could not calculate discounts, I said, "Uh-oh, I need to get you ready for financial independence!"

Frequent Check-ins

As a probation officer, we were responsible for assuring that probationers followed the terms and conditions of their probation. Probationers were under the supervision of the court, and probation officers carried out the authority of the court by making sure that offenders were compliant. The most important goal of probation and parole is to prevent recidivism; in other words, probation officers were charged with assuring that offenders did not re-offend. Probation and Parole Officers used the strategy of checking in to monitor and minimize reactionism. Check-ins are also important for children. Parents should routinely check in on their children to make sure they are doing okay. Check-ins look different during different childhood stages. For an infant, parents are assuring that their babies are thriving by reaching their developmental milestones. Infants who are not looking around or responding to their parents' voices may be a signal that something is wrong. Parents of school-age children are assuring that their children are developing academically. Parents should make sure that their children are working on grade level. At the very least, parents should be in contact with their child's teachers. For adolescents, it is very important that parents don't completely "back off" even if their child is demanding autonomy. Adolescence is a very challenging time. Although teens don't require the same kind of attention, they continue to need parents to be close enough for consultation. Parents of adolescent children should regularly check in by asking their young adult how things are going. I regularly ask my fourteen-year-old how she is doing. While riding in the car, I will ask, "How is your life today?" I may even ask if she is okay or needs anything. Every day, I give her a complete look over. I look at her clothes, hair, and demeanor. It is important to note just in case there is a sudden change. Very often, adolescents suffer in silence. It is easy to miss, even if you are vigilant. Recently, one of my daughters told me that she often went to bed wishing that she did not wake up! At that moment, and unbeknownst to her, my heart stopped beating. We were just lying around talking about life as we often do, and she told me that she believed she had been depressed during her childhood. She said it was her faith in God that prevented her from wanting to take her own life. One thing I do recall is that my daughter often expressed envy about our retired neighbor's lifestyle. When my daughter was in middle school, the school bus would pass by our neighbor's home, and they were often outside gardening early in the morning. My daughter told me that she wished she was already retired. I said, "You haven't even begun your work life." However, my daughter would go on to comment on her desire to be at the end of her life a few more times. I did not recognize it as a sign of depression because her comments were not accompanied by the normal signs of depression, like sadness or irritability. But most importantly, I assumed she was happy because she had all that she needed and most of what she wanted. She had friends, a nice home, good food, we went on vacations, she lived with both parents, she was very bright, and she received a lot of school accolades because of her academic giftedness. How could she be depressed? The answer to that questions is "Because she could be." Depression can be caused by biological, chemical, or social causes. Some signs that your child could be troubled are: extreme mood swings. If you have parented a teen, you are probably thinking that moodiness is a common characteristic of adolescence. However, I am not just talking about grumpiness, shortness in responses, or the occasional, "I don't want to be bothered." I am talking about abrupt changes. When in doubt, consult with a mental health professional.

Lessons from the Field

A friend of mine was raising two sons. She did not see obvious signs of depression, and although he appeared happy, he was a quiet kid. One day, my friend went to run a few errands. She said, something told her to return home before the final errand. She returned home to find her son hanging in her home. If she had completed the final errand, her son would have died. She was able to get him down and call for emergency medical support in time to prevent her son from expiring. In retrospect, the parents saw some signs of depression; however, neither thought that their son was suicidal. These were engaged and loving parents. The point is, parents must act on their suspicions when they believe that there is a sudden change in their child's behavior. Checking in often will aid in seeing sudden changes.

To whip or not to whip (whoop, spank, knock out)

For decades there has been ongoing debate on the merits of corporal punishment. Corporal punishment is physical chastisement in an effort to inflict discomfort at the very least and extreme pain at the other extreme. I never judge parents because as you know, parents do the best they can at any given time with the resources they have. Very often, in the moment, the only resources the parent has available is enough to just slap the child in the head or back. When parents ask me what I think about corporal punishment, I always ask, "what are you hoping to accomplish." Most parents will agree that in that moment that they use corporal punishment, they don't have time or inclination to give a lecture nor are they in a position to "time out." For some parents reading this, they are saying, yes, finally someone gets me. But in response to that lack of time response, I reflect back to the parent that the reason for the corporal punishment is to give a quick solution to what may be a short term problem or even a symptom of a long-range problem.

Since parents never know if they are dealing with a single episodic incident or a manifestation of behavior that may need attention, I suggest that parents always err on the side of caution. And since parents must remain in either the role model, teaching, or consulting role anyway, my response to whether to use corporal punishment is that parents consider if to do so fits in either of their three primary roles. Before you make up your mind whether to spank or not, let me give you just a little bit more knowledge to inform your decision. What happens to a person emotionally when they experience physical pain? I am so glad you asked. Two decades of robust research revealed a correlation between physical punishment and child aggression towards peers, siblings, and parents, juvenile delinquency, and spousal abuse later in life. The research also demonstrated that physical punishment elicits, almost reflexively, physical aggression and conversely, the reduction in physical punishment reduces aggression in children. The research studies also showed that physical punishment has been linked to mental health issues later in life such as anxiety, depression, drug abuse, and overall maladjustment (okay, now I understand what happened to me). In addition to physical and emotional problems associated with physical punishment, the research has also associated corporal punishment with delays in cognitive development and academic achievement.

Although these studies' findings were consistent with the research on adverse childhood experiences (ACE) discussed previously, I had to take a closer look at the research. By examining the research more closely, I found that there were in fact conflicting findings and some research revealed only moderate to minimal adverse effects from physical punishment. However, most importantly, I could not find one study that showed a positive correlation between physical punishment and good behavior or emotional outcomes later in life. I also learned that most instances of substantiated child abuse occurred during episodes of physical punishment; and infants who were spanked were more than two times more likely to suffer an injury requiring medical attention than children not spanked. This made perfect sense to me. Even in my own experience, in most cases where physical punishment was inflicted, the giver was frustrated or angry and the acting out behavior, which was sometimes age appropriate, exasperated the frustration or anger. The spanking allowed the parent to transfer their negative emotional state onto the child in the moment. So the child really just got what was coming to someone else such as a boss who had been micromanaging, a rude salesclerk, a spouse who had upset the parent, the bank teller that could not automatically fix the fees associated with identity theft, the mail carrier who did deliver the check in time to go to the bank, that person on the road that flipped the parent off for no apparent reason moments before. In any event, the research is clear, there is no evidence that corporal punishment leads to positive outcomes later in life but there is convincing evidence to support that spanking, hitting, or whipping kids could cause social, physical, emotional, and academic problems later in life.

I would like to offer a disclaimer for those of us who have applied corporal punishment in due diligence. The research on the negative correlation between corporal punishment and negative outcomes has only been around for two decades, and this information may not have surfaced in some parents' social circles. I know the research wasn't around during my childhood in my social circles, because my friends and I routinely shared similar stories of threats of and actual physical punishment. However, when I think about my childhood and punishment, what was different was the fact that spankings were not random but in most cases scheduled. When I was raised, kids knew exactly what would result in corporal punishment. Very often your parent would warn you that "if you do that again, I am going to whip or spank you." Sometimes when other kids would misbehave other parents would warn that "you better not do that or you will definitely experience physical pain." Pre-warning kids about what would result from certain behavior was a good strategy because it allowed the child to make a choice. Sometimes, our parents would let us know eight to ten hours in advance that corporal punishment was coming.

"When I get home, you are going to get it." Every kid understood what "get it meant." I think having to wait for the eventual doom was more painful than the actual physical pain. For those parents who are bothered by the research findings, it is never too late to change your strategy because you only did the best you could with the resources you had in the moment and now you have more resources.

Lessons from the field

As a probation officer, I was a mandatory reporter of suspected incidents of child abuse. During my career, I executed my responsibility and filed relatively few reports. Needless to say, the number of suspected child abuse reports that probation officers filed did not come close to the actual incidents. It is public knowledge that probation officers are mandatory reporters; therefore, parents and clients are not likely to disclose information that could result in more contact with "the system." Although probation staff are very well trained on how to prepare the reports for suspected child abuse, there is limited training on how to recognize subtle signs of abuse and what questions to ask to solicit the information respectfully and safely. Another reason that some mandatory reporters fail to file a report is because of the knowledge that removing the child from the home could create bigger issues. Most mandated reporters understand that remaining in the home is the best option for children; however, in instances of abuse, there is an immediate need for resources to educate and support parents who may not feel that they have any other options except for physical punishment. Mandated reporters need to have available resources on speed dial so that when instances of abuse arise, mandated reporters will not hesitate to file the report and transfer the parent to an appropriate agency for support.

Parenting: The Choice to Give Up Your Last Shrimp

Parenting is a character builder. If you don't want to grow in this area, you should avoid having children. Parenting will effectively turn you into a philanthropist. When you have a child, you are no longer solely concerned with your welfare. In true meaning of philanthropy, parents are required to generously seek to promote the welfare of others, specifically their dependent children. This could be challenging for some parents who never learned to share, or parents who, for any number of reasons, are still focused on self. There is a popular poster that reads: Everything I needed to know, I learned in kindergarten. The poster displays many of the skills that are essential for not only getting along in the classroom, but also getting along in the larger society. In addition, in social skills such as taking turns and saying thank you and excuse me, one that is magnified is sharing. Perhaps, as early as kindergarten, teachers are preparing their young students parenting skills. When kids are older, it is hoped that they will transfer those kindergarten skills into the workplace and share supplies, space, and resources. As a probation officer, we even had to share official vehicles. This was a challenge because I learned very early in my career that everyone does not adhere to the same values of cleanliness.

None of my sharing experience prepared me for the type of sharing that parenting requires. Not only was I required to share my living space, I also shared my food, clothes, toiletries, and finally my emotions because very often, my children would take my last and final nerve. I guess I would acquire another nerve because my kids would take that one too. I must confess that the sharing of my food was a big adjustment to me. I didn't mind buying enough food for the family; it was taking my food off of my plate that was challenging, especially if it were my last shrimp. I love to eat seafood, in general, but shrimp are my favorite. Sometimes, when I have a shrimp meal with side dishes, I always eat everything and save one shrimp, usually the biggest one for last. Well, because I have been an effective role model, three of my children like shrimp as much as I do. One time, I had eaten all on my plate except that last juicy shrimp. My youngest daughter looked over at my plate and said, "Can I have that?" I didn't need to ask her what "that" was because she was pointing at the lone shrimp on my plate. Although I tried to hide my disappointment, I managed to hand it over. She was young and egocentric, so she didn't care how I felt. It is not until they get older that they understand how selfish it is to take the last bit of food off of anyone's plate. For a few years, I was able to eat all of my food. However, a few years ago, I was blessed with a grandchild. I have a three-year-old granddaughter who, no matter how much she has to eat, will automatically look at your plate and say, "What is that?" Giving up my last shrimp does not bother me anymore because, after raising four kids of my own, I have metamorphosed into a self-proclaimed and proud philanthropist.

Call Me by My First Name

I will conclude the courageous conversations section by letting you know that there will come a time when your kids will see you just for

240

who you are. You will no longer be Mommy and Daddy, Jane's dad, Candy's mother, or Malachi's parents. There is a point when kids grow up and begin to think abstractly. It is at that time that they see you for who you are. For some of you, this section has been a challenge. There were some things written that stung a bit. It's okay because just like getting stung by a bee, you pull out the stinger and you learn to avoid bees in the future. As a parent of four children, I get the discomfort that sometimes comes with enlightenment. Sometimes, you feel validated and other times, there is some embarrassment or even shame for the way you responded without knowledge. I am able to sympathize and empathize with you. I can honestly say that I had no idea what to expect from being a parent. Although I had been around many parents, including my older siblings, it was not until I had my own children that I understood the challenges that lay ahead. Prior to taking on the role of mom or dad, people are just fallible individuals. They have a first, sometimes a middle, and last name. People have a personality that includes strengths and weaknesses. New parents are a totality of their past experiences, as will be the case for the child. Once the baby arrives, people become the mother of baby X or the father of baby Y. Too often, parents fail to make the transition. There is an emotional shift that must take place when one becomes a parent. You cannot stay the same. Your perspective and focus on life must change. You are now the parent of a child. My mother never allowed her children to call her by her first name. We could not even playfully call her by her first name because she felt that to do so was extremely disrespectful. My mother felt she had earned the title of mother and insisted we use it. Since my father was absent, she would sometimes joke that she was our mother and our father. So I guess I could have gotten away with calling her Dad. As I grew older and began to understand that my mother was not just Mom, she was a woman going through her own stages of life. Many of those stages were very challenging, and sometimes her behavior didn't rise to the level of "Mommy." I don't think my mother wanted us to see her, the woman, because then she may not have maintained the respect she desperately needed, especially as a single parent.

However, *it is inevitable that, at some point, children will begin to see the real person in their parents.* Children soon learn that their parents are not super heroes, but instead they are mere mortals with flaws and weaknesses, some of which led to some big personal and parenting mistakes. Parents who plan to have a relationship with their children with respect at the foundation, must understand the need to change and conscientiously discipline themselves in such a way that they are consistently in the parent mode.

When some people learn that they will soon be *promoted* (emphasis mine) to Mom or Dad, they will become more responsible, vigilant, careful, and selfless. These are the good and necessary traits for parents to possess in order to gain the respect of their children. Unfortunately, parents don't always change for the better, and the ability to gain respect is compromised. For some people, raising children will turn them into an alien who is characterized as always yelling, frowning, pleading, and crying. I have met parents who are depressed, pessimistic, and some come across as overall negative. Some parents literally turn into a monster, at least in their children's eyes. Parents who turn into monsters lose themselves during the parenting process. Some parents believe they have to be hard and at the other extreme, some parents feel that they have to be their child's friend. Taking either of these positions to the extreme will also compromise the parent-child relationship. There are times when parents need to be authoritative, and there are other times when the situation calls for the parents to be friendly; however, parents must always remain in the parent mode. To gain a child's respect, parents must take their role very seriously. Parents have the sole responsibility to provide an environment in which their child can grow physically, emotionally, and intellectually. Parents are in charge of guiding their children on a sometimes turbulent path that, if navigated correctly, will lead the child to becoming productive, self-sufficient, and a law-abiding citizen. What that looks like is modeling and teaching proactivity as they plan for their parenting journey. Just like the planning of any road trip, parents must make sure they have all the resources they need. Parents must start with the end in mind. If parents want their kids to avoid the criminal justice system, the parents must work to raise their kids to be productive abstract reasoners who make good choices. Parents should keep a mental picture of their children as independent adults. Parents must unselfishly and unapologetically make sure that their kids have what they need to thrive and avoid traumatic experiences. Parents must model putting first things first by making their child their number one priority and sometimes at the expense of the parent comfort. Parents should avoid an adversarial relationship with their kids and focus on opportunities for a win-win experience. That may mean relinquishing some of the parental power in the moment to reach consensus. Other times, and more often than not, parents will ignore a lot of behavior as long as the overall desired behavior is being performed. I recall working in the juvenile hall. We were trained not to escalate situations, and as long as the detainee was complying, ignore their demeanor. A good example of this was when detainees were directed to go to their rooms as a time-out for misbehavior. Most often, the detainee would be very upset and would verbalize their displeasure as they moved toward their room. Some staff would engage the detainee and argue with them all the way to the door, irrespective of our training to ignore the attitude and verbal assaults if the detainee was complying.

By understanding the three broad phases of development, parents will be able to empathize with their kids by understanding the world through the child's perspective. Having this level of understanding will permit the parents to understand their children instead of always wanting to be understood or win every argument. Parents must work diligently with their kids so that they learn how to adapt to society. There are over seven billion people in the world. Your child is just one of them. Life will not appear fair; children will not always come first. Once they leave the confines of the family incubator, they will join billions of people who want to have it their way. Parents must teach their kids to get along with many people of all shapes, sizes, colors, religions, beliefs, and behaviors. In that way, kids have the freedom to choose their friends and intimate relationships. Finally, parents have a finite period of time to expose their kids to what may turn out to be their gifts. Like Michelangelo, it is not clear to parents at birth what lies beneath the surface of a child. It is the parents' job to expose the child to as much as possible to allow the child to manifest with all of their gifts and glory.

Summary

No Matter What Happens, Remain on the Parent Path

If you have arrived at the end of this book, congratulations. You have demonstrated two of the most important skills of people who do not end up in the criminal justice system. You modeled putting first things first, understanding your responsibility as a parent, and proactivity as you are gathering data for your parenting plan. You are wiser and better prepared to address the challenges and joys that come along with parenting. For some of you this was new information, and for others the book reinforced what you already knew. In either event, you understand that parenting a child is a journey that you begin the moment the child is born. Although at the beginning of that journey, the road seems very long. If you ask any parent of an adult, they will likely advise that the time moves very fast and there is no time to waste. On the parenting journey, parents will find that there are distinct child developmental stages that the parents must navigate using age-appropriate strategies. The parent-child relationship is the catalyst for imparting the life skills and habits of productive adults in their children. The most important parenting strategies are positive role modeling, active and consistent teaching, and ultimately, stepping back and becoming a consultant who, when invited, are prepared to provide honest and sometimes courageous advice. Children do what the people they love do, not what they say, so parents must be the person they want their children to become. It is not sufficient that parents plan to raise kids that avoid the criminal justice system; parents must have a very specific road map that provides positive directions that steer far away from the criminal justice system. The road map includes being proactive, prioritizing, demonstrating adaptation, delayed gratification, or being comfortable with not providing any gratification at all. In other words, just say no. Most importantly, parents must remain on the parent path until the end. Keep chipping away at the clay like Michelangelo.

Departure from the parental role is a common mistake. Some parents take a break from parenting. I am not referring to respite, in which case you take physical and proximate breaks from the kids. Those periodic and short time-outs are important for the mental and emotional stability of the parents and the child. The leave-taking that I am referring to is more akin to a detour from their parental role. I am talking about parents who actually decide that they don't want to parent for a time period. For example, some parents get so involved in their careers that they are not available for their children. Instead of attending back to school-night activities, some parents are at work. Instead of engaging with children after work, some parents bring work home. Instead of family vacations, parents refuse to take time off of the job for fear of losing seniority or promotional opportunities. Some parents may also take a break from parenting to pursue their personal interests. Instead of being at home baking cookies for their child's classroom party, the parent may be out on a date.

Some parents may not actually take a physical break from the parenting role, but although they are there, they fail to actually journey with their children. A parent who is not on the journey with their child is easily frustrated at their child's current situation. They are frustrated at the infant's constant crying and can't wait until she can toddle and at least verbalize what is wrong. The parent of the toddler is frustrated because the child embarrasses him because he does not share and the child is stubborn, saying no to everything. The parent of the young school-age child is tired of helping with homework and becomes very frustrated when she has to help her child with the "new math," especially since the parent "didn't learn that way." The parent of the adolescent is tired of the mood swings and just wants the teenager to settle down and stop acting erratic. For some parents, the most exciting milestone is when their children no longer require constant supervision. Parents want to be able to leave their children at home for long periods of time. Parents want their children to have autonomy so that the parents can be autonomous. Some parents even think that when their children reach adolescence, they can ease up on the rings and be less involved. This is a huge mistake. Children are not old enough for autonomy until they are capable of thinking abstractly.

Allow me to encourage you. It took Michelangelo two years to complete the famous statue of David. Michelangelo worked tirelessly, day and night, until he completed the statue. Parents will invest considerably more time on their works of art (their children) than Michelangelo did on the stature, but I am suggesting that prospective parents change the way they view raising a child and liken the parenting process to creating something beautiful of which to be proud of. It doesn't matter if having your child was the result of years of planning, prayer, hope, or "oops, how did that happen?" It is imperative that parents make a conscious decision to raise their child with unconditional love. When Michelangelo was commissioned to sculpt David, other artists had declined to do the work because of the many imperfections in the marble. You will find that at times, you may not want to work with your child because of what you believe are too many imperfections. It is during that time when the promise of unconditional love must come forth. Focusing on the end product will remind you that something beautiful will soon manifest, just like that statue of David. Finally, if you make a mistake, I mean when you make a mistake, do just like you would do if you fall off of a bike: rather than dragging that bike all the back to the starting point, you get up, remount, and continue moving forward. That's what you will do with your children: you will move forward and away from the criminal justice system.

Acknowledgements

I want to thank all of the families that I was graciously permitted to serve during my 30 year tenure working with criminal justice involved clients. This book would not be possible without the gift of stories and challenges you provided. As Isaac Newton wrote, "if I have seen further it is by standing on the shoulders of Giants." Thank you for allowing me to stand on your shoulders in order to get a better view to help others. You are my giants.

Printed in the USA
CPSIA information can be obtained
at www.ICGtesting.com
JSHW021111151223
53845JS00011B/68